Dear Reader:

The book you are about to read is the latest bestseller from the St. Martin's True Crime Library, the imprint *The New York Times* calls "the leader in true crime!" Each month, we offer you a fascinating account of the latest, most sensational crime that has captured the national attention. St. Martin's is the publisher of bestselling true crime author and crime journalist Kieran Crowley, who explores the dark, deadly links between a prominent Manhattan surgeon and the disappearance of his wife fifteen years earlier in THE SURGEON'S WIFE. Suzy Spencer's BREAKING POINT guides readers through the tortuous twists and turns in the case of Andrea Yates, the Houston mother who drowned her five young children in the family's bathtub. In Edgar Award-nominated DARK DREAMS, legendary FBI profiler Roy Hazelwood and bestselling crime author Stephen G. Michaud shine light on the inner workings of America's most violent and depraved murderers. In the book you now hold, SAFE HARBOR, acclaimed author Brian McDonald investigates the mysterious disappearance of a woman after she meets the man she mistakenly thought was Mr. Right.

St. Martin's True Crime Library gives you the stories behind the headlines. Our authors take you right to the scene of the crime and into the minds of the most notorious murderers to show you what really makes them tick. St. Martin's True Crime Library paperbacks are better than the most terrifying thriller, because it's all true! The next time you want a crackling good read, make sure it's got the St. Martin's True Crime Library logo on the spine—you'll be up all night!

Charles E. Spicer, Jr.
Executive Editor, St. Martin's True Crime Library

ALSO BY BRIAN McDONALD

My Father's Gun

SAFE HARBOR

A MURDER IN NANTUCKET

BRIAN McDONALD

St. Martin's Paperbacks

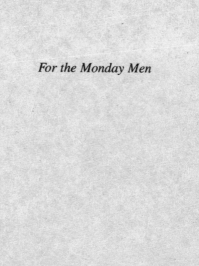

For the Monday Men

INTRODUCTION

I t was on the beautiful and stratospherically rich island of Nantucket that the lives of Thomas Toolan III and Beth Lochtefeld intersected. Within weeks of their meeting, Toolan would be charged with stabbing her to death. Though not wealthy, Toolan lived a life of privilege. He attended private Catholic grammar school, a Jesuit high school, and Columbia University. Growing up in an affluent section of Brooklyn, he was surrounded by families with mountains of wealth. Few knew him well—he was adroit at compartmentalizing and reinventing his life. But when he'd screw up, which he did often, his family and friends would forgive him and finance a fresh start. Tall, handsome, and witty, he was blessed with god-given attributes that should have opened doors to a successful life. But he was also deeply disturbed. Underneath a self-admitted alcohol problem lurked a lethal hatred of women. For much of his adult life, it seemed, Tom Toolan was a homicide waiting to happen.

Then there was Beth. From fairly humble beginnings, Beth worked all of her life toward building a business that eventually made her rich. In that business, she was a Girl Scout in a world that was spiderwebbed with crime. She was a bundle of energy, with circles and strata of friendships that reached all over the globe. Her memorial mass in Manhattan drew over a thousand people; the overwhelming majority of those who attended knew Beth at least well enough to have shared a meal or a laugh with her. But when Beth's head was on her pillow, most of those nights in bed by herself, she was inundated with feelings of loneliness. In her younger days, she ran from lovers, had too much to do, too much to see, to be attached. But as she aged, and needed to fill the aching loneliness, lovers ran from her. Still, it seemed incomprehensible that Beth stayed alone for so long. She was caring, loving, and beautiful.

By the time Beth stopped running, the very uncomfortable thought occurred to her that, at forty-four, she had run too long. Tom Toolan's acumen as a murderer might be suspect, but his timing was horribly superb. He crossed into Beth's life on Nantucket at the exact and only time she would have let him in, an event perhaps foretold many years before in an astrological chart.

But the stars didn't kill Beth. A four-inch serrated fishing knife did, one that was plunged into her over and over as she fought valiantly for her life. One that literally ripped her heart apart.

PART
ONE

CHAPTER ONE

Tom Lochtefeld stood on the Forty-second Street side of the New York Public Library and glanced at his watch. It was late October, and the first of the huge golden leaves from the London plane trees that line Bryant Park gently swirled to the ground. Rush hour had started to wane. It was nearly six. The last of New York City's daytime workforce rushed past him, some disappearing into the subway station, others hurrying down the street toward Grand Central Terminal and trains to the suburbs. He looked again at his watch. His sister was running a little late.

Tom hadn't seen Beth in about six months. Not really that long, considering their circumstances. Tom worked for a Japanese bank in midtown. His was the harried life of a Metro North rail commuter with a family in Connecticut.

Beth had no such parental duties. In fact, she had very few attachments at all. It had been a year and a half since she sold her architectural consulting business. She was subletting the apartment she owned in Greenwich Village and renting a cottage on Nantucket. But she was traveling a lot, to California and Europe. She sponsored a chair at the Allen Room, Jazz at Lincoln Center, but, just recently, a trip to Seville, Spain, to see an open-air performance of *Carmen* had fallen through. She was also trying to sell a book project containing her father's artwork, a book for which she had written the accompanying text.

And then there was romance.

At forty-four, Beth was still single, but, finally, that status looked as though it might change. More than at any other time in her life, a life that she had lived as though she were in a hurry, a life that was by turns joyously brimming and hauntingly lonely, Beth was available for marriage.

Tom Lochtefeld saw her rushing toward him along the crowded sidewalk. She was smiling that thousand-watt smile of hers that always made him feel like a little brother: safe and comfortable. Beth looks great, he thought to himself. She did look good, in the best shape of her adult life. She had been taking classes in aikido, a martial arts discipline, for a year, and had lost over twenty pounds. Her hair was cut short and blond, a color that suited her. The sea air, California's and Nantucket's, gave her a healthy hue. Some of Beth's friends thought it was love Beth radiated.

Brother Tom wasn't so sure.

Beth had called her younger brother several times over the previous month or so about Tom Toolan. At first, his sister's tone was enthusiastic. She bubbled about the relationship. "He's so honest," she had said to her brother. "So forthright." But Toolan's honesty might have been part of a carefully crafted persona. Toolan was a man of acquaintances by design. He liked his secrets. No one, it seemed, knew the whole story of Tom Toolan. He did tell Beth about embarrassing moments from his past, like the time he was arrested for stealing a sixty-pound sculpture from an art show. Toolan, drinking heavily that evening, had slipped the sculpture under his coat and tried to walk out the door. He was spotted by a guard and arrested. In court, his lawyer's defense was that it was a drunken prank. Maybe. But the statue was worth eighty thousand dollars. The story became part of an affected repertoire, delivered with just the right amount of self-deprecation, humility, or humor, depending on the audience. He'd bragged about stealing the sculpture in a bar called the Dublin House, a place where he was a regular. He told the story humbly in group therapy, knowing full well the attention and sympathy he would garner. Toolan used honesty as a device.

◆ ◆ ◆

n subsequent phone calls to her brother, Beth was less enthusiastic about the relationship. There were some very curious things about her boyfriend. For instance, the way he dressed. Initially, Beth thought it debonair, Toolan's penchant for double-breasted blazers and tasseled loafers even for the most casual dates. He often accessorized with pocket handkerchiefs, even ascots. Once he even showed up dressed that way for a date at a jazz club; Beth was wearing jeans and a leather jacket. On another date they met in Central Park for an outdoor opera. Toolan arrived looking like he had just come from the yacht club, everything but the captain's hat. Beth wasn't blind. She knew her boyfriend was a poseur. She could put up with that, she'd told friends. There were worse things in life than being overdressed. That she could live with.

But then there was the business about the refrigerator. Toolan had the superintendent of his building remove it from his apartment. He told some friends that he wanted more room in his kitchen. Others he told that it was a way of losing weight, a battle he'd fought his whole adulthood, a battle that he'd recently begun to win—he'd lost forty pounds. Perhaps it was just another harmless idiosyncrasy, Beth reasoned. Maybe.

There was no rationalization, however, for the pistol she'd come across in one of his drawers. Toolan reacted angrily, telling her to put it back and mind her own business. Beth didn't tell anyone about the gun, at least not right away, and at least not her brother Tom. She didn't want the family to worry, was Tom Lochtefeld's reasoning for Beth's silence about the gun. In one sense, her reluctance to alarm loved ones was an endearing quality—she cared about others' feelings. But as any domestic-abuse counselor will tell you, a hidden pistol trumps all feelings: Unless your significant other has a real good reason, a gun in the home is a flashing exit sign.

Instead of getting out, Beth took a trip with Toolan to California, where the unraveling of the relationship began almost sweetly. Toolan had proposed, which at first flattered

Beth. But they'd only been going out for three weeks, and Toolan proved to be a nightmare of a traveling partner. Two flights were missed because, according to Beth, "he couldn't get his shit together."

Beth told him that it was too soon in their relationship to talk about marriage. Toolan wouldn't take no for an answer. She was so unnerved by his abrupt proposal and cavalier attitude on the trip that she returned home alone. From there she e-mailed friends, exasperated, "He's already talking rings!"

He couched his desire to marry Beth in pillow talk and heated professions of love and forever. But Toolan's motives were questionable from the start. Though Beth wasn't the multimillionaire some news stories reported, she was in solid financial shape. The profit from the sale of her business was considerable. She owned outright a co-op in Greenwich Village that would eventually sell for nearly eight hundred thousand dollars. She had been a savvy investor all of her business life.

Toolan's financial situation was as mysterious as his personality. He worked for Smith Barney, first in Atlanta, then Manhattan. Smith Barney fired him twice. Later, he would be fired from yet another banking job because someone there recognized him from the newspaper stories about his attempted theft of the sculpture. In the months before he met Beth, Toolan told friends he was working from his apartment. "He was always just about to make the big deal," remembered neighbor Mika Duffy. But the big deal never materialized. Toolan was a guy with tastebuds for champagne, but the pocket change for beer.

Though Toolan's wallet might have been light, he had the trappings of a successful businessman. He had a membership at the New York Athletic Club. He rented a thirty-two-hundred-dollar-a-month apartment on West End Avenue, a tony Manhattan address. Toolan told one girlfriend that he had built considerable savings from his broker jobs, and that he drew on the account to pay his bills. But employment records show that Toolan didn't make anywhere near the money that he bragged to friends he made. What's more, he had a significant gambling problem, which included an offshore account for sports betting. He told friends his full name was Thomas Patrick Edward Francis Toolan III. When he said it, he would round off the hard *T* of Toolan making it sound like "Doolan." If there were such a thing as Irish royalty, his full moniker would be as blue blood as you could get. But his phone was listed under only Thomas Patrick. He told the same girlfriend he had it listed like that to keep telemarketers away. Conveniently, though, it also kept the creditors away, both the legitimate ones, and the ones who worked for less reputable lending institutions. One thing is for certain; he had to have help to pay his bills.

Maybe Toolan's biggest asset was how well he thought of the persona he'd crafted for himself. With attention paid right down to the angle of the cufflink, Toolan would look in the mirror and see the Prince of Park Slope looking back at him. Like a stage actor, his costume empowered him, helped him deliver his lines.

Beth, at first, was a willing audience. She enjoyed being the benefactor a bit too much. According to one published report, Beth had promised to back Toolan in a computer imaging business. She had already started to share some of her considerable business contacts with him. According to brother Tom, there was also talk about Beth cosigning a lease on West Side office space for Toolan. Beth was as savvy in business as you can get. But her skills in romance were lacking. She seemed to invest so much in Toolan because of a need to be liked, not from sound, financial thinking.

Beth wanted very badly to be in love for good. For all of her success and glamorous lifestyle, there was emptiness within. For many years, Beth sought to outrun that vacancy. But she was running in place. Like stones, though, models of happiness were set in place all around her: her parents' marriage, her sibling relationships. Beth looked past much of Toolan's flawed character because she knew she was running out of time. In his poignant eulogy, brother Jim recalled Beth telling his wife, Nancy: "All I want is to find a man like my brothers." Before the California trip Beth had told friends and family that Toolan might be the one. "Being forty-four and single and thinking she had met the man she was going to marry, she was very excited," her cousin Eric told a reporter on Nantucket. Outwardly at least, Toolan and Beth gave the appearance of the perfect upscale couple. It seemed they could fit perfectly into a home in Connecticut or Westchester, summering on Nantucket. And what better place than her own beloved Nantucket for a wedding? *The New York Times* calls the island "a destination" wedding spot. The Chamber of Commerce has a pamphlet on wedding services. In season, there are four weddings a weekend on the tiny island. But for Beth it was more than just some public relations firm's spin. Nantucket, in its elegance and perfection, was a place where Beth's dreams had formed. It was part of her soul. More than anything, perhaps, Beth wanted the stars over Nantucket Harbor to light her wedding night.

It was under those stars, back from California, that Beth started to miss Toolan. He'd called a dozen times, apologizing profusely. Months after her sister was dead, Cathy Lochtefeld found a note in some of Beth's toiletries that were never unpacked after the California trip. It read simply: "I love you, Tom." He would gear it back, he promised. It would be different this time, his tone indicated. One thing was for certain; Toolan could talk a satin streak. Beth had told her brother that she was going to give it "the four seasons test," to stay with him a year and see how things progressed. I'll give him a year, she said.

From the deepest part of his heart, Tom Lochtefeld wanted his sister to be happy. He knew she lived a pretty glamorous life: a world traveler with friends on three conti-   But he also knew it was his life she looked at with envy: his kids, the house in the suburbs, a happy marriage. Beth's brother hoped that she would find a man with whom she'd spend the rest of her life. In the most horrible fashion, Tom Toolan would turn that hope into a nightmare.

CHAPTER TWO

That Wednesday, the night he and Beth met Tom Lochtefeld at the Harvard Club, Toolan showed up with his blond hair slicked back and wearing a blue pinstriped suit. Towering, at six foot two, and two hundred something pounds, and with a chin as prominent as a New England senator's, he was quite the formidable presence. Even Beth's brother, no shrimp himself, was somewhat impressed. "I just remember he looked very confident," Tom Lochtefeld said. They sat at a table in the modest oak Grill Room, modest at least in comparison to the main dining room with its soaring forty-foot ceiling. Around them, Harvard grads from decades past laughed, drank, and dined. Beth's brother was taken by Toolan's manners, later calling him a "complete gentleman." They talked about the trip to California but stopped short of discussing the separate returns. Toolan told Tom Lochtefeld about Beth helping him with business contacts. But Toolan was evasive about his employment. And Beth's brother wasn't convinced that Toolan actually had a job. At one point Toolan reminisced about the long-ago summer with the Nantucket Theatre, where he acted a bit, painted scenery, and struck sets. Beth then talked glowingly about a trip they had recently taken to visit Toolan's sister, Tara, in Westchester. Beth liked Toolan's sister a great deal, and perhaps saw in her what she hoped for herself. Happily married, Tara Toolan lived a storybook life, with a family and a swell suburban home, an existence similar to the one Beth's brother lived.

Several times during dinner, Toolan excused himself and left the table for a few minutes. He's trying to quit smoking, Beth explained to her brother. "He knows that I don't like it, and he's trying," she said. "He's trying to make changes." In hindsight, it seemed as though Beth was trying to convince herself, and not her brother, that Toolan was worth her time and trouble.

The three of them had cocktails, but Toolan was on his best behavior. "He treated me like he was meeting her father," Tom Lochtefeld remembered thinking. "Completely gracious."

Outside the Harvard Club a chilly breeze had rustled up Forty-fourth Street. Tom Lochtefeld was headed the two blocks east to Grand Central to catch a train home to Darien. He shook hands with Toolan. "Well, I'll see you again soon," Toolan said casually. Then Tom leaned in and kissed his sister. Beth put on a brave face. She had mentioned Toolan's drinking to her brother, and even to her father, but "she tried to play it down," Tom Lochtefeld remembered. Beth's brother took one more look at his sister as she walked down the street arm in arm with Toolan. It was the last time he would see her alive.

Two days later, on Friday afternoon, Beth and Toolan climbed the steps to the Metropolitan Museum of Art. Around them, students and tourists sat in the bright sunshine. Hanging from the façade of the neoclassical building, five-story-high banners announcing the exhibits, including one of German drawings and prints from the Weimar Republic, flapped in the gentle breeze. In front of the museum, Fifth Avenue was a winding stream of yellow taxis. Beth had been staying at Toolan's apartment most of that week, at least from Wednesday night, when they'd had dinner at the Harvard Club. Earlier in the day, Toolan had suggested an afternoon at the Metropolitan, then maybe have some dinner on the East Side. Partly, it was Toolan's appreciation of art and music that Beth had been drawn to. Just a few weeks before, on Nantucket, Beth looked on proudly as her boyfriend held his own in an art conversation with her artist father. Although not an aficionado like Beth, Toolan even enjoyed the opera. But an afternoon at the museum might also be the thing to take the pressure off, Beth thought. It hadn't been a good idea to stay with Toolan for so many days. His peculiarities, his addictions, were bubbling over and becoming hard to ignore. The smell of cigarette smoke on his clothing and in his apartment made her almost physically sick. The memory of the California trip and all the pressure he had put on her was still fresh in her mind. But Beth was still holding on to the idea that the relationship was salvageable. Besides, the museum had an Andy Goldsworthy sculpture exhibit on the roof that Beth wanted to see. For Beth it would be again like a first date. There would be no pressure, no big drama.

Toolan had other ideas.

After an hour or so of Greek and Roman statues, Dutch Masters and Impressionists, Toolan took Beth by the hand and led her to a quiet corner. Perhaps he chose the shimmering pool in front of the Egyptian Temple of Dendur, which, according to the museum, is a favorite spot for such things. He went down on one knee and took an antique ring from the pocket of his sports jacket. Toolan was no stranger to the position. Several months before proposing to Beth, he was engaged to a woman who worked as a sales rep for a clothing manufacturer. Among other things, Toolan's drinking was the reason for the breakup of that relationship. And there was at least one other woman, in Atlanta, to whom he had been engaged. But for now, Toolan's history isn't as important as the chain of events the proposal would set in motion.

Beth swallowed hard. "Oh, god. Please no," she thought, as she quickly looked away. "Tom, I've already told you it's too early for me, I can't say yes," she said. Toolan rose to his feet, his face flushed.

"It's now or never, Beth," he hissed.

"Then it's going to have to be never," Beth replied.

Toolan tried another tack.

"You don't love me enough to marry me," he said.

"I'm not ready," Beth said, as she turned and started to walk away.

The dialogue might seem a bit soap operish, and it comes second-hand. Beth recounted the scene to her brother in a phone conversation the following day. But the emotions were real and building. Beth hurried to the exit of the museum. Once at the door she realized she had checked her coat. Flustered, she searched her pockets for the coat check. Meanwhile, Toolan was following quickly after her, his saccharine words giving way to orders for her to stop and listen to him. When Beth finally had her coat, she ran full-out for the door. Toolan took off after her, his hulking frame producing a wake of startled museumgoers. He caught up with Beth as she was climbing into a cab on Fifth Avenue. He forced his way in after her.

The cab scooted south on Fifth for three or four blocks, then turned right onto the Seventy-ninth Street transverse. According to one source, at some point during the ride across Central Park Toolan realized he had lost the ring. He must have dropped it running after Beth. He went into a rage in the backseat of the cab. Beth had experienced Toolan's anger before. One night, on Seventy-ninth Street, Toolan was drunk and put her in a headlock. In the cab, she was frightened. But she still felt she had some control over the situation. Otherwise she could have screamed, jumped out at a light. Instead, she decided to ride it out with him. Go into his apartment, get her stuff, the Palm Pilot, some of her clothing, and then walk out of Toolan's life for good. Inside Toolan's apartment, however, Beth quickly realized she'd made the wrong decision.

Several hours later, in Darien, Tom Lochtefeld kicked off his shoes, opened a beer, sat back on the couch in his living room, and put his stocking feet on the coffee table. It had been a tough week at work, and he was looking forward to a bit of TV and relaxation—as much as one can relax in a house filled with kids. Just as he was settling in, his phone rang. He sighed, pushed himself up, and walked the twelve or so feet to the kitchen. It was Beth's cell number on the caller ID. He picked up the receiver. Beth's voice was deliberate, measured. "We're trying to work things out," she said slowly. At first Tom was confused at the non sequitur. But then he realized Beth was talking about her and Toolan.

"I'm staying here tonight," his sister said. "We're trying to work things out."

Tom has gone over the conversation he had with his sister that Friday night innumerable times. Over and over, he's asked himself why he didn't fully understand the peril Beth was in. Why couldn't he have just said: "Beth, if you're not okay, just call me 'Little Bro' or cough or something, anything to signal me." But the notion that Beth was in physical danger was not even close to his radar screen. Just that week he had had dinner with Toolan and Beth. Yeah, Tom Lochtefeld thought, Toolan was a bit of a pompous ass, but a captor and tormentor? Previous to Friday night there was no way Tom could have come to that conclusion. If he had, the consequences would have been frightening for Toolan. Beth's little brother was an all-county fullback and defensive end on his high school football team. He'd played fullback for Harvard. At forty-one, he was still in terrific shape. He would have ripped Toolan's door off the hinges had he known what was going on behind it. At one point Toolan had snatched Beth's suitcase and thrown it against his television, smashing the screen. At some point during that night, Toolan told Beth he was going to kill her.

What Tom Lochtefeld didn't know was that Beth had called his house earlier that evening, while he was still making his way home by train. Tom's mother-in-law, who was staying for the weekend, picked up the phone. She told her daughter, Nancy, that she was concerned about Beth's tone. Beth told her that she was breaking up with Toolan and she wanted to spend the night with Tom and the family. When Tom heard about this call, he was more surprised than alarmed. "It's gone from the 'four seasons test,' to 'I got to get out of here,'" Tom remembers thinking. And now she was on the phone, sounding very strange, telling him she was working things out. Tom didn't know what to think.

Though he would do anything for Beth, the fact that his sister was staying in New York meant that he didn't have to put on his shoes and coat and drive to the train station to pick her up. "We're trying to work things out," Beth repeated.

"Okay, whatever you want, that's fine," Tom said, and he hung up the phone.

Just as he settled back on the couch, the phone rang again. Back in the kitchen, Beth's caller ID was again on his phone. Tom slowly shook his head. But this time when he picked up the phone he heard the deep, unmistakable voice of Toolan. Now it was getting really strange, Tom thought.

"I just wanted to let you know that I love your sister very much," Toolan said.

What was I supposed to say to that? Tom remembers thinking. On one hand, he was glad that his sister and her boyfriend seem to be working things out. But on the other hand, he was getting a little fed up with the high school making-up, breaking-up thing he'd been dragged into.

"I want you to know I love your sister very much," Toolan repeated. "We're trying to work things out."

Beth's brother had reached his limit.

"Good luck," he said, and hung up his phone.

CHAPTER THREE

Saturday night.

In the early evening of the following day, the roof deck of the New York Athletic Club was deserted. Toolan walked toward the five-foot-high walls that enclose the space. The view before him was spectacular, like looking down on the universe, the city lights like clusters of stars below him, the dark rectangle of Central Park spread like a black carpet outlined with shimmering headlights and street lamps. To the east were the lights of the high-rise condominiums of the Upper East Side, to the west, the new Time Warner Center and Lincoln Center. Toolan knew the view well. His father was a longtime member of the club, and as a child of twelve or thirteen, Toolan would stand at almost the same spot and throw pieces of brick and stone at a glass atrium some twenty floors below. But this night, all Toolan saw was the street straight down—twenty-four floors.

The best estimate is that Toolan had been drinking all day. He had awakened in the claustrophobic confines of his West End Avenue apartment, his despondency overwhelming. He was in an alcoholic purgatory, half drunk, half hungover. He sat on the edge of his bed, his head hanging, his blond hair matted and twisted, his eyes glazed as he looked at the cell phone in his hands.

The night before he had kept Beth captive. The gun was still in his apartment. He was drinking throughout the night. His tone with Beth alternated between drunken maudlin and frighteningly threatening. He didn't pass out until the early morning hours. Beth then quickly gathered her stuff and slipped out.

When Toolan came to and realized Beth was gone, he began a furious volley of calls to her cell phone. Beth picked up the first time. A mistake, she knew. Though a baritone, Toolan had a way of putting on a little boy's voice. The innocence had worked before. Not this time. In that first call, Beth told Toolan that it was over. She let the rest of his calls go to voice mail.

Still, he kept calling all day. Time after time he listened to Beth's recorded voice, her perky message. His head pounded from a horrible hangover headache, but worse than the physical pain was the emotional anguish. As Beth's voice came from the phone, perhaps his head played an inner recording of self-hatred, a tape playing over and over, louder and louder. Somewhere inside this self-hating monster he'd become was a good person who had lost control of his life. In high school, he'd put on a clown costume and performed at children's parties. He had once dreamt of being an actor and a writer. His eyes, raw-red, swelled with tears. It just hurt too bad, and the only way he knew how to stop the pain was to start drinking again.

He was first seen in the taproom of the New York AC about noon on Saturday. In the evening, after hours of drinking, he staggered to the elevator and took it to the twenty-first floor, where the squash courts are located. The elevators go no higher. From there he unsteadily climbed a thin staircase to the atrium on the roof.

In one way, it would have been appropriate for Toolan to end his life by jumping off the roof of the building. The mortar was just dry on the Central Park South clubhouse on that Black Monday in 1929 when captains of finance jumped off roofs all over the city.* However much Toolan professed true love for Beth, there is a pretty strong case that

---

*According to *The Year of the Great Crash, 1929* (1991) by historian William K. Klingaman, asphyxiation by gas was the most common method of doing oneself in, although there was considerable variety.

money was at least part of his motivation. Beth was the quick fix for him. In business, she was everything he was not: successful, hardworking, and, in a business that has a history of corruption that goes as far back as the city itself, as ethical as one can be. Among Beth's clients, many of whom became her friends, were the very elite of architecture, fashion, restaurants, and the arts. Beth walked comfortably in a world that Toolan salivated over. Maybe, on some level, he did love her. Maybe. But it certainly didn't hurt that Beth worked and lived in affluent circles.

There was a soft breeze that evening, and it rippled at his clothing. How could things have gone so wrong in his life for him to deem it over at thirty-seven? Hundreds of feet below, life announced itself with car horns. The bottleneck of Seventh Avenue at Fifty-ninth Street was yellow with taxis in the backseats of which couples laughed or fought or silently stared out the windows. But on the roof the only sound he heard was the voice inside his head, a voice that told him he didn't deserve to live. For most of Toolan's adult life, privilege and position had held safety nets each time he fell. For a few moments it seemed as though this time there would be no soft landing. Below was only concrete. Then, according to several sources, a longtime friend of Toolan's saw him climb the staircase and followed him out onto the roof. There, he literally talked Toolan down from the ledge, and, unwittingly, set in motion a chain of events that found Beth dead and Toolan charged with killing her.

The cab pulled up in front of Toolan's building on West End Avenue at about eleven o'clock at night, just as Mika Duffy, a neighbor of Toolan's, was coming home from walking her dog, a Sussex spaniel. The friend from the Athletic Club had taken Toolan home in a taxi. Duffy knew Toolan fairly well because they both were dog owners and would often run into each other in the lobby with their pets.

Toolan had tried to open the front door to his building, but couldn't get the key in the lock. The friend had taken the keys from Toolan, and Duffy remembers him still holding them when she entered the lobby. Toolan looked desperate, a man who had abandoned all hope. The friend wouldn't let Toolan into the elevator with Duffy. "I guess he was afraid Tom would throw up," Duffy said. Instead, the friend propped Toolan against the wall. "He couldn't stand up," Toolan's neighbor remembered. "He was leaning against the wall, with his head down," she said.

The next morning, Sunday, Toolan was awakened by the steady buzz of his intercom. The sound came from somewhere very close, but very far away—a late summer bumblebee inside his skull. It was painful to open his eyes. The throbbing in his head had to be unbearable. In the lobby, his father, Thomas Toolan Jr., was leaning on the button. Someone, most probably a friend who had escorted Toolan home the night before, had called the father to alert him that his son was on a drinking binge. According to one source, Mr. Toolan had driven into Manhattan from his Park Slope apartment. Apparently, it was not unusual for the elder Toolan to try to rescue his son from the clutches of a binge.

Six months before, Toolan was at the Dublin House, a bar around the corner from his apartment, in a condition that was described as "really cooked," according to the bartender who worked that night. The bartender thought there might be more to Toolan's high than just beer. The word around the bar was that a guy Toolan was hanging out with was a "scumbag," Dublin House–speak for a heroin junkie. That night, Toolan wore the same dead stare as his pal. At one point, Toolan staggered toward the door. The bartender called to him. There was the not-so-small matter of a forty-two-dollar bar tab, no easy feat at a two-dollar-a-beer joint like the Dublin. Toolan put on an act of patting all his pockets as though he was searching for a roll of money or a wallet. Coming up empty, he told the bartender that he had to go to an ATM. The bartender suspected Toolan was not coming back, not that he was overly concerned. Toolan was a regular. He'd get him to pay the tab the next time he came in. But there was finality to Toolan's condition that night. Ten years behind a bar matches any psychology degree, and in the bartender's estimation Toolan was looking over the edge into a very dark place: the bottom of addiction. Ten minutes after Toolan left, the phone behind the bar rang. The professorial, older-sounding voice on the other end of the line asked if Tom Toolan was at the bar. The bartender made a smart-assed comment about Toolan running out on the tab. The phone conversation ended there. But three minutes later, the phone rang again. It was the same odd voice. The man identified himself as the person who had just asked for Tom Toolan, but this time he added he was Tom Toolan's father. The bartender both felt embarrassed for being so dismissive to Toolan's father, but also embarrassed *for* Toolan's father. The elder Toolan asked if his son had been drinking. How Mr. Toolan found out that his son was on a bender is not known. But the bartender confirmed he was. In a worried tone, Mr. Toolan then asked the bartender to have Tom call if he came back to the bar. Not surprisingly, Toolan didn't return to the Dublin that night. In fact, he would stay away for six months. The bartender happened to run into him on the street several days later. A contrite Toolan apologized and told the bartender that he was on the wagon.

Mr. Toolan had watched his son party himself out of prestigious Colby College in Maine. He saw him lose at least two banking jobs because of his drinking, one for threatening to punch a boss at a cocktail party. Toolan's parents had tried to get him help for his drinking numerous times. Just recently, he had been scheduled to go to a drug and alcohol rehab in Antigua. Toolan told Beth that he'd been in three alcohol detoxes. But the Toolans also seemed to hold on to the hope that their son would grow out of his problem as though it were some kind of teenage phase. In the language of recovery, they were enabling his addiction.

Toolan spoke to his father over the intercom, telling him he'd be right down. He then managed to shower and change while the elder Toolan dutifully waited. The plan, one imagines, was to get Toolan back to Park Slope where his parents could nurse him off the drunk. Maybe there had been quick plans made for another detox or rehab.

Toolan had other ideas. On the street, a car had double-parked in front of Mr. Toolan's car. The younger Toolan saw his opportunity. He told his father he would find the owner and have him move the automobile. As Mr. Toolan slid in behind the wheel, his son walked around the corner of the building and headed toward the Dublin House. As he sat in his car and realized that his thirty-seven-year-old son had run away from him like a schoolchild, perhaps Mr. Toolan decided enough was enough.

CHAPTER FOUR

Toolan's final hours of innocence saw him transform from a delusional man with a serious drinking problem to an accused murderer. If the accusations were true, it's hard to say what tipped the cards in the end. Was it pure bloodlust? Had he truly always been a murderer waiting to happen? Was he losing his mind because of a desperate financial situation? Was it something deeper, perhaps from his childhood (of which more will be explored later)? Or was it just the alcohol? Either way, it was just after noon when Toolan ordered a Miller Lite and a shot of Ketel One vodka. There were perhaps ten or so patrons already bellied up to the oak bar, a gathering that the regulars at the Dublin House call "Sunday mass." Terry Bradshaw and Howie Long blabbed away on the NFL pregame show on TV over the bar. Though the vodka began to ease the pain, Toolan's head still pounded from his hangover. He had a self-hatred that was palpable. Horrible glimpses of Friday and Saturday exploded in his thoughts like a montage from a psychological thriller. Each sliver of memory jolted him like a bolt of electricity: the night before on the roof of the club, Friday night holding Beth in his apartment, Friday afternoon on one knee in the museum handing her an engagement ring. But there were large segments of the two previous days he couldn't remember at all.

An "alcoholic blackout" is a severe amnesia that occurs during a drinking episode. Blackouts can last for hours and sometimes, though rarely, as long as a few days. Perhaps the scariest element of a blackout is that the person experiencing one can appear perfectly normal to the outside world, often performing tasks and carrying on conversations in a seemingly sober way. For at least part of the extended drunk he was now on, Toolan was in a blackout. In several forums, group therapy for one, he had admitted that he blacked out often when he drank. Though, in a court of law, an alcoholic blackout does not absolve one of criminal culpability (the condition occurs as a result of a voluntary act), whether the person in a blackout knows the difference between right and wrong is debatable.

But Toolan's pathology went beyond alcoholism and alcoholic blackouts. He had a depraved and at times violent history with women. He exhibited characteristics of antisocial personality disorders: borderline and narcissistic. On that gray afternoon, in that darkened bar, perhaps he turned a desire for self-destruction into something much worse. Up until that point he was content to kill himself. Then, as the booze and beer slid down his throat, did a dramatic change occur within the electrical currents, the synapses and neurotransmitters of his brain? Perhaps he hadn't given up on suicide. Perhaps he was still going to end his life, but not by jumping off a roof. Was he going to end his life by ending another's? He lit a Marlboro Light and looked again at himself in the barroom mirror. Someone strange smiled back. "I should buy a hat," he thought.

Toolan certainly didn't look sober. But he had a way of carrying himself with a sort of drunken dignity that could be slightly endearing, and nonviolent, at least according to the bar patrons at the Dublin. His head was murky, but as he drank the shot of vodka and chased it with a Miller Lite, the hangover began to recede. He felt his power return. At two hundred and twenty pounds he was quite capable of killing.

Manhattan was overcast and chilly. A raw wind blew miniature twisters of leaves and papers across Seventy-ninth Street. Toolan walked down the few cement steps to the side-

walk and hailed a cab, folded his six-foot-two-inch frame
into the backseat and directed the driver to LaGuardia Airport. The trip from the West Side to LaGuardia on a Sunday
afternoon, when the traffic is light, takes no more than a half
hour. Toolan looked out through the grimy window at the
grayness of Queens as the cab raced over the Triborough
Bridge. He could feel the knife in the inside pocket of his
topcoat, and an evil sense of purpose strengthened. It's possible that Toolan put the knife in his jacket when his father
came to his apartment. Or he might have stopped on the way
to the airport. It doesn't really matter when he put it in his
coat. Only the reason he put it there matters. In some ways,
it seemed inconceivable, the thoughts that now so easily
played out in his mind. He seemed to still have much of that
good Saint Saviour Catholic schoolboy, the Xavier High
School freshman, with the guiltless blue eyes and sandy,
tousled hair and the tie knotted tight to his collar. His face
still held some of the angelic innocence that had mostly disappeared from his heart.

By the time Toolan entered the airport terminal he
had his bearings. He carried his topcoat folded over
his arm as he entered the gate. He was instructed by
a Transportation Safety Administration screener to lay the
coat on a conveyor belt to be x-rayed. The screen showed the
outline of a large serrated knife hidden within the topcoat.
Did he actually think they wouldn't find it? Toolan gave two
different explanations to two different security employees.
To one he said he didn't know it was there, as if everyone
carries a kitchen knife in case they're invited to turkey dinner. To the other, he said his sister had given it to him for a
fishing trip. One airport source told the New York *Daily
News* that it was obvious that Toolan had been drinking but
"was coherent enough to get on a plane." A background
check of Toolan's criminal history produced "nothing that
would jump out on him and say, we got to hold on to this
guy," Luis Martinez, a spokesman for the Port Authority of
New York and New Jersey, told *The Boston Globe.* Accord-

ing to Martinez, there were no prior arrests on his record. The Port Authority police detained Toolan for about forty-five minutes, long enough for him to miss his flight. He was given a misdemeanor summons to appear in Queens, New York, District Court for possession of an illegal weapon. Considering the importance of security in today's world, the decision not to arrest Toolan is curious, to say the least. But, according to one police source, over three thousand knives are confiscated each year at LaGuardia. Regardless, the decision not to arrest Toolan let a man who twenty-four hours later was accused of murder go free. Minus the knife, Toolan walked out of the terminal building, got into a cab, and headed back to Manhattan. A Port Authority police spokesman said that police can't speculate as to a person's intentions. Toolan's trip to Nantucket might have been delayed, but his intention to get there was still firmly in place.

The Sunday mass crowd at the Dublin had dissipated and was somewhere resting peacefully. In their place were a few of the regular night crew. Toolan knew them well. As he walked into the dark bar, he was greeted with a chorus of "Where you been?" He smiled his boyish grin and assembled a story of having fallen asleep at the airport and missing his flight to Nantucket. His appearance was essentially the same, the topcoat and scarf. But there was one glaring addition. He now sported a brand-new tan fedora. The hat became a topic of bar banter. "You have to be kidding with that hat, Tom. In here?" said his bar pal, George Gross. Someone else came to Toolan's aid. "I think it's a nice hat," the patron said. "In this place it's ridiculous," Gross shot back. Through it all, Toolan just smiled, the hat cocked at a jaunty angle on his head.

Nothing in Toolan's demeanor gave away his intentions. He ordered a Miller Lite and to those within earshot continued his explanation of where he'd been. Maybe it was for the bartender's sake, the same fellow who had served Toolan earlier in the day. He said that he had missed his flight, and that his girlfriend "was going to be pissed at him." George Gross, who had hung on since Sunday mass, saw little difference in his friend's demeanor that evening: "He might have seemed a little down, but that might be me looking back," said Gross. Toolan and Gross talked about the football games and the World Series game being played that night. Gross has no recollection of Toolan being preoccupied or angry. But Toolan had never shown an angry side to Gross. "He was pretty laid back. Nothing seemed to bother him too much," Gross said. One evening, Gross remembered, Toolan even played the peacemaker. "A couple of people were acting up," Gross said. "When the ruckus started, Tom held one of the guys back. Me or one of the other guys held the other back."

Toolan ordered another Lite. At some point, a woman with a small dog came into the bar and sat next to him. According to Gross, Toolan started up a conversation, talking about Jack, his white German shepherd. Uninvited, the barman offered his opinion: "There is no dog like that," he said. "I'll go to my apartment and get him right now," Toolan answered. "No dogs allowed," the barman bellowed sarcastically. "I'm bringing my dog in here, too," Toolan announced. "Get the fuck out of here," the bartender said with mock annoyance. The moment dissolved into good-natured laughter.

Perhaps the best insight into Toolan's personality was offered by Kostas Ladopoulos, the owner of the New Wave Café, just down the block from the Dublin. "He knew everybody," Ladopoulos told *The New York Times,* "but you never saw him with anybody." For Toolan, the perfect stage was the Dublin. There no one cared who you were or what you were pretending to be. As long as you paid your tab, and didn't pick any fights, you were allowed to play any role you wanted. The Dublin was also a place where guys went, alone, to drink their loneliness away. Here, too, the bar was a perfect setting. Toolan's bluster aside, there was a forlorn man inside the blue blazer. Below the act, he was as lonely as Beth, and needed someone in his life just as much.

At times, Toolan talked to Gross and others at the Dublin about his dating. But it was never about one particular girl. Gross never knew him to be in any type of serious relationship. On rare occasions, Toolan would escort a woman into the bar. One night, Toolan introduced his date to Gross. She was pretty, Gross remembered, tall, with blond hair similar to Beth's. Toolan said that they were going to a nearby restaurant for dinner and asked if Gross wanted to come along. Gross declined. "He seemed to be happy with her," Gross remembered. "She seemed to be having a good time, too."

But Toolan liked to tell the boys at the bar about his conquests. He'd often begin a monologue with the same opening: "I was banging this chick, see . . ." It became almost Toolan's catchphrase amongst the regulars at the bar. "Who knows if he was with the girls," Gross wondered.

Without question, Toolan could be exceedingly charming. He had what another Dublin patron, Bruce Kelly, called "a Dean Martin banter," or a "radio announcer's voice," as one news article said. His style was soft and reassuring and more rounded at the edges with each beer he drank. According to Kelly, Toolan at times talked in a conspiratorial manner, lowering his voice, drawing you close to him. It was in this manner that he continued the conversation with the woman with the dog at the bar.

He told her about his girlfriend on Nantucket. He professed his love for Beth and said something about straightening things out. He swigged the bottle of Lite beer empty and ordered another. The woman with the dog provided a sympathetic ear. Patrons remember that Toolan became weepy at one point. He did have his soft, cuddly side. George Gross remembered a snowy Christmas night in 2002. Gross had just fought his way back in a blizzard from a family celebration at his brother's house in New Jersey and was sitting in a quiet Dublin having a beer. Not too much later Toolan walked in the door. The two bachelors sat next to each other swapping family Christmas stories. Toolan had a new digital camera, perhaps a Christmas gift. He was aglow showing

Gross pictures of his three- or four-year-old niece, the daughter of his older sister, Tara, ripping open presents. As the Christmas snow piled up on the street outside the Dublin, Gross was touched by his wisecracking friend's affection for the child. "He talked about the bunch of gifts he'd given his niece," Gross remembers. "A proud uncle."

Time slides by at the Dublin, especially when the beers keep coming. The Red Sox had the television now. Winning four to nothing, the Sox were about to go up two games to none in their World Series against the Cardinals. In the stands, Fenway fans were bundled against the cold. All over Nantucket, televisions were tuned in to the game. In bed in the guest bedroom in her brother Peter's house, Beth was snuggled under a comforter reading *Potluck at Midnight Farm,* a book about food and family on Martha's Vineyard.

CHAPTER FIVE

A light fog that morning clung to the island like a damp beach towel. Nantucket was in a dreary lull. The rich and summer folk were long gone, and scallop fishing season had not yet begun. Beth walked from Peter's house holding hands with Zuzu and Sam. She helped her niece and nephew into the 1999 Subaru Forester Wagon that she had bought used the previous March. Her first stop that morning was Zuzu's school, then Sam's kindergarten, where he would attend a half day. After a hug good-bye, Beth watched as they scampered into the schoolhouse.

Beth had flown into Nantucket two days before, on Saturday morning. Soon after she arrived at Nantucket Memorial Airport, she had stopped at the Nantucket Police Department. There she inquired about an order of protection against Toolan. She inquired, but she didn't take one out. It was as though Beth was involved in an inner tug-of-war.

One part of her was scared to death. Just a few months before, Beth had sent a letter to an aikido sensei on Nantucket. In it she wrote of a constant dread she'd carried her whole life. It was the reason she began taking aikido classes. Part of that training was defending oneself against a knife attack. But an even bigger element of aikido was learning to face one's fear. According to a family member, Beth had her astrological chart done at a fair while she was in high school, and the reading frightened her so much she never forgot it.

But another part of Beth wasn't going to let Toolan dictate how she was going to live her life. As a kind of compromise, a character trait Beth displayed all her life, she took some information about a domestic-violence crisis center on the island called A Safe Place and walked out of the police station. "Don't think that officer isn't here today, beating his head against the wall, wondering what question he couldn't have asked her," the island's police chief, William Pittman, later told the New York *Daily News*.

From the police station, she went to her brother's house. She didn't want to stay alone in the cottage on Hawthorne Lane, and there was nowhere in the world where she would feel safer than staying with her older brother. Peter was perhaps her closest sibling, and something of a protector. They had spent two years together at the University of Notre Dame, Peter being one of the big reasons Beth chose that school. Anyhow, staying at Peter's was no hardship. Though Beth was close to all ten of her nieces and nephews, she saw Peter's children the most. Many characterized Beth's relationship with Zuzu as special. There are photographs of them playing dress-up together. That weekend, Peter happened to have company from Amsterdam. One of the guests wrote on a memorial Web site for Beth, on meeting her that weekend:

"Last weekend I met Beth at the house of her brother Peter and his family. It was so nice seeing her love for the children and their love for her. How she was sitting there on the *banc* [sic] reading the same book three times because the children wanted her to do so. All the three of them sitting on her lap. I feel happy that I have met her. . . ."

A photo accompanies the submission to the Web site. In it Beth has the book spread in her lap and is surrounded by the kids. It's one of the only pictures taken of Beth where she isn't smiling.

By Monday morning, Beth decided that she'd stayed away from the cottage long enough. Toolan had left some clothing there, and Beth wanted it out. She didn't want any reminder of him. How could she have not seen this crazy side of him, she asked herself. She should have run for her life the moment she found the gun in his drawer. "Beth was the kind of person who threw herself completely into a situation to try and make it work out," her brother Tom once said. Certainly Beth worked hard at everything she did. She built her business by refusing to quit. Over her computer she had a quote from William the Conqueror: "You don't have to succeed to persevere."

Toolan leaned back on the headrest as the nineteen-seat U.S. Air commuter plane rumbled down runway thirty-one at LaGuardia. As the turboprop broke free from the tarmac and lurched skyward, Toolan closed his eyes. His placid exterior belied the homicidal rage within. The plane banked as it climbed. Outside the window the South Bronx, especially grungy in the overcast morning, slipped out of view like the picture of an old black-and-white television with a vertical roll. Long Island Sound below was dark green and polished smooth. The aircraft bounced as it broke through the low ceiling, a cottony mattress seen from above. It had been chilly that morning, dipping into the midforties. But the air was moist and motionless. Toolan had dressed in a blazer and camel-hair topcoat, accessorized with a silk scarf and the light-tan fedora, the coat, scarf, and hat stowed in the overhead compartment. In some ways, he was a Fitzgerald character—Gatsbyesque, but without the money or the heart. Still, he always dressed as though he had just closed the deal of his life. He had a number of ex-fiancées and ex-girlfriends, but he seemed to have the same staying power in relationships that he had with jobs.

Under the cloud cover lay the southern coast of Connecticut, then the Rhode Island shore, where the plane turned toward the open sea. There was a dull, constant ache at the base of his skull; his stomach was in a rolling sea of acid. Over the last three days, his nourishment had been a couple of slices of pizza and perhaps a few bar peanuts at the New York Athletic Club. He didn't want food to allay the effects of the beer and vodka drunk he'd been on. He smelled of it, the booze, and the cologne he tried to cover it with. One of his bar pals said that the fragrances Toolan preferred "smelled like your grandmother's toilet water." Though ragged, he was still handsome. Blond hair sprouted from the top of his head like a handful of wheat, but was darker and combed back on the sides. His eyes, hazel eyes that changed from green to blue, this morning were like star sapphire, but with period-sized black pupils. A fine stubble was beginning to show on his prominent chin.

The drone of the engines felt like someone was sandpapering the insides of his head. Still, he smiled as he made small talk with the passenger next to him. No matter how hungover, or drunk, he liked to chat. This trait endeared him to barflies and girlfriends alike. Below the banter, his thoughts were on the previous Friday afternoon—two days and a lifetime ago, and the subtext was murder. How embarrassing it was for him: on one knee at the museum only to have his proposal turned down. Just who did she think she was? He was seven years younger than her, for God's sake. He was doing her a favor. An anger that was almost primal fought its way into his consciousness. He thought about a fishing supply store he knew on the harbor. There he would be able to buy the knife he needed, one with not too long a blade, something sharp and easy to control. The engines on the Beechcraft began to power down. Only thirty minutes after the plane had taken off, it began its descent. Toolan looked out the window and saw the wisps of fog like a white bird's nest around the island. He would rent the car, go right to the fishing supply store, and buy the knife. Then he would drive to Beth's cottage. There he would set things straight. He would make her realize that she had made a big mistake. He turned to his seatmate and smiled and said something about how beautiful Nantucket looked from the air.

I n the secluded cottage on Hawthorne Lane, Beth Lochtefeld wrapped a few of Toolan's things in brown paper. She addressed the package to Toolan's West End Avenue apartment in Manhattan. She hoped that this was the last piece of business she would have with her new ex-boyfriend. Somewhere in the deepest reaches of her soul, however, she could feel him coming for her.

A few sprinkles of rain dotted the windshield of the Subaru as Beth drove to Parcel Plus. As her brother Tom would say later: "I will forever find it ironic that Beth had the integrity to do the right thing and return the guy's items the day after he held her captive and threatened to kill her."

At Parcel Plus, a salesgirl remembered asking her if she wanted to insure the package. "No," Beth reportedly replied. "This is just going back to my psycho ex-boyfriend."

A t approximately the same time, at ten minutes after ten, Toolan walked across the tarmac from the small U.S. Airways commuter plane. He held his topcoat close against the wind, a silk scarf flapping at his neck, the fedora at a rakish angle. He was memorable. "He looked like Hugh Jackman coming out of the Waldorf," said Dave Murphy, rental car agent. Toolan approached Murphy and asked about a reservation. "He seemed so nice, so gentle," Murphy said. Toolan had made a reservation, but it was for the day before. In a soft voice, Toolan told Murphy the same tale he told the gang at the Dublin. "I don't believe what happened to me," he reportedly said. "I fell asleep. I was sitting in the Nantucket section and nobody woke me up." According to the Nantucket *Inquirer and Mirror*, Toolan told the rental agent that he was on the island to "straighten out some type of situation." Murphy told that paper that Toolan's manner belied what he was about to do. "There was no indication that he was here to murder anyone," he said. Murphy couldn't find Toolan's reservation. An agent at an adjacent counter overheard the conversation and looked in her company's system. There was Toolan's reservation for a Ford Escape SUV.

◆ ◆ ◆

B eth pulled into the gravel drive of Hawthorne Lane. Her landlady was working in the yard of her house about fifty feet from Beth's cottage. Barbara Kotalac is part of an established Nantucket family. Her son, Rick, owns Brant Point Marine, a fishing and boating supply store on the harbor. Barbara was fond of Beth, and the feeling was mutual. Beth had signed the lease on the cottage the previous March, and Mrs. Kotalac was under the impression that Beth was planning on staying there for the long term.

Barbara Kotalac brushed the dirt off her gardening gloves as Beth climbed out of the Subaru. Her tenant hadn't been in the cottage for at least a week, and Barbara asked how she was doing. Beth explained that she had just dropped off her boyfriend's clothing at Parcel Plus. Barbara gladly lent a sympathetic ear as Beth told her that she was breaking off with him. Though Toolan had been to Beth's cottage, Barbara had never met him. The two women chatted for a few minutes. But Beth had things to do. She had promised her friend Patrick that she would transfer slides of some of his sculpture to the computer. She had promised her parents, due back that evening on the five o'clock ferry from a trip to Upstate New York, that she would prepare dinner. Beth also mentioned to Mrs. Kotalac that she had to pick up Sam at one o'clock.

Beth shrugged and smiled, as if to say "just another nutty day," and turned to walk down the path to the cottage. Barbara Kotalac went back to gardening.

Inside the cottage, Beth went to the guest bedroom that she used as an office. The cottage was a bit musty with the island scents of salt and heath. Beth had a cleaning lady who came over at noon on Mondays, but Beth had called her and told her not to come. It was almost twelve-thirty. One of the reasons Beth had taken the cottage was its isolation. After twenty years in Manhattan, the quiet of Nantucket seemed very attractive. But as she sat at her desk, the silence was unnerving. She looked at her watch and wished that it were time to pick up Sam.

◆ ◆ ◆

Toolan drove the Ford Escape to Washington Street. He pulled into a nearly empty permit parking lot. From there he walked across the street to Brant Point Marine. The back of Rick Kotalac's shop faces the harbor. A cold rain continued to spit and blow off the water. To Toolan's left as he walked in was a glass case filled with sporting knives. He saw what he wanted right away. He pointed to the Frost fishing knife with a four-inch serrated blade and an orange handle. It cost him $13.95. The clerk who sold Toolan the knife told the New York *Daily News* "He looked a little weird."

In the cottage, the aroma of navy beans, thyme, onions, garlic, and pork, ingredients for her parents' dinner, cassoulet, hung in the air. While the ingredients simmered, Beth was in the guest bedroom finishing her project. The aroma and the busy work were comforting; it kept her mind off of being alone. It kept her mind off of him.

Toolan took a left out of the parking lot and turned left again at the Lion's Paw home furnishings onto Main Street. The SUV bounced and shimmied on the cobblestones. He passed Murray's Toggery, its window filled with shirts of Nantucket red and pants with embroidered little whales. He drove past the three identical brick captains' homes. He turned left again around the Civil War monument. On Milk Street, he drove out of town into the open land overgrown with scrub oak. He passed the arrowhead of land of Prospect Hill Cemetery. He slowed and turned on to the gravel drive of Hawthorne Lane.

Barbara Kotalac was still working in the yard when Toolan pulled in. She turned and looked at the incongruous sight before her: a man in a topcoat, dressed, she said, "like a New Yorker."

In his baritone voice, Toolan asked if there was anyone in the cottage. Imbued with a New Englander's suspicions, especially toward someone from New York, Barbara said she didn't know. The Subaru was parked in plain sight.

◆ ◆ ◆

Perhaps the killer twisted the knob to the front door and it opened silently. Maybe he could hear the click of Beth typing in the guest bedroom. She was at her computer. The bedrooms in the cottage, he knew, were at the end of a long, narrow hallway. The layout of the cottage would essentially trap Beth; it was the reason she couldn't escape.

The killer held the knife in his hand and raced down the hall. His mind was set. He knew there was a chance that he would lose his courage or, worse, that Beth would get by him. He needed to do this quickly, to get it over with. Beth heard his footfalls, and pushed away from the desk. By then the killer was through the doorway and coming at her. She instinctively crossed her hands in front of her face. With the first rip at her, the blade deflected off the band of Beth's Rolex watch, the knife nicking the flesh of her left arm. Again, then again, the killer sliced at her. Beth flailed back at him. At least one of the killer's first jabs sliced Beth deep, because there was a great deal of her blood left on a single bed she had in her office. But at some point early on in the attack, the killer backed off for a second. Beth was able to get by him to the hall. The killer grabbed at her head from behind. His palm ripped on the back of Beth's earring. Beth was ten feet away from the front door. Every muscle in her body coiled. She knew her life depended on reaching that doorway.

PART
TWO

CHAPTER SIX

In the spring of 1969 in a village in the northwest corner of Westchester County, the Lochtefeld family piled their suitcases on top of the blue Chevy Bel Air station wagon and headed toward the Massachusetts coast and their future new summer home. In the back of the wagon, along with the children in descending order—Jim, Peter, Beth, Cathy, and Tommy, who ranged in age from twelve to six—was a spare tire, ironing board, art supplies, and the family dog, a red and white Brittany spaniel named Fitzgerald, after JFK. The night before the trip, like a Christmas Eve in June, Beth had trouble sleeping because Judy Lochtefeld, Beth's mother, had told her and the other children that they were going on a boat to an island. Late into the night the Lochtefeld children lay awake with thoughts of rolling ocean waves and distant shores. With sunrise still an hour away, the Chevy wagon backed out of the driveway at 72 Oregon Road in Peekskill, New York. As the tailpipe scraped, the memory of that first trip was imprinted in the collective Lochtefeld family memory.

The story of how the Lochtefelds first discovered Nantucket goes something like this: Beth's father was then a young and struggling fine arts professor at Marymount College in Westchester. With five young children, John Lochtefeld was looking for both an inexpensive vacation spot and a chance to sell his artwork to a summer throng. His first attempt with a seasonal art gallery was in the beach commu-

nity of Lavalette, New Jersey. Though John had been to the
Jersey Shore many times, he had never before tried to sell art
there. He quickly discovered that the working-class, one-
week-a-year family vacationers who frequented the Shore
weren't much of an art crowd. So in the fall of 1968 John
decided to try a gallery in Bay Head. Still on the Shore, but
halfway between New York City and Atlantic City, Bay
Head was a bit more upscale than Lavalette. The situation
wasn't perfect, but John was anxious to get started on his
summer plan. He signed a lease, but fate had other plans.

Sometime during that year, John's brother-in-law, Jimmy
Crecca, came into a bit of money from a land sale. Looking
to reinvest the windfall, Jimmy had heard about real estate
bargains on Nantucket (a far cry from today). He called his
brother-in-law and asked him if he'd like to take a trip to the
island to have a look around.

It was December when John stepped off the ferry onto
Nantucket Island. With the summer crowds long gone, and
the arrival of the island's current zillionares still years away,
the Nantucket that John first experienced was magical. With
its coastal health and its ever-present fog, it seemed as en-
chanting as *Brigadoon*. They stayed in the White House, a
boardinghouse right next to the building that was once the
home of George Pollard, the captain of the whaleship *Essex*
on which Herman Melville based *Moby-Dick*.

That first night, John walked the cobblestone streets of
Nantucket and noticed the shuttered, gray-shingled art galleries. A dreamy idea began to materialize. If the natural
beauty, history, and art community of the island were con-
spiring, it was perhaps the Nantucket night sky that convinced him. That velvet blackness punctuated by brilliant
stars would inspire John's artwork for the next thirty years.
The next morning, John walked into the office of an island
real estate broker and was shown a place down by the wharf.

For the Lochtefeld children, the high point of that first
trip to Nantucket was the ferry ride. The *Nobska* was
a two-hundred-foot-long "coastal steamer" that

seemed to have had sailed right out of a bygone era. In fact, it had. The *Nobska* had been ferrying folks for forty years, except for a short stint in the navy during World War II. During the war, a German U-boat fired a torpedo at the steamer but missed because it went beneath the shallow hull. The ferry was also used as a hospital ship during the Normandy invasion. One story has it that a New Bedford, Massachusetts, soldier was taken aboard the ship after being injured on Omaha Beach. Reviving in the familiar surroundings of the *Nobska*, the soldier thought he was either in heaven or hallucinating that he was home.

To the Lochtefeld children, the boat seemed as big as the *Titanic*. The prized viewing spot was the ship's prow, where a garbage can with a swinging-door lid provided a platform. The children fought for their turn sitting on it. Unlike Leonardo DiCaprio, though, he with his arms thrust out to cut through the wind, Beth held on for dear life as the boat bounced off the chop. But she acted brave and smiled at her siblings.

The trip from Woods Hole to Nantucket took some three and a half hours. Beth and her brothers and sister passed part of the time playing explorer or ship captain or cards. They stole sugar cubes from the concession stand and giggled wildly as they ran along the deck. In those days, the ferry stopped first at Martha's Vineyard, and then sailed on to Nantucket. At both stops, local children dived off the pier and swam up to the boat. Passengers tossed coins from the deck, and the island children dived for them.

Soon, from the top of the garbage can, Beth could see a tiny bit of land rising out of the dark-green, choppy horizon. As the ferry rounded Brant Point and entered the harbor, she first saw the church steeples and widow's walks of Nantucket.

The gallery John had rented was right off Harbor Square at the foot of Lower Main Street on the Straight Wharf. It was a former sail loft, with a space for the gallery on the first floor and two bedrooms above.

The Lochtefeld boys slept up in the eaves, the girls, Beth and Cathy, in one bedroom, and John and Judy in the other. Each morning they'd awaken to the screams of seagulls pulling apart the garbage behind Cap'n Tobey's Chowder House across the alley.

Nantucket in 1969 was a far different place than the ultra-rich theme park it is today. There were none of the twenty-room "cottages," as one *Boston Globe* writer calls them, the mansions that dominate Surfside and every bit of the island's high land. In *Town & Country*, writer David Halber-stam described Nantucket of the late sixties like this: "In the great houses along Hulburt Avenue, our showcase street that runs along the harbor, the houses were, as they always had been, a little worn down, with bathroom sinks stained green by the relentless drip of the water—a reminder of plumbers never summoned."

The Lochtefelds' first summer on Nantucket coincided with the completion of a renovation to the waterfront that would ultimately change the destiny of the island. The con-struction, restoration, and repair of downtown and the wharfs were the brainchild of Walter Beinecke, the so-called Green Stamp King and a kind of Nantucket version of Don-ald Trump. Beinecke's Sherburne Associates began buying up the downtown property in 1964. His vision wasn't all that popular with longtime islanders. When the Lochtefelds ar-rived, islanders still wore protest buttons that read "No Man Is an Island," and "Ban the B." But the truth was, the wharves had been in utter disrepair. And if the business of Nantucket was to thrive into the future, it needed to attract a wealthy clientele, which, as Beinecke's plan progressed, was exactly what it began to do.

All of this high finance was lost on Beth, her brothers, and sister. For the Lochtefeld children, the Nantucket water-front was right out of a dream, filled with pirates and magic and the greatest hiding spots anyone can imagine. Only a few steps away from the gallery, and under a wooden arch-way, stood a band shell that on Sunday nights was home to a

one-hour-long community concert. Children would march
around to the strains of "Georgie Girl" or John Philip Sousa.
The rest of the week the band shell was the haunt of the
Lochtefeld kids. Most of the day was spent playing fort, but
there was work to do, too. Each morning, they would use the
band shell as their workshop to sand their father's sculptures. Surrounding the band shell, rows of hydrangea grew.
In the spring those bushes would burst into pink and blue
flowers. But it was the large, thick green leaves of the hy-
drangeas that were most important to the children. For hide-
and-seek there was no better cover.

When the bandstand lost its thrill, the Lochtefeld kids
would wander over to the Crow's Nest gift shop. There they
would play Shoot the Moon or spend long moments watching the movement of the sixties lava lights, or the hippies
who bought them. For snacks, they'd invade the Penny
Patch, where they ate homemade fudge, rock candy, and
Turkish Taffy. On one corner of Harbor Square was a restau-
rant called Le Crêpe. That first summer on Nantucket, Beth,
Cathy, and Tom befriended the restaurant owner's sons,
Yves and François. That the French boys didn't speak any
English proved to be no obstacle to having fun. (The following summer, Yves and François spoke perfect English.) On
Sundays, after nine o'clock mass at St. Mary's, Judy
Lochtefeld would prepare a picnic lunch and the family
would go off to the beach. Sometimes John would take Beth,
Cathy, and the boys to Smith's Point to fish for blues. There
is a picture of Beth taken after one such expedition. She
wears shorts and a T-shirt and a grin that seems to swallow
her ears. In her hand, she is holding a bluefish that is a third
her size. As recently as a year before she was murdered,
Beth told her brother Tommy that the picture captured one
of her proudest and happiest moments.

All Lochtefeld children learned the fine art of bicycle
building. With the bicycle rental places updating their stock
every few years, the town dump had no shortage of parts.
The Raleigh three-speed was the most prevalent model, and

those parts were interchangeable with just about every other bike. They also learned to swim at the Children's Beach, a rectangle of sand on Nantucket Harbor. There lessons were held regardless of whether it was high or low tide and the odor that accompanied the latter. Emily, the Red Cross swimming teacher would demonstrate the technique of the crawl and the breaststroke on the safety of the sand. As they grew older, they learned lifesaving skills, where they would have to jump off a float fully clothed, shimmy out of their pants, then make an improvised life vest by tying off the cuffs and filling them with air. In those days, it wasn't only the summer kids who took lessons, but some of the islander children, too.

Nantucket is the most insular of societies. Unless you're born and raised on the Nantucket, you're never really accepted as an islander. There is an old Nantucket tale that goes like this: A baby was born on a boat just pulling into Nantucket Harbor. The boy spent every day of his life on the island, becoming a minister. He helped the island's sick and poor, married hundreds of Nantucket couples, and was a pillar of the community until his last day. When the modest obituary ran in *The Inquirer and Mirror* the headline read: "Off-Islander Dies."

But it was, perhaps, during the swimming lessons that the Lochtefeld children began to be considered as close to islanders as you can get. At the Children's Beach, they swam with the Almadobar boys, the Fee kids, and Ricky Bretschneider, who years later would become Nantucket's sheriff. After swimming, all of the children would play baseball on the square of grass behind the beach. When the sun went down, they would sit next to each other and watch the outdoor movie projected on the side of the old shed.

Beth knew everyone, and everyone knew Beth. A chatterbox, she often embarrassed her sister, Cathy, with her openness. The Lochtefeld children were allowed to hitchhike when they reached middle-school age, and hitchhiking is a

favorite mode of transportation on Nantucket. In the backseat of strangers' cars, Beth would not only tell her life story,
but the whole family's story. "Beth would tell them everything," Cathy said.

John called his gallery Shore Bird and themed some
of his artwork to match the name. On pieces of drift-
wood he would paint piping plovers, dunlins, and
sandpipers. Or he would carve sculptures of the shorebirds
out of maple he brought from his yard in Peekskill.

Though John's work was unique, Nantucket might not
have noticed it for some time had it not been for the artist
who lived next door. Bobby Bushong was like no one the
Lochtefeld family had ever encountered. Gay, proud, and
portly, Bobby would often don a tuxedo replete with a top
hat for occasions no grander than its being Tuesday. His skin
was so fair he was almost see-through. When not decked out
in a tux, he wore lace shirts and skimpy shorts that showed
off a pair of legs that better belonged on a Formica table.
Brother Tommy swears he remembers once seeing Bobby
and his friend Buddy coming back from the beach wearing
only dress shirts. Tom was not completely sure until Bobby
and Buddy lifted their arms to wave and their shirttails came
up.

Bobby liked an occasional cocktail. One story about his
drinking has an indelible place in Nantucket lore. He was
pulled over for driving erratically. At the time, Nantucket
police had acquired the services of two police dogs to help
root out people bringing drugs onto the island. The cop who
pulled Bobby over was one of the K9 patrol, his dog in the
car beside him. When Bobby went to court, the judge asked
him to tell what had happened. Bobby said he had been
pulled over by two policemen; one surprisingly, was wearing a fur hat.

Bobby convinced John that he should have an art opening
on the island, "with lots of vodka," he said with his pro-
nounced lisp. And although Judy didn't exactly appreciate

the way Bobby longingly gazed at her husband, she, too, thought it was a good idea.

For Beth, and the other Lochtefeld children, after the initial culture shock, Bobby proved a source of endless entertainment. The kids would watch and listen in rapt wonder as Bobby would have one his many fights with Buddy. Often, saltshakers or dinner plates would fly out of his kitchen window. But he also became a good friend to the Lochtefelds. He wouldn't hear of the children calling him Mr. Bushong as Judy had insisted; instead, it was "Uncle Bobby," and "Uncle Buddy."

For the rest of Beth's life, some of her closest friends were gay men. No doubt, her happy memories of Uncle Bobby had something to do with that.

From the opening of his gallery, John framed works for other artists. He had bundles of moulding material sent from Rockland County or Long Island. His glass suppliers delivered regularly.

Everyone in the family pitched in at the gallery. Along with sanding the sculptures for an hour each morning, Beth and her siblings helped make the frames. First they would cut the joints, using a forty-five-degree miter saw. Then they would block the frame, and, with Elmer's Glue, fasten the sides. Next, they would sink holes and nail the frame together. Finally, they would hide the holes and seams with wax. The family worked like an oiled machine, but the children didn't mind. They knew that their stay in Nantucket depended on their father's summer business. For them, the work they had to do was the smallest of sacrifices. As the island became stratospherically rich, the Lochtefeld kids' feet stayed firmly on the ground.

Beth was never happier than when she was on Nantucket. In the years to come, her life would encompass rings and rings of friends, hundreds of them from all over the globe. But only one bond in Beth's life came anywhere near the one she had with her family. Nantucket was never a resort for Beth. From that first trip when the tailpipe on the Bel Air wagon scraped the driveway, to the swimming lessons with the Fee kids and Ricky Bretschneider, to the nights in the middle of August when she would lie on the porch and gaze up at the Perseids, the midsummer shower of shooting stars, and for the rest of Beth's life, Nantucket was her summer home.

CHAPTER SEVEN

Beth was born Elizabeth Anne Lochtefeld at seven thirty in the evening on April 4, 1960, in St. Vincent's Hospital in Erie, Pennsylvania, the third child of John and Judy Lochtefeld. John then taught in Mercyhurst, a small all-women college in Erie. In 1964, John took an art professor's position at Kutztown State Teachers College, and the Lochtefeld clan moved to a small town called Topton in the Amish Country of Pennsylvania. In Topton, Beth attended kindergarten in a school called Long Swamp Elementary. The Lochtefelds rented a fieldstone Dutch colonial that had a summer kitchen John used as a studio. The landlord lived just down the road on a farm complete with pigs and horses. The man also owned huskies, and in the winter would treat the Lochtefeld children to dogsled rides. Though the surroundings were storybook, John and Judy yearned for their own place, no matter the sacrifice.

In the summer of 1966, they'd get their wish. John was offered a job at Marymount College, a small all-women school on a pretty campus overlooking the Hudson River in New York State. On August 15, 1966, the Feast of the Assumption (the family had attended mass that morning), the Lochtefeld family moved into a house of their own in Westchester County.

Though the town in which Beth grew up is only forty miles north of New York City, it might as well have been four hundred. The landscape of the town of Cortlandt then was mostly rural, a combination of woodland and farmland

and the beginnings of housing developments that brought an influx of families. (It hasn't changed all that much today.) But the history of the area is rich. The Western European view of it began in 1609. In a quiet cove in the river that would bear his name, Henry Hudson anchored the *Half Moon* and became the first white man to set foot on the land that eventually would become the city of Peekskill. The history of the surrounding town of Cortlandt began in 1677, when Stephanus (Jacobus) Van Cortlandt, a merchant and the first American-born mayor of New York City, began purchasing the land there from several tribes of Indians. There are houses and cemeteries in Cortlandt that date to the Revolutionary War. The city of Peekskill was a strategic headquarters of General George Washington, and Abraham Lincoln made a brief stop there on his way to be inaugurated in Washington, D.C. But the area is perhaps best known for being the birthplace of the Crayola crayon, Mel Gibson, and Pee-Wee Herman.

The Lochtefelds lived in a shingle-style home, brown with white trim, on Oregon Road, a winding, relatively busy route. The owners of the house before them were a handicapped man and his wife. Ramps for his wheelchair were built next to the steps. The whole neighborhood knew the sound of the school bell attached to the house next to the back door. The sound of that bell would have the Lochtefeld kids scampering home.

Beth attended Van Cortlandtville Elementary School and Walter Panas High School. She did the things then that little girls growing up in the 1960s did in upper Westchester County. She rode her bike down a secluded street, one that later in the sixties would be dubbed Reefer Road, stopping to inspect a lizard or strange insect that caught her eye. Sometimes she fished with her brothers off Pumphouse Bridge, less than a half mile's walk from her backyard. Beyond the bridge was what the Lochtefeld children called "a mountain," but was really just a steep, heavily wooded slope, part of the Hudson Highlands, the foothills of the Catskill Mountains. On those wonderful snowy days, when school had been canceled, she'd join the rest of the neighborhood kids with their Flexible Flyers, and head down the double dip of Lockwood Hill in the back of a neighbor's house on Smith Road.

Beth took piano lessons and sang in chorus in school. She ran track and played intramural volleyball, though she'd be the first to tell you she wasn't the greatest athlete. There is a story on her memorial Web site about a volleyball game in which the ball landed between Beth and a teammate, both of them thinking the other would make the play. For a moment the teammates exchanged a silent stare, neither knowing whether to accept or assign the blame. Then Beth cracked up laughing, breaking the tension.

All of the Lochtefeld children were in scouting; the boys were Cub and Boy Scouts, Beth and Cathy were Brownies and Girl Scouts. Judy Lochtefeld, once a Girl Scout herself, was a troop leader. Not to be outdone, John, for a while, led the boys' Boy Scout troop. Obviously, five children separated by six years is an enormous financial drain, and scouting was the inexpensive way to keep the kids entertained. Beth and her sister went on hikes and sold cookies. Most times, John used the family Bel Air station wagon to commute to school in Tarrytown. So when Beth was twelve, mom took command of an old Opel sedan, which chugged along on a few cylinders less than the full complement. With the troop, Judy piled the mileage on the Opel. They went on trips to the Amish Country in Pennsylvania, to Philadelphia and Washington, D.C. As a Scout leader, Judy was enthusiastic, and her enthusiasm rubbed off on her girls. Beth and Cathy excelled at scouting, and both rose to the highest level: First Class Scout.* When Beth was a sophomore in high school, she received a letter from the then new president of the United States, Jimmy Carter, congratulating her on her achievement. Though Beth was extremely proud, she mostly kept the letter a secret. Being a Girl Scout in high school wasn't the coolest thing that could happen to you.

*In 1980, the Gold Award replaced First Class Scout as the Girl Scouts' highest recognition.

Much of Beth's work ethic came from her mother. Judy Lochtefeld had graduated from Michigan State University, where she obtained the antiquated degree of Homemaker. When her children were old enough to take care of themselves, she took a job as a substitute teacher in the local school system. Later, as the children began leaving home for college, she went back to school to obtain her master's degree and became a full-time teacher in the elementary school. Organized and supportive, Judy would often tape motivational slogans on the refrigerator, like "When the going gets tough, the tough get going." But she also had a sense of humor. She liked to tell the story about an introduction to a first-grader who thought he heard "Mrs. Octopus" rather than Mrs. Lochtefeld.

Also hung on the refrigerator was a "chore sheet," and each of the Lochtefeld children was expected to do his or her part. Both the boys and the girls learned how to wash and mend their own clothing. Beth made some of her own outfits. No one would ever confuse Peekskill of the seventies with John Travolta's Brooklyn. The disco fashion of platform shoes, gabardine pants, and printed shirts never did quite make it that far north. But, from very early on, Beth had her own sense of style. In middle school, several times a year, Beth and four or five of her friends would shun the usual sweaters, corduroys, and hiking boots of the day and wear real, honest-to-goodness, dress-up dresses. "Even the teachers would remark about how nice they looked," said John Gaccione, a childhood friend of Beth's.

The Lochtefelds spent each Christmas Eve with friends of the family, the Casperians and the Boyles, who, like the Lochtefelds, had a gaggle of kids. Sherri Casperian and Nancy Boyle were among Beth's best friends. Aram Casperian was a principal in the local school system and Judy's boss when she was a substitute. Later, when Judy was teaching full-time, Mr. Casperian was school superintendent. Mr. Boyle was in the cement business. Usually the Christmas Eve get-together was held at his home, an enormous converted barn with a master bedroom in a silo, and a game room that had a pool table, air hockey, and a stereo that would be played much too loud for the parents' taste. Though Nancy Boyle represented Peekskill's upper crust (in Peekskill, "upper crust" and "down-to-earth" can occur simultaneously), Beth's relationships were never based on what someone had, or where they came from. Her practice of judging people on their merits and not their race or economic echelon, came, perhaps, from her father.

The town of Cortlandt has a history of racial divide. In 1949, a riot exploded after a Paul Robeson concert held at Lakeland Acres, just north of Peekskill.

In the summer of 1970, an uproar occurred in Cortlandt over foster care of a few children who had resided in a St. Joseph's Orphanage in Peekskill. St. Joseph's announced that it was placing some of their wards in a private home in an affluent section of Cortlandt called Evergreen Knolls. One hundred and fifty local residents gathered in a show of protest against the plan. When Beth's father read of the protest, he sat at the kitchen table and typed out a letter to the editor of the Peekskill *Evening Star*, which read in part:

To the Editor:
   You wonder what reasoning leads to such an action. Is it the cost of removing a small parcel of property from the local tax rolls. The cost to any of us doesn't amount to much, perhaps a fraction of what most of us spend on beer or cigarettes in the course of a year.
   Is it the children themselves? I see them almost daily in our community. They deliver this newspaper, they are in the local Boy Scout troop, they play on our public school athletic teams and you see them at the local parish church on Sunday mornings. From what I can observe they are rather normal kids who are trying to grow up. They seem to be doing a rather decent job of it.
   I think some of us find our lives a little richer for having known them.

One wonders what these petitioning residents say to their own children as they work to exclude a handful of homeless children from their neighborhood.

John F. Lochtefeld
Peekskill

Patti Engel was in Beth's Girl Scout troop, and was a close friend to Beth throughout their school years. Years after the controversy, Patti would marry one of the boys who lived in the foster home. Edwin Sambrana, Patti's husband, cut Mr. Lochtefeld's letter out of the paper thirty-five years ago, and has kept it since.[†]

In the eighth-grade chorus, Beth had an African-American friend named Jeffrey Cuffee. In the days before the big yearly chorus recital, the young soloist had trouble hitting the high note. It seemed the harder he tried, the more his voice would crack. Jeffrey was painfully shy, and had trouble fitting in with the white students in chorus. But Beth never let someone's shyness get in the way of a possible friendship. At first, he was taken aback by Beth's boldness. But soon he looked forward to their chats before and after practice. They were also in the same honors classes together, and there a real friendship formed. The day before the recital, Jeffrey was disconsolate, ready to quit. But Beth, weaned on a childhood of positive slogans from her mother, would have none of her friend's negative talk. "You can do it," she said in a pep talk that afternoon. Beth reminded him how beautiful a voice he had, that all he had to do was open his mouth and let it free. It was hard not to be swayed by Beth when she had a cause. The next night at the recital, Cuffee hit the note perfectly, with only one slight variation. Jeffrey's voice had changed overnight, and he hit the note with a beautiful bass, not the soprano as planned.

◆ ◆ ◆

[†]Patti and Edwin Sambrana are still married and live in Maryland, and they supplied a copy of the letter to the author.

Though Beth loved her summers on Nantucket, at the end of each school year she'd go through pangs of separation anxiety: She hated leaving her Peekskill friends behind. One of Beth's best friends all through middle school and high school was Karen Russo, who remembered that she and Beth would cry at the end of each school year. But Beth would promise Karen she would write, and write she did, as many as eight letters over the course of the summer. "Sometimes it was just a note telling me about something fun she was doing," Karen remembered. "Sometimes the letters were a couple of pages long." At summer's end, she'd go through the same pangs with her Nantucket friends. Twice a year, every year growing up, Beth would have to say good-bye to her entire world.

CHAPTER EIGHT

By the time Beth entered high school, she was tall and just on the fuller side of slender with blond hair cut in a kind of wing style that was made popular by *Charlie's Angels,* blow-dryers, and curling irons. She wore oversized aviator glasses, some with sparkly frames, and had a way of bounding when she walked, "like Tigger," said Karen Russo. As is usually the case with girls in high school, boys became a major part of the experience.

Beth's first real love was the star fullback for the Walter Panas Panthers. Outwardly, at least, it looked as though Beth and Tony Maresco were a mismatched pair. As outgoing as Beth was, Tony was reserved. "He had the goods," said Karen Russo. "He just didn't flaunt it." Beth was fair and blond, Tony had a full head of black hair and a five o'clock shadow that would arrive sometime in the early afternoon— his nickname was the "Java Man." And Beth was about 5'9", at least an inch or two taller than Tony.

They did have some things in common. They were both honor students and took the same classes throughout high school. There was, at least on Tony's part, something of a friendly academic rivalry, a competition in which he usually finished second-best. Beth ranked consistently among the top students of her class. Tony, no slouch himself, would come in at number ten or twelve on the academic ladder. They shared an interest in music; both played instruments. Here, however, Tony had the better of Beth. While Beth never really mastered the piano, Tony was a professional

guitarist—if you can call professional a series of gigs at
VFW halls playing Sinatra and Tom Jones tunes while wearing leisure suits with ruffled shirts.

Tony first declared his interest in Beth before football
practice one day. John Gaccione was the center on the team,
and he and Tony were having a conversation in the locker
room. The topic was the approaching fall dance, an event to
which Tony didn't have a date. John Gaccione was perhaps
Beth's best male friend. They'd known each other since seventh grade. "People had the impression we were more than
just friends," John remembered. Uncharacteristically, John,
who was as reserved as Tony, and perhaps even shyer, played
matchmaker. "Maybe Beth Lochtefeld would like to go with
you," the center said.

It's not clear whether Tony's trio performed at that dance,
or at another one, but Tony clearly remembered that his
band's Cream medley with the big "I Shot the Sheriff" moment usually brought the house down. Maybe it was the
sight of Tony on stage that stirred something in Beth. From
the fall dance on, she and Tony were inseparable. "When
you saw one, you pretty much saw the other," remembered
Karen Russo.

They might have been together all the time, but they were
hardly ever alone. Friday nights were the nights out with the
gang. Beth and Tony might ride in Tony's green '72 Ford
Pinto with two hundred thousand on the odometer down to
the Peekskill riverfront. There they would meet up with
Jimmy Fleitz, Karen Russo, John Gaccione, slip Marshall
Tucker or Lynyrd Skynyrd into the eight-track, and crank it
up when "Can't You See" or "Free Bird" played. Most of
these trips were beer-free (at least sources would have you
believe), for fear of getting busted and tossed off the football
team. But the gang did laugh at the jerks who drank too
much beer and played roughhouse on the train tracks. Sometimes, Beth and Karen would go to Huckleberry's, a restaurant in nearby Yorktown Heights, where they would share
some appetizers and talk about their boyfriends. Other

nights were spent at a bowling alley down on Route 202, or in the new mall across Route 6, where they saw *Star Wars* and *National Lampoon's Animal House* in one of the movie theaters.

When there wasn't football practice, volleyball, lacrosse, student government council, or some other after-school activity, Beth, Tony, and the others would head to Onofrio's Pizzeria, where they still spun the dough in the air like the old-time places. One evening at Onofrio's, Beth realized it was getting late and suggested they'd better "hit the road." For the giggles, Jimmy and Tony ran right out the door and started slapping North Division Street, causing something of a traffic jam.

Tony liked being with Beth's family almost as much as he liked being with Beth. The fact that John Lochtefeld tapped the maple trees in his yard late each winter amazed him. "He would make maple syrup and maple candy," Tony remembered wistfully. You could set your watch on Tony being at the Lochtefeld house on Sunday mornings when Judy would make stacks of pancakes. "It was the first time I had real maple syrup," he said.

He also clearly remembers a rhubarb pie that Judy and Beth made from scratch. It seemed to Tony, every time he went to the Lochtefeld home the family was engaged in some activity: John and the boys framing pictures, Beth, Cathy, and Mom in the kitchen baking. "It was so interesting being around them," Tony remembered. Tony especially took to Beth's younger brother, Tommy. They would talk about lacrosse or toss the football for hours.

Saturday night dates with Beth were often spent going no farther than the couch in the Lochtefeld living room. There they'd watch TV or play Monopoly with the family. It wasn't like they wouldn't go out. They did. But Tony once made the mistake of telling Beth's parents that he was taking their daughter to see the movie *Taxi Driver*. The tale of a twisted cabby played by Robert De Niro, and a twelve-year-old prostitute, portrayed by Jodie Foster, didn't sit well with

Beth's parents. "That idea got shot down pretty quick," Tony said. But any acrimony on John and Judy's part would disappear when Tony showed up on Saturday evenings at St. Columbanus and attend mass with their family.

As is their wont to do, the days and nights of high school flew by. Beth often wore Tony's football jacket, with the word "Captain" stitched on the sleeve. Tony gave her his varsity ring. There was talk, as there always is in high school hallways, of Tony and Beth being the perfect couple and destined to be together forever. Beth brought the best out of Tony. Though quiet to the rest of the world, Tony found it easy to open up to Beth. There were long, lingering moments at Onofrio's Pizzeria. They held hands, and stole kisses behind the school, and, no doubt, a bit more. Beth and Tony double-dated often with Jimmy Fleitz and his girl, the evening festivities confined to bombing around in the Pinto or Jimmy's '65 Buick Special. Perhaps it was in the back of the Buick, or on one of the walks behind the school, where Tony began to think about a life with Beth. But Beth's vision of the future wasn't so constrained. There was too much to do, too much to see, to even think about settling down. Sure she loved Tony. But they were only in high school. There was still senior year to think about. Beth and Tony's senior year would be one talked about for a very long time.

CHAPTER NINE

Appropriately, the tumultuous year began with the bonfire. Held annually before the homecoming game against rival Lakeland High School Hornets, it was more than a ritual, it was a rite of passage. For a week beforehand, classmates would gather logs, wooden ladders, election signs, street signs, and anything else that would burn and wasn't nailed down. In Beth's junior year, the students stretched the limits of flammability. They found the carcass of an old MG in the woods behind the high school, hooked it up to a chain, and pulled it from the trees. That afternoon a bunch of the football players pushed the MG onto the woodpile. Somehow the local fire department got wind of the plan and showed up before the fire was lit. "Obviously, they weren't going to let us set it on fire," remembered Tony. Some of the team members then pushed the MG down an embankment where it came to rest next to the football field. It stayed there as a kind of monument to past glory for at least two home games. As it happened, the Walter Panas Panthers were lucky to play any games that year.

Rooting for the Panthers could be heartbreaking. Not that they were bad; on the contrary, they were a pretty solid team with a winning record Beth's junior year. But the students and players never knew how long the season would last. In that junior year, the school budget failed to be approved by voters three or four times, threatening the suspension of all after-school activities. With little industry in the area, most of the burden of paying for education fell on the homeowners—a good portion of whom were retirees. Because the local taxes were so high, the welfare of the football team garnered little sympathy, at least within the community. As far as the students were concerned, football was paramount to the success of the school year. The games were faithfully attended. Even the halftime shows were elaborate, with a marching band, twirlers, and a panther mascot. Despite the budget battles, the Panthers completed the season Beth's junior year. They weren't so lucky the next fall.

T*he New York Times* summed up the 1977 teachers' strike in Beth's senior year best: "The action by the 450-member Lakeland Federation of Teachers produced some of the stiffest jail sentences and fines ever meted out to teachers. It produced a dramatic taxpayer reaction to increasing education costs . . . And, as it droned on, the bitterness multiplied until many saw it as an insurmountable obstacle to a return to normal."

It got pretty nasty.

It was the first teachers' strike within New York State in which the Taylor Law, forbidding public employees to strike, was invoked. Teachers were fined two days' pay for every day they were on strike. Union leaders and teachers were thrown in jail for thirty days. There were incidents of striking teachers hurling themselves in front of scabs' cars. One striker was run over and had to be taken to the hospital. Fistfights between substitute and striking teachers were commonplace. As were pushing and screaming matches at school board meetings. Students of Walter Panas staged sit-ins and, in late October 1978, a student walkout, in which, according to some who were there, Beth and her pals participated. Substitute teachers tried hard, most acting out of concern for the students rather than monetary remuneration. Even Judy Lochtefeld crossed the picket line and taught at the middle school. She didn't think the children should suffer. But some of the substitutes were substandard. "A substitute teacher asked me to define some term in trigonometry, and I made up the definition—she said I was right," one high school football player was quoted as saying in *The New York Times*. Other temporary teachers made up their own grading systems or taught classes in which they had little or no training.

But what was at stake for Beth, and the other members of her gang, was more than just scholastics, even college admissions. The strike risked school memories that would last the rest of their lives.

At first it looked as though the work stoppage would end the football season and the activities that surrounded it. Substitute coaches tried their best, but the season, one that was filled with promise, sputtered, then stalled. The Panthers lost the first game 2–0, on a safety. The strike had taken the heart out of the team. Tony, who was "All-County" that year in football, remembered that, though the substitute coach was knowledgeable about the game, circumstances limited the team's offense. "It was Tony to the left, Tony to the right, Tony up the middle," he said.

Every morning, students walked past the picket line. They saw their favorite teachers and coaches angry and locked out. The students couldn't help but feel bitter and targeted. One afternoon, the substitute football coach asked Tony to move his pickup truck in the parking lot. Purely by mistake, Tony got in the wrong truck, one owned by another substitute. The teacher thought Tony was a striking teacher looking to vandalize his pickup. There were a few scary moments with heated threats before the misunderstanding was straightened out.

"I think the most difficult part during the strike was when buses had to pass through the picket line," said Fran Sullivan Shultz, an English teacher at Panas for over thirty years. "It was most difficult for everyone."

Although Beth might have participated in the student walkout, according to one person close to the family, "The Lochtefelds were not into civil disobedience." But Beth wasn't about to stand by and let her senior year dissolve.

That year she was the vice president of the student council.
She took her position seriously. During the strike there was a
series of meetings between teachers, school board members,
and taxpayers, most of which were less than civil. The most
vocal were the retired members of the community. It was to
this crowd that Beth decided to speak her piece.

The meeting was held in Lakeland Middle School. The
auditorium was packed, with the crowd spilling out into the
hallway. Beth had worked hard on the speech the night before. She was nervous. But she was steadied by resolve. Her
cause was just. For her and her classmates, this meeting
wasn't about teachers' salaries or higher taxes; it was about
saving senior year. Some of her classmates had gathered
outside the school with signs, one of which read: NEGOTIATE
NOW. SCHOOL IS FOR EDUCATION, NOT FOR LABOR DISPUTES.
The inside of the auditorium hummed like an enormous bee-
hive. Beth climbed onto the stage. Her voice cracked a bit as
she began. She said that a big, important part of everyone's
high school career was the football season, and the bonfire.
Just the mention of the football season, and the thought of
the pinch in their pockets it caused, brought forth from the
crowd a cascade of catcalls and hisses. The derisiveness
gained intensity until it drowned out Beth's words. The
strike had to be settled for football to resume, for the bonfire
to be lit. This crowd wanted no part in settling the strike.
They didn't want to pay one cent more in taxes. What was
most disturbing was the rudest of the jeers directed at Beth
came from students' parents and elderly residents of the
town. Tears began to well in Beth's eyes. She looked around
for help. At first, no one came to her aid. It was unexpected,
this repulsive reaction. Her classmates sat in the back row of
the auditorium in shocked silence. Maybe it was lucky that
Tony wasn't there. His dear girlfriend held the paper on
which the speech was written tight to her chest. With her
cheeks streaked with tears, Beth began to shake. "It was
sad," said one person close to Beth who was in the auditorium that day. "She completely fell apart." It was not until
several moments later that the school principal, William

Spinelli, came to her aid. He put his arms around Beth, told her not to pay attention to them, and helped her off of the stage.

In the spring, in a show of solidarity, teachers, students, and even some of the community put on *Camelot,* the musical. The show was performed at what is now the Van Cortlandtville Elementary School auditorium. The casting was unusual. A student played Lancelot, a reading and music teacher was Arthur, the superintendent and assistant superintendent of schools were dressed as castle guards. But Walter Panas was far from being "a most congenial spot," as the song goes. "It was a defining year for the kids," said Ms. Sullivan Shultz. "I believe they grew up more quickly that fall than they would have during any other year."

In the end, there were no winners. The teachers settled for a mere one percent pay raise. When the strike was finally over—it had lasted an incredible forty-one days—the substitutes were ungratefully told that day to clean out their desks and to be out of the school by lunchtime. They weren't even allowed to pick up their paychecks. Animosity amongst teachers toward the school board lasted for years. But it was the students who suffered the most.

Youth is resilient, though. By the time the Christmas break came, the strike had lodged itself somewhere deep in teenage gray matter. Though Beth would always remember that horrible moment in front of the school board meeting, she, too, wouldn't dwell on it. For one thing, Judy Lochtefeld wouldn't let her. No doubt a motivational slogan or two was taped to the refrigerator urging Beth to move on. Plus, there were other things to think about. Beth was in the chorus, and there were Christmas and spring concerts. And, there was the senior class production of *Hello, Dolly!* in which Beth performed. The school treated the cast and crew, which included Tony and Jimmy Fleitz, who worked the spotlights, to a Broadway performance of the show starring Carol Channing. To the show Beth and the rest of the students wore T-shirts that read "Hello, Dolly" on the front, and

"So Long, Dearie," the title of one of the show's songs, on the back. When Channing was taking her bows, a Panas student ran up to the stage and handed her a T-shirt. The star proudly showed both sides of the shirt to the delirious crowd. Beth gushed about that moment for weeks.

Beth also took on the job of senior editor of the yearbook *Paw Prints*. More important, there was the prospect of starting college the following fall. Tony and Beth talked often about colleges. Tony had his sights set on West Point. There he would play football and ready himself for a military career. Beth's college dream was one stirred by stories from her brother Peter and her father.

In the spring of senior year, Tony played lacrosse and Beth was busy with student government and putting together the yearbook. One of her jobs was to poll the students for categories like "Class Clown" and "Most Likely to Succeed." Beth and Tony were chosen "Best Couple," and no one thought the contest was rigged. The picture in the yearbook shows Tony dipping Beth backward; both wear mischievous smiles. Under Beth's graduation picture in the yearbook she lists Nantucket and "the brave and crazy wings of youth," a line from Jackson Browne's antinuclear anthem of the midseventies. In fact, Jackson Browne played the constant theme in Beth's life then. Her favorite album was *Late for the Sky,* with Browne's mellow sound and haunting words a comfort to her.

The senior prom was held at Colonial Manor, a local restaurant and catering hall. Beth wore a red dress that she made herself. To the best of his recollection, Tony wore a blue tuxedo. (The tuxedo was actually fuchsia.) Beth and Tony, Jimmy and his girl, drove that night after the prom across the Bear Mountain Bridge and up the winding road to the summit of Storm King Mountain. There they opened a bottle of champagne and toasted the stars. As they finished the bottle the sun came up over the Hudson Valley. From that vantage, you can see down the Hudson River for miles. Like their future, it seemed welcoming and limitless. Fueled by adrenaline for the occasion, they piled back into the car and drove north to Lake Taghkanic, where they spent the day.

Beth and Tony's relationship would last through the summer of 1978, but would begin to wane when both went away to school. As is the case with many high school romances, college would prove too large of an impediment. According to Tony, their parting was mutual but "maybe more mutual for her." According to friends, Beth told Tony she was breaking it off in a letter. By then Tony had begun classes at West Point and Beth was already at Notre Dame. Regardless of how or when, both knew it was inevitable. Beth and Tony were smart enough to know that there was too much distance, and too much to explore, to stay a couple. What was obvious to friends was that Tony took the breakup harder than Beth. The summer following the split, Tony and Jimmy Fleitz hitchhiked all the way to Nantucket to visit Beth. It was an interesting journey that included a ride with a beer-swigging truck driver of questionable intelligence and an eight-mile walk to the Woods Hole ferry.

Once on the island, however, Beth and the Lochtefelds opened their house and hearts. At the end of their stay, Tony and Jimmy pooled all their money, about eight bucks, and bought the ingredients to make a lasagna from a recipe of Tony's father. Somehow Tony remembered the proportions correctly, and the extended family enjoyed the meal.

If Tony saw Beth again after that Nantucket trip, he can't remember it. In the years that followed, their lives took them in different directions. Tony left West Point after only a semester. He would later marry, have children, and eventually move to California. For Beth, it would be first Notre Dame, then the brightly lit skyline of Manhattan that beckoned. High school romances, however, don't fade easily. When Tony talked of Beth recently, there was an unmistakable wistful quality in his voice. According to family and friends, Beth, too, thought of her high school sweetheart often. Apparently, those once-in-a-while smiles lasted the rest of Beth's life.

CHAPTER TEN

Throughout the sixties and seventies, the neighborhood in which Tom Toolan grew up was as upwardly mobile as an escalator and a model of gentrification. Not everybody was thrilled with Park Slope's metamorphosis, however. Some native Brooklynites grieved when local saloonkeepers took down neon Rheingold beer signs and hung ferns in their windows instead.

Still, if you had to pick a neighborhood in New York City in the 1970s to spend your childhood, Park Slope would be a pretty good choice.

A little history: In the 1850s, a railroad magnate named Edwin C. Litchfield owned most of the land that is now Park Slope. On it he built an Italian-style villa, which overlooked his expanse of property that sloped all the way to New York Harbor.

In 1860, the City of Brooklyn forced Litchfield to give up twenty-four acres of his land—and the villa—because of a planned five-hundred-and-fifty-acre park. Brooklyn hired Central Park architects Frederick Law Olmsted and Calvert Vaux. The main entrance to Prospect Park, Grand Army Plaza, was patterned after the Arc de Triomphe. In later years, Prospect Park would include the Brooklyn Museum and Brooklyn Botanical Garden.

After the Brooklyn Bridge was built in 1883 connecting Brooklyn to Manhattan, Park Slope became home to the upper reaches of German and English society. Mansions were built alongside Prospect Park. Thomas Adams Jr., the Chiclets candy king, was one of the more notable mansion owners. Your distance from the park measured your wealth. Three- and four-story single-family homes called brownstones housed Irish and Italian immigrants who worked as servants for the parkside gentry.

In the 1950s, white flight from the neighborhood left a large portion of the brownstones to be converted into rooming houses. But the downturn of property values in Park Slope would last less than a decade. In other sections of Brooklyn, public housing projects fostered poverty and crime. No projects were built in Park Slope. By the early sixties, what became known as the Brownstone pioneers, some of whom were artists and teachers, bought the houses at prices as low as twenty-five thousand dollars and began long-term renovations. As the brownstones were returned to their original condition, detailed with wainscoting and beveled glass, property values exploded. By the 1970s the brownstones had increased fivefold in value. In 1973, parts of the neighborhood near the park were designated a historic district, ensuring that the housing would look the same forever, and that boosted property values even more. By the 1980s, Park Slope was one of the most desirable neighborhoods in New York City. Wall Streeters flocked there; so did professionals, doctors, and lawyers. The wealth of the neighborhood formed an impenetrable wall, keeping the black and Hispanic inner-city residents at bay. Throughout the 1980s and into the 1990s, Park Slope would remain remarkably isolated from the incendiary events that surrounded it: the crack cocaine devastation of inner-city Brooklyn neighborhoods like Bedford-Stuyvesant and Brownsville, the Crown Heights race riots. There was no limit to how high real estate prices would go in Park Slope. There a number of lucky Brooklyn schoolteachers became millionaires just by being in the right place and buying at the right time.

The children of those brownstone pioneers were afforded schools and comforts that their hardworking parents never

dreamed of. The children of the wealthy who moved into
Park Slope already had a sense of entitlement in place. In
simple terms, some of the Park Slope children of the 1970s
were just plain spoiled brats. Park Slope, as one real estate
writer put it, is a small town with a cosmopolitan agenda.

Both Toolan's father and mother were teachers. In
1967, Dolores Toolan, Tom's mother, started a private school in a local church on Carroll Street, a
quaint Park Slope block lined with brownstones. The school
actually began as more of a day-care center for prekinder-
gartners. Mrs. Toolan's oldest child, Tom's sister, Tara, was
then three years old. It was an ingenious way for Dolores
Toolan to work and raise a daughter at the same time. Necessity is not only the mother of invention, it often generates
money. The timing of Mrs. Toolan's idea was perfect. As the
neighborhood became more affluent, the Carroll Street
School gained in stature and enrollment. By the midseventies, the Carroll Street School had expanded to the sixth
grade. Outgrowing the church basement, the school moved
to a building down the block on Carroll Street. The school's
growth was only beginning.

In 1982, the hundred-year-old Berkeley Institute, a prestigious Brooklyn preparatory school, came to the Carroll
Street School with an offer. The partnership formed the
Berkeley Carroll School. To give some idea of how competitive enrollment to the school has become, applications for
the preschool program of the Berkeley Carroll School are
made available six months before the school year starts. Parents of prospective "students," three- and four-year-olds,
sleep in cars and sleeping bags outside the school office the
night before the applications are made available. And appli-
cation by no means guarantees admission.

As the founder of the Carroll Street School, then director
of admissions of Berkeley Carroll, Dolores Toolan found
herself in a unique position to help influential people. Years
later, Toolan would boast that his mother counted her

Prospect Park West neighbor and United States senator Chuck Schumer among her closest friends.

Tom Toolan would grow up in an atmosphere of intense social climbing.

Sources paint a confusing picture of Toolan's relationship with his mother. On one hand, people close to Toolan describe him as a devoted son who often spoke of Dolores in loving terms. He told at least one girlfriend that his mom, in her younger days, resembled Marilyn Monroe. He liked to tell the story of how his mother wouldn't give up when she first became interested in his dad, no matter how "hard to get" Mr. Toolan played. Years later, at dinner dances at the New York Athletic Club, Toolan would watch with tender pride as his father led his mother gracefully around the dance floor. Toolan was supposedly quite a dancer himself. One girlfriend of Toolan's remembers him constantly on the phone with his mom. But other friends say his relationships with both his mother and father were frosty at best. Several times, in group therapy, Toolan made mention of his mother's age as a factor in keeping them apart. Dolores Toolan was thirty-eight when she gave birth to her son. To the group Toolan described both his parents as detached, aloof, and with divided attention. The Carroll Street School brought money and prestige to the family. But it also brought the hot light of scrutiny by Park Slope society. To his group, Toolan said from a very early age he was expected to behave and purport himself as a child of privilege should.

Those who knew him as an adult say that Toolan talked in a constant monologue about his childhood. He waxed eloquent about playing stickball, and he called Prospect Park his "backyard." As many of us do, he inflated some of the tales. As a kid, he said, he roamed the streets of Brooklyn, even wandering into neighboorhoods outside the imaginary walls around Park Slope, trying to be perceived as a little tougher, a little more streetwise, than he actually was. He'd tell people he was from Brooklyn, but conveniently leave out that he was from a section of the borough as docile as any bucolic suburb. But, years later, a girlfriend did believe him when he told her that he was introduced to heroin on the streets of Park Slope in his early teens. She said he told her he that he used the drug on and off into his adult years.

In the fall, Prospect Park West is covered by a gold and red canopy of changing leaves. In the winter the bare limbs of the trees hang over the street like the bones of giant skeletal hands. By spring, the Norway maples convert the thoroughfare into a lush, green tunnel. With Prospect Park on his left and the stately homes and apartment buildings on his right, a young Tom Toolan walked to school dressed in a uniform of gray flannel trousers, blue button-down shirt, plaid tie, and a sweater with St. Saviour School insignia. He was always neat and pressed, his hair short but with a blond cowlick. Like the other kids, he carried his books in a knapsack on his back.

For a Catholic family of any means in Park Slope, there was no other choice but to send your child to St. Saviour. Going to school there was as much a part of growing up as going to mass on Sunday.

And, on Sunday, the Toolan family attended a packed mass at St. Saviour, a small but beautiful church with a soaring ceiling, hundred-year-old stained glass windows, and iconic murals. Squeezed into the pews alongside them where folks with names straight out of a Dublin phonebook. But as the neighborhood became more affluent, the blue-collar Irish Americans of other sections of New York City looked upon their rich Park Slope cousins as lace-curtain, an unflattering term that implies forgetting one's simple roots.

Still, lace curtain or no, the School Sisters of Notre Dame, the nuns who staffed the school, condemned any self-importance. The nuns took no nonsense, made sure their charges learned the basics by rote, and lectured at length on the penalty to those who strayed from God's narrow path. It was a lesson Tom Toolan would forget.

◆ ◆ ◆

The Toolan family first lived in a modest apartment at 44 Prospect Park West. In the 1970s, coinciding with the popularity of Mrs. Toolan's school, the family moved up the block to a building at 35 Prospect Park West.

They traded up.

The land on which 35 Prospect Park West stands was owned by the Tilyou family, who also owned the famed Steeplechase Park in Coney Island, Brooklyn. The building faces Prospect Park, and is just a couple of blocks from the park's ornate entrance. Emory Roth, a Hungarian-born architect and the preeminent builder of fashionable apartment houses in New York City, designed the building. Much of the elegance of Park and Fifth Avenue in Manhattan is credited to Roth (Emery Roth & Sons were coarchitects of the World Trade Center). Throughout the building's existence, Brooklyn's elite have called it home. The doyenne of the Tilyou family, Mary E. Tilyou, lived there until she died at 103 in the 1950s. Another longtime resident was John L. Smith, the chairman of the board of Charles Pfizer & Company in the days when the drug manufacturer became a giant selling penicillin. Part owner of the Brooklyn Dodgers, Smith might have been able to see Abe Stark's HIT SIGN, WIN SUIT sign in right-center in Ebbets Field from the window of his apartment. Frank Frackenthal, acting president of Columbia University, lived there, as did a plethora of Brooklyn bank presidents, prominent physicians, and well-known lawyers. James M. Fawcett, who represented the Lindbergh baby killer, and James B. Donovan, who negotiated the exchange of a Soviet colonel for American U-2 pilot Francis Gary Powers during the height of the cold war, both lived in the building.

While the fortunes of the brownstones that surrounded the building dipped and climbed dramatically, 35 Prospect Park West was always a solid fortress of wealth.

Perhaps Toolan's closest childhood friend was Jim Mannix. The Mannix family lived three floors above the Toolans at 35 Prospect Park West. Almost identical in age, Toolan

and Mannix were, physically at least, a mismatched pair.
Classmates in high school, the childhood friends once posed
for a photograph of the staff of the school paper. Toolan is at
least a foot taller than his pal. Where Mannix is full-faced,
with a mane of dark hair, Toolan has wavy blond hair and his
face is long and thin.

Without exception, tenants in 35 Prospect Park West were
at least upper-middle class. But even in a building of afflu-
ence, the Mannixes' wealth stood out. Jim Mannix's father
was driven to work in a limousine. The driver was a black
man by the name of James who wore a chauffeur's uniform,
complete with cap. James was often at the disposal of the
younger Mannix, and, by extension, Toolan. Mr. Mannix accumulated his wealth by savvy real estate investments, and,
possibly, gas station ownership. By all accounts, he was extremely well liked in the neighborhood. He kept a pocketful
of green shamrock key chains, which he would hand to people he'd meet during his daily travels. The younger Mannix
seemed to inherit much of his father's pleasant characteristics. He also had his father's sense of commerce. In high
school, along with Toolan, Mannix started his own business,
performing as a clown at children's parties. They were paid
twenty-five or thirty dollars for each gig.

Toolan perfected some magic tricks for the act, including
pulling a rabbit out of a top hat. Team Mannix and Toolan
had business cards made up, and apparently the act was
good enough to keep them busy for a few years. But on at
least one occasion Toolan showed that his clown had a spite-
ful side.

Mannix had called Toolan one day about a job at a party
that came up that same afternoon. Toolan told his friend that
he was busy with other things and couldn't work. According
to a friend who happened to be in the Mannix apartment that
day, Mr. Mannix suggested that the friend take Toolan's
place. Arrangements were made for Toolan to leave his costume on the back of the kitchen door that led to the stairwell.
The friend didn't open the garment bag until James, the
chauffeur, dropped young Mannix and him at the party.

When he did, instead of a clown costume he found the bag filled with rotten fruit, milk containers, and empty cans. Annoyed that the friend was taking his place, Toolan had filled it with kitchen garbage.

Toolan changed dramatically in high school. Physically, it was as though his grammar school body was made of taffy and, by high school, someone had begun to pull it at either end. He was nearly six feet tall as a freshman, and couldn't have weighed more than one hundred and twenty pounds. He was nearly a head taller than many of his classmates. His ears protruded, and though his face would quickly fill in and become handsome, as a freshman he looked as though he still carried a comic book rolled up in his back pocket.

He attended Xavier, a Jesuit high school in the Chelsea section of Manhattan. It couldn't have been the easiest of transitions for him. No longer did he walk the few gentle blocks to St. Saviour. Instead, it was a long subway ride for a skinny kid wearing a white shirt and tie and crimson blazer. Subway crime was rampant then in New York; this was the era of Bernard Goetz, the "subway vigilante" who shot four black youths who tried to mug him. A skinny, rich kid in a crimson blazer had to have his share of run-ins. Mr. Mannix, however, would come to the rescue. James was directed to drive Jim and Toolan to school.

Though he managed to dodge subway ruffians, there would be no getting around the hardscrabble kids of his high school. Xavier has been around for over one hundred and fifty years. In its early days, it was called a "military day school." In 1935 it became a junior ROTC school and gained a reputation for its scholastics and rifle team. The most famous rifleman the school produced was Antonin Scalia. According to a profile of the Supreme Court associate justice in *The New Yorker*, Justice Scalia would ride the subways from Queens to Xavier with a .22 carbine on his lap.*

*Xavier switched to air rifles in 1994.

The Vietnam War greatly diminished the school's military focus, and in 1971 the fulltime ROTC became optional. But even in Toolan's time students were expected to participate in a short-term ROTC program.

Coming from Park Slope made Toolan something of an outsider at Xavier. For much of its history, the high school drew the sons of working-class Irish-American, Italian-American, and, later, Hispanic students. Many of the students came from Stuyvesant Town, an East Side housing project built by the Metropolitan Life Insurance Company in 1943. Traditionally, the alumni of Xavier filled the ranks of New York's police and fire departments, federal law enforcement agencies, and brokerage firms. In the days, months, and years after 9/11, the school mourned no fewer than sixty alumni or close family of alumni killed in the attack. One mass for the school's dead drew fifteen hundred into the small, adjacent church. According to *The New York Times*, a police officer assigned to direct traffic outside the church happened to be a Xavier alumnus. In a spontaneous moment, the cop held a megaphone to his mouth and led the crowd gathered on the steps in the Xavier fight song.

According to several of his classmates, Toolan didn't try to hide his Park Slope pretensions. "He could put on airs," said Lawrence Rivera, a fellow Xavier student said of Toolan. "He knew he was in the upper league, it was part of his upbringing." When a Caribbean student was elected senior class president, Rivera remembered Toolan said something to the effect that "I can't believe that someone *like him* could get elected."

Xavier is a small school, with an enrollment of only twelve hundred or so. Often, bonds formed there last for the rest of the students' lives. But Toolan's allegiance was more to Park Slope than Xavier. His closest friends were Mannix and a fellow named Walsh, both of whom lived at 35 Prospect Park West.

Steve Doran[†] was one of the few friends Toolan made at Xavier who was outside the Park Slope circle. He remembered Toolan as a "shy, geeky" kid. "He wasn't the guy who would get the girl," Doran said. But Toolan would shed his shyness at Xavier, and he did so right in front of Doran's eyes.

As long as there have been saloons—and a legal drinking age—getting served in a bar has been a rite of passage for underage teenagers. In New York City, in days before Rudy Giuliani had a chance to scrub it clean, Times Square had at least a dozen places where kids could go to have phony ID made. And even though neither Doran nor Toolan looked anywhere near twenty-one, the legal drinking age then, there were plenty of establishments that would glance past the rosy cheeks to the green in the wallet. They first wanted to go to the Palladium, which was then the biggest, most popular club in the city. But the Palladium was notorious for its hard-edged bouncers. Worried that their phony ID wouldn't stand up to scrutiny, Doran and Toolan passed on the mega dance club and headed down the block to a smaller, less discriminating place. Their plan succeeded. They were let in without so much as a second look. Once inside, the boys tried to appear both cool and inconspicuous, a task that was difficult on both fronts—they were, after all, only thirteen. For Toolan, this was an experience of immense proportions. He was literally just months removed from St. Saviour Grammar School, his interaction with girls, perhaps, limited to a school dance chaperoned by nuns. Now, as the strobe lights flickered on his face, he looked out intently on the dance floor. In front of him, young women suggestively dressed in disco spandex gyrated to the pulsing music, and, perhaps for the first time, he experienced what he had only in prepubescence giggled and snickered about. On this night, or one just like it, Toolan slipped into his sexuality, and he liked the way it felt.

Emboldened by the seductive atmosphere, Toolan waved to the bartender and ordered two black Russians. In a gulp, the vodka and Kahlua concoction went down his throat, the heat from it spreading through his body like a fever. Then an amazing thing happened. In that moment, the shy, geeky kid didn't feel so shy and geeky anymore. Instead, fueled by booze, confidence surged within him. He felt sexy and powerful. As Doran watched in disbelief, Toolan approached a girl and asked her to dance. "He was like someone else," Doran remembered thinking. Toolan still stumbled over his words, and the girl, some eight or ten years older than he, laughed at the absurdity of his request. But it didn't matter. Alcohol had helped him conquer his fear. And from that moment on, every significant relationship Toolan had with a woman was lubricated with it. Those same feelings of confidence and power that alcohol gave him that first night replicated themselves over and over again. Ultimately, doing so in the most horrible of ways.

Toolan drank that night as though he was feeding something that had been starving. By midnight he was drunk and out of money. The two freshmen walked unsteadily out of the club. They parted company, and Doran took the subway home to Queens. Toolan flagged a cab.

It would be Monday morning when Toolan told Doran the story of his trip home. He had the cabby pull up to the side entrance of his apartment building, on Garfield Place. Once there, he told the driver that he didn't have money. He said he would have to go up to his apartment and bring some back down. But he had no intention of coming back down. Once he was safely inside the lobby, he told the doorman that the taxi driver was crazy, that he had tried to rip him off with a phony surcharge. After waiting patiently for some time, the driver became suspicious. In a building like Toolan's, the doorman's priority is to keep all undesirables away, no matter how justified they are. The doorman did his job. The cabby lost his temper and began to pound on the locked door. In the elevator, Toolan could hear the pounding as he was whisked to the fourth floor. Even back in the early eighties, the cab fare from Fourteenth Street to Park Slope, with tip, was twenty dollars. Plus, it cost the driver all the wasted time with which he could've been picking up other fares. Toolan laughed as he told Doran the story at school.

◆ ◆ ◆

Toolan's high school yearbook tells the story of an above-average student in an above-average school. In 1991, the U.S. Department of Education recognized Xavier as a "School of Excellence." According to the yearbook, Toolan's accomplishments included working for the school paper all four years. In his senior year he was the associate editor. A member of the French Club, Toolan was its president in his senior year. In the photograph of the French Club in the yearbook, Toolan towers over the other three members and the Jesuit moderator and looks almost Kennedyesque with his wavy blond hair and angular face. He has a small mouth with thin lips formed into a tight smile, like a parenthesis lying on its side. He wears an unbuttoned dark blazer, white shirt, and striped tie. His hands are thrust into the pockets of his khaki pants.

According to the yearbook, he belonged to the Drama Club all four years. He is not, however, listed in the cast of either senior production: *One Flew Over the Cuckoo's Nest* or *The Royal Hunt of the Sun.* He also does not appear in the group photograph of the senior council, which he listed under his graduation picture as part of his accomplishments. Like Beth, he made the National Honor Society. But Doran remembered Toolan "just skating by." (Academically, and otherwise, Toolan was obscured in the shadow of his older sister. When Toolan was in high school, his sister had already graduated magna cum laude from Yale University and was working on a master's degree in biology at Fordham University. She was also married, the ceremony held at a chapel in St. Patrick's Cathedral. The event was reported in *The New York Times,* a sure sign of social prominence.) Toolan told at least one girlfriend that he played football in high school, but the yearbook says that he played only tennis for Xavier.

Under his graduation photograph, Toolan quoted Thoreau: "If one advances confidently in the direction of his dreams . . . he will meet with a success unexpected in common hours."

Perhaps there are no more formative years than the four of high school. You first enter the school building in freshman year as a child. And though your transition to adulthood is probably not completed by the end of senior year, your experiences in school are imprinted on your character and stay with you for the rest of your life. Nothing in Toolan's yearbook indicates that he was anything but a normal kid in an all-boys high school. Like most documents, however, there is a much larger story behind the printed words. In Toolan's case it was a couple of short paragraphs explaining Xavier's foreign exchange program. It would be in Paris that the worst part of Toolan's character would form.

CHAPTER ELEVEN

They had met at the house on St. Louis Boulevard that Matt Bresnahan shared with several other guys who went to Notre Dame. The house wasn't in the nicest of neighborhoods. Part of the newly named Rust Belt, South Bend is the town that produced the Studebaker, an automobile whose fortune was short lived. Studebaker's demise, and other businesses that failed, left parts of South Bend stripped and on the blocks for decades. The ghetto location, however, didn't stop Matt's house from garnering a reputation as one of the university's premier party places. Though it fell a bit shy of the craziness portrayed in John Belushi's *Animal House,* Thursday nights at the St. Louis Boulevard dwelling were so popular that complete strangers would approach Matt on campus and ask if the party was on.

Matt was actually sitting in a tree when Beth walked into his life. The night before the party there had been a dangerous late-summer storm. Lightning had provided Matt's perch. On its side, the large pine covered just about the whole backyard. The weather had cleared, and above Matt was a canopy of black velvet, glistening with stars. As he sipped his beer, a pretty girl dressed in shorts and a sweatshirt appeared. Matt was taken by Beth's "natural look," absent of makeup. What he didn't know was that by junior year Beth had begun to wear contacts. Still, her dark blond hair was full and just short of shoulder-length and, according to Carolyn Elliott, a dorm mate of Beth's, she had "nice, long legs." Beth and Matt sat together in a crook of the tree for

most of the evening, except, when every so often, Matt ran
back to the house for beers. In the course of sharing a six-
pack, they found out about each other. After the basics—
where they had grown up, what year of school they were
in—the conversation became interesting. Matt was en-
thralled with Beth's stories of Nantucket, and he in turn regaled her with stories of growing up in Chicago. He
explained how proud he was of his collection of T-shirts; his
favorite was silk-screened with pictures of beer bottles from
around the world. There was even a beer called Matt's, he
exclaimed. Somewhere during that night, a feeling came
over Beth. Matt looked to her more like a college freshman
than a senior. He was just shy of six feet and about one hundred and sixty-five pounds—in good shape from almost
daily Frisbee games. "Matt was a baby face," remembered
Carolyn Elliott. Before the end of the night, no doubt, there
was some necking; nothing too hot, or too heavy, just
enough to whet a college kid's appetite. And when Beth
asked Matt if he'd like to stop by her dorm the following
day, he couldn't believe his good luck. "I was like, 'Holy
shit!' 'Wow!' I was the goofy guy jumping around when the
pretty girl asked him out," Matt remembered.

Matt was a little nervous in the girls' dorm room in Badin
Hall on the South Quad of the university grounds. In 1972,
Badin was the first Notre Dame dorm to house female students. The school went coed that year, accepting three hundred and twenty-five young women into its male universe.
Six years hadn't exactly brought Notre Dame up to speed as
far as equal rights were concerned. The university was still
run by the mores dictated by the football field and the Roman Catholic Church. For instance, in Beth's time, women
were not allowed to send their dirty clothes to the university
laundry. Instead, the women's dorms, like Badin, were
equipped with a Laundromat. An unforeseen result of this
laundry segregation was the popularity of the women's
washing machines among the male students. Though nobody would mistake Badin for South Beach, it did have a
certain buzz. Because a computer chose room and dorm

mates randomly, the school's living quarters were haphazard by definition. A guy walking into Badin would encounter a high level of feminine energy and might even find girls in several stages of dress. Matt remembers meeting several of Beth's dorm mates, Charlotte Wolf, Delia Thomas, and Carolyn Elliott. Even in all the activity, even with all things to divert his attention, it was easy for him to focus on Beth. He liked what he saw.

There is a certain immediacy to autumn in northern Indiana. As winter descends inexorably from Canada, every last bit of warmth becomes precious. The snowfall in South Bend is over seventy-five inches annually. An ever-stiffening breeze tries to hold on to September into November but invariably gives way to December. As red and golden leaves tumble across the winding walkways of the campus, couples hold each other closer than in schools in more temperate climates. Sweaters and bulky sweatshirts excite the imagination. There is a necessity to body warmth.

There is perhaps no better place to frame a college romance than Notre Dame. Beth and Matt picked a pretty good year as backdrop. For one thing, the Fighting Irish football team was ranked number one in the nation for a good part of the season. Only a disappointing loss to rival Southern Cal kept the Irish from playing for the national title.

Together, Beth and Matt attended pep rallies and after-game parties. There was a road trip to the Michigan game, which the Fighting Irish won on a last-second field goal. Perhaps learning the trick from her older brother, Peter, Beth knew the routine of getting on line first to score tickets for the games. For Matt, Beth was almost as much fun in a room filled with his rowdy buddies watching the game on TV as she was alone on a romantic walk. Almost. Though Beth liked football, and all the hoopla that surrounds it at Notre Dame, the biggest event that year for Beth was the Jackson Browne concert.

By the time the first snowflakes swirled to the ground, Matt had fallen. Beth was like no one he had met before.

Over and over, throughout Beth's life, friends, lovers, and acquaintances alike would echo the same refrain: Beth had a way of looking at you, listening to you, that made you feel special, like you were the only one that mattered.

Beth, too, was smitten. She would brighten in Matt's company. And though she enjoyed hanging out with the whole gang from St. Louis Boulevard and Badin Hall, she especially liked the moments alone with Matt. "Matt was sweet to Beth," Carolyn Elliot remembered.

By Beth's junior year, she had begun to tire of Notre Dame. There was a sophomoric naughtiness that Beth was a bit too mature for. At this school, Billy Joel's "Only the Good Die Young," with the line "Come out, Virginia, don't make me wait You Catholic girls start much too late" plays like a theme song at mixers and house parties. The university's view on sex follows the dictate of Rome. In a recent edition of *Du Lac,* the student handbook of rules and regulations, Notre Dame's position on the matter is stated like this: "Because a genuine and complete expression of love through sex requires a commitment to a total living and sharing together of two persons in marriage, the University believes that sexual union should occur only in marriage. Students found in violation of this policy shall be subject to disciplinary suspension or permanent dismissal."

As one university biographer writes, the eponymous Virgin Mary hovers over the school. "Touchdown Jesus," the hundred-foot-high library wall mosaic, with arms outstretched as if he's signaling a touchdown, gazes upon the two hundred million yellow bricks that make up the football stadium. The iconic golden dome itself is a replica of the one in Rome.

Under its vestments, Notre Dame is like a sleepaway camp. A big part of going there is seeing what you can get away with. Joe Pelicane, a classmate of Beth's, put it this way: "There were kids that would go to the library. There were kids that would go to mass every night. But there were guys who were drinking beer and smoking pot and trying to take girls' clothing off."

Throughout her adult life Beth would, now and then, stop into a small Catholic church in Greenwich Village, opting for the traditional mass, or the "smells and bells" mass, as she called it, rather than the folk masses geared to attract the young. But Beth's view on Catholicism was one that was filtered through her own set of beliefs.

The young men and women who are attracted to South Bend are overwhelmingly good kids, from good families. Just about everything the university does fosters and enforces this image. The parietals of the school are as antiquated as they are voluminous. *Du Lac* is nearly 300-pages long. At one point, Beth told family members that she was disgusted that a school she was paying for would send the bills—even her report cards—to her parents.

Beth was far too worldly, had spent too many summers on Nantucket, for the kegger mentality of Notre Dame. Though she didn't mind draft beer, she'd much prefer a glass of wine. Beth believed that a subdued house gathering, with a home-cooked meal, beat a packed college bar or a mixer any day. In her senior year, Beth moved with a few dorm mates to an apartment above a flower shop called Kagel's. Bill Arzbaecher, now a criminal defense attorney in Sacramento, lived down the block from them. "The girls above Kagel's had parties like you have after college," he said. "More intimate—but large—I remember candles, it being a warm, inviting place to go."

At Christmas 1981, Matt went back to Chicago and Beth went back east. He sent her a dozen roses and spent long sessions with her on the phone. Beth's Christmas gift to Matt was a sweater. Big and bulky, it was as functional as it was unsentimental. Matt wore the sweater often every day.

By then, Beth had a practical view of the relationship. She saw the big picture, the long term. Matt was a senior and about to graduate. Beth was a year behind. She knew that a romance with someone out of school was unrealistic and limiting. As with her feeling for Tony, there was just too much to explore, too much to do. She wasn't about to be tied to a phone cord talking long-distance to a boyfriend.

But there was also a part of Beth that ran from people who wanted her too much. After Beth was murdered, someone very close to her said she was afraid of repeating her parents' relationship, and the sacrifice they had made. Her mother was just about Beth's age when she married. John Lochtefeld was only a few years older than that. Beth knew firsthand the struggles and constriction of marriage and family. She especially was aware of how her father had forgone a full-time art career for the sake of his family. Beth liked Matt plenty, just not enough to constrict her life.

J ust before Matt graduated, there was some talk, but no firm plans, about his visiting Beth in Nantucket. By August, however, Matt's summer wanderings were limited to a few trips to Wrigley Field. His was a kind of summer of decompression. He didn't want to jump just yet into the workforce, so he knocked about with some of the pals he grew up with. He called Beth regularly. Sometimes, after a few too many Buds, he sloppily professed his everlasting love. Though Matt wouldn't allow himself to believe it, the reality was that the distance, both physical and emotional, was compassionately putting his relationship with Beth to sleep.

Still, removed from the rest of the world, Nantucket has a way of holding the inevitable in suspended animation. And as fate would have it, Matt would get a whole month with Beth on the beautiful and romantic island. And though time would sprint by, the memory of that Nantucket August would last forever.

O ne of Matt's house buddies at Notre Dame was taking a job as counselor in an upscale camp in New Hampshire. He was looking for company on the long car trip. Matt jumped at the offer. New Hampshire is a heck of a lot closer to Nantucket than Chicago. How hard could it be to talk his pal into a little side trip?

Beth met Matt and Matt's friend on Cape Cod and the trio took the ferry across to the island. Matt had planned only to stay about a week. The Lochtefelds offered to put him up. In 1973, John Lochtefeld moved his family and studio to a free-standing building on Fair Street, just off of Main Street. The gallery/studio was on street level with two apartments above. During the summer, the floors of the kitchen and family rooms at 4 Fair Street would be filled with as many as a dozen weary bodies sleeping in comforters and sleeping bags. For the friends of Jim, Peter, Beth, and Cathy, the Lochtefelds' Nantucket home was like a youth hostel. A family story tells of how Beth's brother Jim arrived on the late ferry with a half dozen friends. Beth was sleeping in the small bedroom off the kitchen and didn't hear them come in. When she awoke during the night to use the bathroom, her first step landed on a bearded face.

But a spot on the Lochtefeld floor proved not to be necessary for Matt. A friend of Jim's happened to be looking for a roommate. The friend, Tom Laughlin Kelly, who went by the moniker "the Lock," had taken a job as a summer mailman on the island.

With a chance to be near Beth, and just twenty-one, having no real plans, Matt jumped at the opportunity. August on Nantucket was a whole lot better than August in Chicago. With the Lock, Matt moved into a converted garage and Beth got him a job washing dishes in a place called Easy Street. Considering his circumstances, the name of the restaurant was most appropriate.

Beth was then working as waitress at DeMarco, a well-known restaurant on the island. Her shifts coincided with Matt's. Both of them had to be at work at four in the afternoon. Both were finished around midnight. Summer restaurant work is hard—there's never a slow night. Still, there was always enough youthful energy left for them to meet after work at one of the late-night gathering spots in town.

Once a week or so, there was a clambake on the moonlit beach. Days were spent under the sun, sometimes with Beth's sister, Cathy. All were avid body surfers, and the best body surfing on the island was at Nobadeer Beech, where there were no guards and a dog or a beer cooler wouldn't draw any attention.

But maybe the best time Matt had on Nantucket that August was discovering the island with Beth as his guide. Beth knew every gray shingle, every cobblestone on Main Street, and the history of Nantucket as well as most. On their ambles through town, she would show Matt the shipowners' houses on Pleasant Street, built at a high vantage from which they could keep an eye on their floating blubber factories. She explained how the sea captains lived on Orange Street because it had the best view of the harbor. "She'd point out the famous houses and tell me the story of the widow's walks," Matt said. The roof platforms on the houses called "walks" were built to extinguish chimney fires. But most had telescopes through which captains could spy far into the sea. It was on these walks, too, that Quaker wives would anxiously watch for the return of their husbands' ships. The term "widow's walk" was born from this practice, as too often sailors' wives waited for ships that never returned. Beth loved the tender sadness of the widow's walks. In a way, she thought of Nantucket in the same fashion: beautiful, but sadly all alone out at sea. "She talked about Nantucket in very romantic terms," Matt remembers.

CHAPTER TWELVE

Weathered and rough, the island of Nantucket is the face of a whale captain's wife, her chin jutting proudly into a breeze off the Gulf Stream, her stare fixed on the open sea. Some twenty-four miles off the coast of southern New England, Nantucket's nearest neighbor to the east is Portugal. Nantucketers call their island "the Rock," though it is more a sandy crescent or an "elbow of sand, all beach, without a background," as Herman Melville described it in *Moby-Dick*. It is only fourteen miles long and, at its widest, about five miles across. And it's getting smaller. In 1984 a lighthouse at Great Point on the northern tip of the island fell into the sea. Over four hundred feet of land that once separated the lighthouse from the ocean had disappeared. The island's open-sea vulnerability has left it a target for disastrous storms, including "the Perfect Storm," which in 1991 did extensive damage to the Old North Wharf and flooded the streets in the town of Nantucket. A good part of the time the island is shrouded in fog, which is the reason for the island's other nickname, "the Gray Lady." In summer it's a bit cooler than the mainland, and warmer, supposedly, in winter. This is due to the North Atlantic stretch of the Gulf Stream, first charted by Benjamin Franklin whose mother, Abiah Lee Folger, was born on Nantucket.

The island's first inhabitants were the Wampanoag Indians. Melville wrote that according to Indian legend an eagle swooped down on the coast of New England, snatched an Indian baby in its talons and carried the child out to sea. The parents followed in a canoe and finally came upon "natock-ete," which means "faraway land." There they found the dried bones of their child in an ivory casket.

In 1641, disregarding the three thousand or so Wampanoag living there, England declared itself owner of the island. The Crown then deeded it to a Martha's Vineyard merchant named Thomas Mayhew, who turned around and sold it to nine reputable residents of Cape Cod. The negoti-ated price of the island was thirty pounds sterling and two beaver hats. One of the buyers was Thomas Macy, a clothier. Macy, whose descendants would open a department store on Thirty-fourth Street in Manhattan a couple of hundred years later, supplied the hats.

Though primarily a business deal, the Nantucket nine also sought freedom from the tyranny and the fanaticism of the Puritans in Massachusetts. Mary Coffin Starbuck, the daughter of one of the Nantucket originals, Tristram Coffin, was the first to convert to the Society of Friends.

The historical independent spirit of Nantucket's women partly comes from the Quaker belief in the intellectual equality of women and men. This independence also comes from the fact that sailors' wives were left to fend for them-selves for years at a time. In fact, women performed most of the political and business managing of the island's affairs. The image of a Quaker wife is dutiful, hardworking, and for-ever faithful.

But, as Frank Conroy notes in his Nantucket memoir, *Time and Tide,* when Quakers lived and reigned on Nan-tucket, there was also an unmistakable sexual undercurrent, one that survives and flourishes right up until today. An adver-tisement in the paper of the whaling days read: "Nervous ? I will spend the night with thee. 25 cents." A ceramic phallus, called "He's at home," was popular with sailors' wives.

The early settlers of Nantucket raised sheep and farmed the island. But a natural phenomenon altered Nantucket's destiny: Whale carcasses washed ashore. As Nantucketers realized the benefits of blubber, they were soon pushing fishing boats into the surf in search of the animals. Never has there been a better example of the unbounded imagination that results from supply and demand economics than the whaling business of Nantucket. With each passing year, in an ever-increasing whale-oil market, whale ships were built bigger and eventually rigged with onboard blubber-rendering factories. What started with the fishing of whales within sight of land became around-the-world seagoing voyages of three, four, and five years. From the tiny port of Nantucket, whaling ships sailed around Cape Horn deep into the Pacific Ocean.

In the early 1800s Nantucket was, perhaps, the richest fifty square miles on the planet. By then, whale oil had become what petroleum is today, and Nantucket was the Saudi Arabia of its time. By 1820, there were 140 whaling ships sailing from Nantucket Harbor, each with owners who were millionaires many times over—multimillionaires in a day when a multimillionaire was the equal of today's billionaire. But unlike the flaunting of the incomprehensible wealth of Saudi princes—or the obnoxious money of the island's present inhabitants—the Friends of Nantucket lived with a fervent modesty. It was this modesty that imbued the island with its lasting charm. Houses were built with lumber and other parts of old whaling ships. Quarter boards with names of ships were pulled from hulls and nailed on homes. (Most of the trophy houses on Nantucket today feature quarter boards.) Many years later, the frugal nature of Friends would give the island its remarkable quaintness, a genuine theme that has been fabricated innumerable times in seaside resorts throughout the world.

Nantucket's position as the center of the universe would not last. In *In the Heart of the Sea: The Tragedy of the Whaleship "Essex,"* Nathaniel Philbrick describes the island's fate: "Relentlessly acquisitive, technologically advanced, with a religious sense of its own destiny, Nantucket was, in 1821, what America would

become. No one dreamed that in a little more than a generation the island would founder—done in, like the *Essex,* by a
too-close association with the whale."

A myriad of circumstances combined to end Nantucket's
whale-oil riches. By the mid-1800s, Nantucket whalers had
depleted much of the world's sperm whale population.
Whaling expeditions were expensive and a huge gamble for
ship owners, as more and more often they were unproduc-
tive. The mainland ports of New Bedford and Salem could
utilize the burgeoning railroad to distribute its catch,
whereas Nantucket was isolated out at sea. In addition, in
1846 a fire that started in a whale-oil storage left the wharf
and town in cinders. Outside events also affected the island.
The adventurous personality of the Nantucket whaler was
particularly susceptible to the promise of riches in the California Gold Rush, which depleted much of the island's man-
power. The Civil War drew many men, who found their
deaths not in the briny deep, but in the killing fields of Virginia and Tennessee.

Then, in 1859, the death knell for the whole of the whaling industry rang in Titusville, Pennsylvania. There a man
named Edwin Drake drilled sixty-nine feet into the soft
earth and struck oil. Wells sprang up like summer dande-
lions. Crude oil saved the sperm whale, but doomed the
whale-oil industry and, for a while at least, Nantucket along
with it.

During the last half of the 1800s, Nantucket's fortune
steadily declined. Boardinghouses and waterfront
saloons that catered to seamen closed, as did gro-
cery and dry goods stores and other businesses that sup-
ported and depended on the whale-oil industry. It seemed
that the island was destined to return to days of sheep graz-
ing. But there was one natural resource that Nantucket had in
abundance, and it was a resource that could never be bested:
the summer sun and the island's natural beauty. It didn't take
long for the leisure class to discover the island. As Nathaniel

Philbrick wrote: "The Gray Lady began to exchange her Quaker bonnet for a bathing costume. . . ."

In 1845 Nantucket's newspaper, *The Inquirer,* predicted the island's future as a summer resort: "Every day's experience convinces us that our little island is destined to become *the* watering place of the country, to which the wealthy, and fashionable, and health-seeking thousands . . . will fly, for relaxation or pleasure during the summer months."

Where, just decades before, the white sails of whaling ships covered the horizon beyond the island, the late 1800s saw steam-powered pleasure liners, filled with day-trippers and sunseekers, motor into Nantucket Bay. One of these, the *Gay Head,* made its maiden voyage to Nantucket on July 8, 1891. The interior of the 203-foot steamer was finished in black walnut and maple and appointed with a Neapolitan-style gold trim, cherrywood seats. There were ten private staterooms aboard and a fifty-foot social hall. Though the *Gay Head* was much more luxurious than the Nantucket of that day, it portended the future riches of the island. Nantucket would become perhaps the first *historical* pleasure destination in the United States—a theme park of sorts of the island's not-too-distant glory. Even back then the houses of Greek Revival from the golden era of whaling wealth, Federal architecture from the island's long trading partnership with England, and the modest Quaker homes that lined the maze of narrow streets and alleys made Nantucket into a kind of living diorama. In his memoir of Nantucket, Frank Conroy describes this section of Nantucket this way: "It is not a museum, people live here, but as quiet, calm, and peaceful as anyone could wish. One finds oneself walking softly, talking softly, without consciously deciding to do so. I have visited and seen many lovely towns across America, but nothing has taken my breath away like old Nantucket." The captains' houses, with their widow's walks, which had fallen into disrepair, were reincarnated. The only thing missing were the widows themselves.

But even more than the quaintness of the village, perhaps,

it was the island that drew the crowds and money. On Nantucket, there are salt marshes that contain incredibly complex ecosystems. Plants, mosses, and berries that grow on Nantucket are seen nowhere else in the world. Roses and beach plums grow wild. Nantucket is home to several species of birds on the endangered list, including the osprey, short-eared owl, northern harrier hawk, and the piping plover. On the south shore, waves seem to break right out of a fog bank. The sheer beauty of the island is astounding.

Throughout the twentieth century, the island's popularity dipped and crested in conjunction with historical events: the world wars, the depression. Periodically, it would be "discovered" again by new money who would claim Nantucket as their playground. Their claims were unfounded. On Nantucket there is always someone who has been there before you.

Nantucket is like an exclusive club. Your influence in the club is measured by the length of your membership. The charter members are the first settlers of the island, names that are still found in the Nantucket phone book, names like Folger, Coffin, and Macy. In this island fraternity, blacks stand next. These members trace their ancestors to Cape Verde and Portugal, the harpooners on the whale ships. Then comes the first influx of money, the idle rich of the Gilded Age. The great-grandchildren of these members still walk Nantucket (in the summer) dressed in faded red shorts embroidered with tiny whales. Like the rest of the country, the club loosened its standards during the sixties, and an influx of hippies and pirates pitched tents. The children of these members are now rich from Nantucket real estate, having bought or built when land was still dirt and not gold. By the eighties, the money of the membership becomes fresh and sticky: These are the masters of the Wall Street universe who lit *The Bonfire of the Vanities*. There is a substratum of these people; the lesser of this lot spend July on the island, the greater spend August. Finally, there is the new, new money, the stupid cash that today tries to bully and buy.

Though the island might be quaint, the longer your membership in the club, the less quaint you are. Both the history of the whaling wealth and Quaker stoicism helped form personality traits of islanders that endure today. The writer Ralph Waldo Emerson, a frequent visitor to the island, called this state of mind "the Nantucket nation."

For all the old members care, new money can come and go as it pleases. The newcomers can never really own anything on the island. True islanders have always known that there is one immutable fact about Nantucket: It belongs to the sea.

CHAPTER THIRTEEN

By the end of August 1981 Beth prepared to go back to Notre Dame and her senior year. With no such commitment, Matt decided to stay on Nantucket for a few weeks longer. As they had with Tony Maresco, the Lochtefelds took a liking to Matt. He was comfortable hanging around the Fair Street studio, even, now and then, helping with the framing. He played his share of Monopoly and enjoyed Sunday family dinners. The studio was always filled with friends and extended family. To Matt, it seemed Beth's family included just about everyone on Nantucket.

Matt became especially friendly with Beth's brother, Tom, and the two took a side job late that summer painting a house. Each day, as the sun glistened, Matt marveled at the expanse of the ocean; each night he'd count his blessings, along with the glimmering constellations in the limitless black sky. "It was the best summer of my life," Matt remembers.

Matt and Beth spent one final weekend together, on a trip to Beth's brother Jim's place in Boston. When Beth left for school the following week, there were no tearful good-byes. As far as Matt was concerned, the summer's end didn't mean the end of his relationship. "My girlfriend's at Notre Dame," Matt would explain to those who asked when he'd show up at places solo.

For Beth, it was a different story. In some ways, Beth fit right in with the history of independent women on the island. From Lucretia Mott and the Quakers' belief in intellectual equality to the strong-willed whaling wives to the modern lady islanders, Nantucket has never been a place where women depended on or even needed men. Beth started working when she was thirteen at the Nantucket bakeshop. Though she took out a student loan for part of her tuition, she was paying her own way at Notre Dame.

In mid-September, Matt went home and began his delayed job search. After a few weeks, he landed a position with the city of Chicago, working in the data-processing center. It was an entry-level job and "mundane," by his own estimation. Each weekend was a reprieve, and would find him on the highway to South Bend. He still held out hope. But by November, he, too, realized his relationship with Beth was just about out of gas.

Beth had moved off-campus with Carolyn Elliot and two other Notre Dame students, Maura Welsh and Maribeth Faccenda. The girls' apartment was on North Michigan Street. Unlike Matt's apartment on St. Louis Boulevard, Beth's place over Kagel's was in a nice neighborhood right next to Memorial Hospital. The apartment had an unusual layout, with a stairway in the kitchen that led right down to the back of the flower shop. "We'd just walk down the stairs to pay our rent," Maura Welsh remembered.

Beth and Maura were both in relationships that were waning, which made their friendship even stronger. "We were inseparable," Maura said. "The boyfriend thing, then the no-boyfriend thing." One day Maura came home to see a dozen roses sent up from Kagel's sitting in a vase on the kitchen table. Just as Maura was opening the card, Beth walked in. "Are they for me?" Beth asked. "No," Maura replied. "They're for me." "Thank God," Beth said, rolling her eyes. Then, on second thought, she added, "Oh, I mean, that's too bad." The uncomfortable moment dissolved into a giggle. The girls then stowed their schoolbooks and went down the block to wash the thought of their ex-boyfriends away with a beer.

The roomies took full advantage of their newfound freedom. There was a trip to Chicago for a Grateful Dead concert, and at least one Fighting Irish away game. They took turns cooking "real dinners" like pot roast and roasted chicken. Beth and Maura took a spring break trip to Fort Lauderdale that wasn't exactly your average college kid's vacation. For one thing, Maura's father came along.

Maura's family owned a duplex, four-bedroom condominium in Fort Lauderdale. At first, it was just to be Beth, Maura, and Maura's father as chaperone. But Maura's father had grown up in a large family. "He always needed people around," Maura explained. So he invited six of his cronies, ranging in age from their early forties to midfifties, to come along. "There was no hanky-panky," Maura insists. But a couple of the guys thought they were in college again. They took the girls parasailing and speedboating in the Lauderdale canals. Every night they went to a different restaurant. They even went out clubbing. "We didn't spend a dime," Maura remembered.

As senior year rolled by, Beth became more disillusioned with her school. She had gone to Notre Dame to follow family tradition. Her father had studied fine arts at the university. Years later he would joke that most people didn't even know the Notre Dame of that era had a fine arts program. He would say that the program made up for its diminutive stature with enthusiasm and a couple of very good art professors. And having brother Peter in school with her had kept any homesickness at bay. Beth liked the fact that she would share her alma mater with her dad and brother. But in her last year at school, with Peter graduated, a good deal of her initial motivation had worn off. There was narrow-mindedness present at Notre Dame that rubbed against the core of Beth's personality.

In senior year, a close male friend of Maura's confided to her that he was gay. By her own admission, Maura didn't know how to handle the situation. "I was just a little Indiana girl," she said. Maura went to Beth.

It's perhaps no big surprise that a testosterone-driven, Catholic environment like Notre Dame had a very crowded closet. Beth's sophistication made her the perfect confidante.

"She told me to take a breath," Maura said. Beth and the fellow struck up an immediate friendship, and soon he was over at the girls' apartment just about every day. Following Beth's example, Maura resumed her friendship, and did so on a deeper level.

Throughout Beth's adult life she counted gay men among her very best friends. No doubt, the fun memories of Uncle Bobby on Nantucket had something to do with that. But Beth had also worked for years in the restaurant business, and later built her own business in an industry filled with designers and architects, two worlds that, stereotypically at least, are heavily populated by gay men. Without the sexual component, there wasn't the emotional baggage that would weigh Beth down. She was high-energy, always on the go, up for adventure. Beth was drawn to the arts, good food, and wine. The finer things in life were more attractive to Beth than some straight boys' lives of bars, beer, and bowling.

Kevin Yoder met Beth in his freshman year at Notre Dame. The two would become fast friends, then, much later, best friends. In his eulogy of Beth at St. Bartholomew's Church in Manhattan, Kevin remembered the day Beth walked out of the late-summer afternoon glare in South Bend and into his life: "A tall woman in blue corduroy and a white cotton shirt walked toward me with a smile that seemed as wide as the Grand Canyon and twice as deep," he said.

"The fact that I was from California intrigued her—new worlds always intrigued Beth," he continued. "To my West Coast, she was East Coast—the Hudson Valley and Nantucket, with a father who was an artist and a brother already at Notre Dame. My suburban California upbringing seemed so mundane in comparison."

For the first six weeks of school, Beth and Kevin were glued together. At hyper speed, Beth shared all her plans with Kevin. She told him that she was going to Innsbruck, Austria, for a year. A little while later, she changed her mind but held to the goal of being fluent in German. Kevin's birthday fell during those first six weeks and Beth was working in the cafeteria, clearing trays. "Beth gave me a present in the dining room," Kevin remembered. "Nothing special—a swiped dessert, a food services hat, and a homemade card full of references to things we shared those first few weeks. I kept that card and hat for years." In his eulogy,* Kevin told about how Beth would camp out for football seats for herself and her friends. "In the first six weeks I knew her," he said. "Beth accomplished more than most people did in their first year of study."

Kevin called Notre Dame "a world controlled by the orbits of specific social circles." Beth and Kevin would remain friendly throughout their time at school, though not as intensely as in those first weeks. At the Jackson Browne concert in junior year, they were able to get their hands on a gas-powered golf cart from a nearby golf course. They drove it all over the concert grounds that night. But after graduation their lives drifted apart.

When Beth made a friend, it usually meant forever. Sometimes this phenomenon was as the result of hard work on Beth's part. Year in, year out, she would send birthday and Christmas cards or make periodic phone calls to keep in touch. But sometimes it seemed that fate conspired with her to keep people from fading away. Four years after school, and having not been in touch all that time, Beth and Kevin met on a street in Greenwich Village. It was like the early days at Notre Dame again, only this time the intensity of their friendship wouldn't last just six weeks. Outside of her family, for the rest of her life, Kevin would be Beth's closest friend.

As the fantasy of the university shrank to size, Beth began to look at a life beyond Notre Dame. "We knew we were going to become adults when we graduated," Carolyn Elliot remembered. "I don't think there was any question she was going to work hard. She was so in-

---

*The text of Kevin's eulogy appears on Beth's memorial Web site. Kevin was contacted for this book, but declined to be interviewed.

tense," Maura said of Beth. "She had grand ambitions, so much energy," Carolyn Elliot said. Beth's major was American studies, with a minor in German. Often Maura would peer into Beth's bedroom to see her roommate sitting cross-legged on her bed surrounded by stacks of research material, books, and posters for some project she was doing. Notre Dame is not an easy school. In later years, when *U.S. News & World Report* would publish its annual college scholastic rankings, the failure of Notre Dame to reach the top twenty-five would be taken as hard on campus as not being in the top twenty-five in the AP football poll. What's more, it was even more competitive for female students. In Beth's time there, there was a slow-growth policy for women applicants. Because the number of women who were applying was so large, the small number of female students admitted were, scholastically, in the very top of their high school classes.

For Beth, the harder the challenge, the more she loved it. She would later explain that the reason she'd do homework on her bed was because she'd have to finish to have a place to sleep. Her system worked. Beth would go on to graduate from Notre Dame with honors.

On his last visit to see her at the university, Matt said Beth seemed "businesslike." "She said that it was nothing I had done, but that she wanted to feel free to flirt," he remembered. Though Beth came straight to the point, Matt also remembers that her words were tempered. She was tactful and loving, he said.

According to her roommates, Beth didn't think of her breaking up with Matt as a life-changing decision. "They were dating. She just didn't want to date anymore," said Maura. "She had more to explore," said Carolyn Elliot.

Matt and Beth held each other for a lingering moment. She smiled brightly and waved when he turned back to look. Their eyes glistened a bit from tears.

By all accounts, Beth didn't have a steady boyfriend the rest of her time at Notre Dame. "I think she might have had a date or two," Maura said. "But I don't remember any guy interesting her very much. You move in a large pack. You don't want to waste any time."

There is a picture of Beth dressed in her graduation gown at a party just after the ceremony. Her cheeks are full and her hair short in a kind of hairdo made popular by Olympic skater Dorothy Hamill. Classmates surround her: a guy with a *Welcome Back Kotter* mustache and Afro, and a fellow drinking a Bud. It's hard to read into a captured moment, but her smile, set in her square, Pilgrim jaw, seems to be one of relief or anticipation. Beth wanted to see every corner of the world—at least the corners that served good wine. In the photo it looks as though she couldn't wait to start.

For Matt it was hard trying to put Beth behind him. For a few years, there was an annual Christmas card and the occasional phone call. But then there was no contact at all. Still, Beth was kept apprised of Matt's situation through the grapevine. She knew that he was married, and, one by one, heard of his children. Periodically, someone would give Matt updates on Beth's life, too. He knew she did well in business and that she traveled a great deal.

Matt always had a feeling that he would see Beth again. And he did, almost twenty years later. In July 2004 Matt took his wife and family on a vacation to Nantucket, where they met Beth. Three months later she was murdered.

CHAPTER FOURTEEN

Except for the first Lochtefeld in America, Henry Melchior Lochtefeld, who emigrated from a German area near the Dutch border in 1832, the Lochtefelds stayed for generations pretty much where you put them. Henry found his way to the virgin forests of Ohio, settling in a town called Maria Stein. The Lochtefelds were and are Catholic, a decided minority in Germany and in the part of America in which they settled. Both their religious belief and the language they spoke, *plautdeitch*, or Plattdeutsch, kept them insulated from the outside world. There are still Lochtefelds to be found in the Maria Stein phone book.

Beth wasn't about to stay put. Her wanderlust began in her junior year of high school, when she traveled to Germany. There were several reasons for the trip, including the wedding of a close friend of the family's. But Beth was the only one of the Lochtefeld children studying German in high school, and her parents thought it would benefit her most. Besides, she'd get a chance to see where the Lochtefeld family came from.

The trip to Germany opened Beth's eyes to a world she longed to explore. She traveled with school chum Patti Engel and stayed in Germany for six weeks. To some extent, Beth already knew how wide the world was from her summers on Nantucket, which has had an international population since white people began to live there. Just as her great-great-grandfather Henry had, Beth saw the planet on a smaller scale than most. She was determined to circle it a couple of times.

I n the spring of 1983, Asia became the first leg of Beth's lifelong journey around the globe. Though Beth had only a cursory grasp of some basic Japanese phrases, her plan was to teach English in Japan. She became disillusioned there after only a short time and left for Hong Kong. She told friends that she didn't like, as a tall blonde, the way she stuck out in the crowded streets. To one friend Beth confided that the Japanese men only came up to her boobs. To her family Beth said that Japan was cold, literally. She said the walls were paper thin, and provided no defense against the cool evenings. But the main reason she went to Hong Kong was English was spoken there, and she wouldn't feel as isolated as she did in Japan.

Raucous, smoky, and on the ground floor of the Bank of America in Hong Kong, the Bull and Bear was not for the timid or the delicate. As many as twenty-five waitresses and bartenders worked behind the bar and at the tables in the dining room, and they had their work cut out for them. Along with British, American, and Chinese businessmen, the English pub drew a steady clientele of American marines and Scots guardsmen, both stationed nearby.

As she had at DeMarco four years earlier, Beth walked into the Bull and Bear one afternoon and asked for a job. She was interviewed by the owners, an elderly British couple, who were nice enough, but a little out of touch with the two-fisted clientele. The waitress's uniform was a long brown skirt, crepe de chine blouse, and a gingham apron, an ensemble meant, no doubt, to evoke the pub wenches of days of old. Though the outfits were not the most evocative of attire, the girls still spent much of their working hours slapping guys' hands away.

One of the waitresses at the Bull and Bear with whom Beth became friendly was Hilary Collins. Though a Scot from Aberdeen, Hilary had much in common with Beth. They share a wanderlust and the love of a good laugh. Hilary remembers Beth as the first person she'd ever met with a Visa card. Most of the girls who worked the Bull and Bear were there for the short term, just to make some quick money and move on. Hilary and Beth were no exception. But they crammed as much fun into their time together as they could. "If anybody offered you a drink, you took it," Hilary remembered. On Sundays, when the bar was closed, Beth, Hilary, and some of the other girls would hop a boat and head to Lantau Island. Now a resort for Hong Kong's wealthy, with a Disneyland about to open there, Lautau then was a set for an exotic movie. Largely undeveloped, it featured waterfront houses on stilts, a feral herd of water buffalo, and mysterious mountains. "The rich and famous live there now," Hilary said, "but then it was the retreat for the Bull and Bear." Most of the time the girls' destination was Mr. Wankie's, a Chinese restaurant where the best dish, somewhat appropriately, was giant prawns.

While working the Bull and Bear, Beth dated a Scots guardsman. Hilary doesn't remember the name, rank, or serial number of the guy. But the soldier left a lasting impression on Beth. One night, with perhaps her standards lowered by a few pints, Beth allowed herself to get talked into getting a tattoo.

It was a rampant lion from the Scottish royal standard. Beth had it strategically placed, and kept it a secret from all but a privileged few (no doubt the Scottish soldier had a peek).

After a few months working the Bull and Bear, Beth and Hilary were eager to move on. They backpacked along the Great Wall, and in all spent six weeks in China. Hilary, not at all shy, met a man who invited her and Beth back to his home in a Chinese commune. "Better make sure your wife approves," Hilary warned him. As it turned out, the man's wife did approve, and what's more was a diplomat and arranged for the girls to have entrée to places and events they would have otherwise not been able to see. They toured the Forbidden City, at a time when tourists were strictly forbidden. They ate a traditional twenty-course Chinese banquet. "It had all sort of strange pieces of animals," Hilary remembered. They were also able to obtain a visa to travel on the Trans-Siberian Railway. They bought two tickets to Moscow.

The train ride took six wondrous days. What Hilary remembers most is the smell of the Russians' uncured sable coats. "You had to hold your nose and run through the indigenous coaches," she said. Still, the two young explorers watched through the window as they passed the Great Wall. At the Chinese border, they waited impatiently while the carriages were moved with hydraulic lifts onto the broad-gauge trucks of the Russian rail system. Soon, the Gobi Desert and the Ural Mountains were rushing by. They saw tumbling streams, tranquil mountain lakes, and forests that seemed to date from the beginning of time.

On the train, Beth met an Englishman by the name of Mark Andrea. He called Beth "Miss America." On Beth's memorial Web site, Mr. Andrea recalled a moment on that trip when "we passed over the Chinese border into Mongolia. There was a Mongolian nurse, fully dressed up, inspecting our Health Certificates (Immunisations etc.). Beth didn't have any, so, with a twinkle in her eye, she handed over some official-looking papers and smiled. It worked. Beth had correctly worked out that the Mongolian couldn't read English. Cheeky and smart!"

In Moscow Beth and Hilary spent the first night taking naps in Moscow Station until police moved them along. The second night they decided to stay in a hotel. Since Beth had the Visa card, she booked the single-occupancy room. Beth went up alone, opened the window, and threw her coat out to Hilary. The coat was meant to fool the hotel workers into believing that Beth and Hilary were the same person. They didn't want the front desk to discover that there were two of them sleeping in the room. Remarkably, the scheme worked, and both girls slept soundly that night.

They only had a forty-eight-hour visa, so the next day the two traveling pals parted company at Moscow Station. Hilary caught a train to Berlin. From there, Hilary left for Scot-

land, and Beth flew home to the U.S. Hilary called the parting "quite emotional." It would not be the end of their
friendship. Over the years, Beth and Hilary kept in touch
with letters and calls.

In all, Beth spent nearly a year traveling through Asia. In
some ways, the trip marked Beth's coming-of-age; the tattoo
perhaps was her private reminder. "Beth had grand ambitions, so much energy, and there was a big, wide world out
there," said Carolyn Elliott, Beth's roommate at Notre
Dame. It had started with the trip to Germany in high
school. Now she'd seen much of Asia. Life was an adventure. Beth was going to squeeze all the passion she could out
of it.

CHAPTER FIFTEEN

I n 2004, real estate sales on Nantucket topped one billion dollars on seven hundred and seven transactions. That averages out to $1.6 million per transaction. The highest-priced home sold for $16 million, the lowest, $400,000. Recently, a half acre of land—without the house—sold for $1.7 million.

Among the more notable of those who call Nantucket their second (third, or fourth) home are H. Wayne Huizenga, founder of Blockbuster and the owner of the Miami Dolphins. According to *The New York Times,* Huizenga recently bought, for $2.5 million, the house next to his house just to gain more privacy. According to the same article, Richard Mellon Scaife, the publisher and heir to the Mellon banking fortune, bought an extra house for his staff. Michael S. Egan, who began Alamo Rent a Car, built a baseball field next to his island home.

Nantucket has old money that dates to the Gilded Age attached to names like Du Pont and Vanderbilt, and new money that replicates itself with broadband speed. The island is literally littered with senior partners and CEOs.

The poster boy of unintelligent wealth was, until recently, Dennis Kozlowski, the Tyco chairman who bilked his company out of $600 million and lived on Nantucket like a pharaoh. Well documented is Kozlowski's lifestyle, so we won't give space to it here. But a reminder of Kozlowski's wealth still exists on the island. In the waiting room for emergencies at Nantucket Cottage Hospital is a mural of his *Endeavor,* a rare, 1930s-vintage yacht. Ostensibly, the mural is the way the hospital said thank-you for Mr. Kozlowski's donation.

Maybe the best example of inflated prices on Nantucket deals not with a piece of land, but rather a painting. The story goes something like this:

A husband and wife who own a home on Nantucket were antiquing in the Berkshires one recent winter. In a small shop they came upon an old painting of the Nantucket Yacht Club. The wife loved the piece and thought it would look terrific hanging in their island home. The husband wasn't so sure. The price was the deciding factor; the shop owner wanted four hundred dollars, and both husband and wife thought the cost was too dear.

That spring they were back on Nantucket. One day they wandered past a gallery just off Main Street. A painting in the window caught their eye. Inside the gallery, their suspicions were confirmed: It was the same painting of the yacht club they had seen in the Berkshires. The small price tag on the frame read $40,000.

In an article for *Town and Country* (July 1999), David Halberstam wrote that Nantucket was the "target for the young, stunningly wealthy winners of Wall Street." He called the money on Nantucket "stupendous." Writer Frank Conroy, who lived on the island for over forty years, wrote that Nantucket was a "status symbol much more potent than the Hamptons, or Palm Beach, or indeed anyplace on the East Coast." Neither writer is prone to hyperbole. Calling the wealth on Nantucket stupendous is an understatement.

Last Fourth of July, more private jets landed at Nantucket Airport than in all flights combined at Boston's Logan. Pick any summer day and as many as two hundred and fifty Challengers, Gulfstreams, and Citations land on the island. Nantucket Harbor is to million-dollar yachts what the Easter Parade is to hats.

◆ ◆ ◆

There is another Nantucket, one whose inhabitants have a far more fundamental attachment to the island, and whose appreciation of Nantucket has more substance than a pricey ocean view. In one respect, Nantucketers can be separated into two distinct groups: those who are served, and those who serve (and a few pirates and lady pirates). Beth's summers on Nantucket were not about private jets and million-dollar yachts. Hers was more box kites and the annual summer regatta, where children raced sailboats they made themselves. And though Beth grew up on Nantucket as a server, her time on the island was far richer than those she served.

At fourteen, Beth's work résumé began. Her first job was at the Nantucket Bake Shop. Just a little cedar shack on Orange Street, the bakery was about eight blocks from her father's gallery, a distance she'd walk or ride on her bike before the first light of day. A photograph of Beth from those days is posted on her memorial Web site. In the picture, Beth wears a blue bandanna, aviator glasses, white short-sleeved shirt, and her hands covered with dough. She is standing in the back room of the bakery, next to the dough mixer, opening a package of cream cheese. Her lips are pressed in a cute little grin.

Several Lochtefeld family stories survive from that time. One of them concerns the manager of the bakery. A wizened curmudgeon, the woman demanded that Beth and her coworkers twist-tie the plastic bags of bread with three full twists. After hearing the instructions innumerable times, one of Beth's coworkers asked: "Clockwise or counterclockwise?" Beth worked as an expeditor of sorts. She was in charge of putting the rolls and buns into the ovens, a job for which timing was of the utmost importance. One side benefit of her lofty position was that Beth got to take home broken cookies and other treats in a white bakery bag that she called the "bro bag." Her younger brother Tom especially liked the pieces of napoleons and butter crunch cookies.

In the summer of 1979, after her freshman year at Notre Dame, Beth went looking for a more substantial summer job. The money at the bakery was fine for her high school years, and the broken cookies she brought home were a nice perk, but Beth was now a college girl. She needed to make some real cash for school. In the beginning of the summer, Beth took a job as personal assistant to an island artist. But a little more than halfway through the summer Beth became ill with pneumonia. She recovered, but with less than a month left in the summer, she was out of a job and a little desperate. About the same time, a new restaurant opened just a few blocks from her father's studio.

The building that had just finished being renovated was a three-story Federal-style wooden structure on India Street in the middle of Nantucket's historic district. India Street is cobblestone and is still lined with gaslight poles. The building dates to the 1840s and survived the Great Grease Fire of 1846, which, on a hot July night, began in whale-oil storage and destroyed over three hundred buildings in Nantucket's center. By the midseventies, the building served as a bed-and-breakfast. The house was divided into small rooms, with a number of potbellied stoves and fireplaces. The walls were lattice board sealed with horsehair plaster. Though imbued with a certain charm, the building had fallen into disrepair. But the price was right, and Don DeMarco, along with his brothers, Dennis, David, Douglas, decided to buy it.

The first order of business was to get the place in shape. Except for some plumbing and electrical work, the DeMarco brothers did most of the labor themselves. During the summer months they would also hire vacationing kids looking to make a couple of bucks. This ragtag team would sometimes number eight or ten. The DeMarcos had material shipped from the mainland, including twenty-foot lengths of ten-by-ten-inch hardwood beams from an old sawmill in Shrewsbury, Massachusetts. The renovation took nearly three years. For most of that time, the thought of turning the place into a restaurant didn't even occur to them. But the DeMarco brothers' timing was superb, in that it coincided with a boom on Nantucket. Somewhere along the line they realized that a restaurant just might be successful. In remembering those days, Dennis DeMarco said: "I couldn't believe what people would pay for a dish of pasta. My mother could feed us for a week with that."

DeMarco Restaurant opened for business in July 1979. The opening had been delayed for several months by Nantucket's infamous bureaucracy. Half the summer was over before all licenses and certificates were issued. Some of the delay had to do with conforming to the numerous guidelines in the historic district. Other delays can be traced to the DeMarcos' off-islander status. At one point, the island selectmen, Nantucket's legislative body, issued a liquor license that was good only until ten at night, a time when most of the restaurants on the island were just hitting their stride.

Those who know the restaurant business will tell you that timing and location can overcome many mistakes. Such was the case with the DeMarco brothers' restaurant. By their own admission, the brothers were a bit naive. The only exposure they had had to the food-service business was through their father, who had once been a cook in an Italian restaurant in the Mohawk Valley in central New York State. "We were rookies," Dennis recalled. Still, their restaurant was a success from the moment the doors opened.

Over the prior three summers, Beth had noticed that renovations were under way. When the trucks began to deliver stoves, refrigerators, and other kitchen equipment, she knew what business the DeMarcos had in mind. And, even at nineteen, Beth had good business sense. She figured rightly that the DeMarco Restaurant would be a place to make some good money. As soon as Beth felt well enough, she walked into DeMarco, and the course of her life changed.

A schoolteacher by profession, Dennis DeMarco assumed the role of DeMarco general manager. He remembers vividly the day Beth, dressed in T-shirt and jeans, walked into the barroom.

"Mr. DeMarco?" Beth asked. "I hear you're looking for someone to bust some suds."

Yeah, that's right, Dennis answered, a smile on his face.

"Well, I'm your man," said Beth.

When can you start?

"How about right now?"

That afternoon, Beth, still pale and weak from extended bed rest, began her career at DeMarco as the pot washer. She wouldn't stay "busting suds" for long, however. After only a couple of days, she realized the real money to be made was in the front of the restaurant, not in the back. Again, she went to Dennis DeMarco.

"Look," Beth reasoned. "I can keep the kitchen clean during the day and work on the floor at night."

Beth then had the confidence of a cardsharp and the smile of a Girl Scout. It was just about impossible to say no to her. "We let her do exactly what she asked," Dennis DeMarco remembered. That very night, Beth was bussing tables in the dining room. Once she was working the floor, it was only a matter of time until she graduated from bussing tables to waiting on them.

Though opening a restaurant on Nantucket in 1979, even one with barely adequate food, was a sure thing, the food at DeMarco was quite a bit better than that. DeMarco's first chef had been a literature teacher in New York City. While in Florence studying the Renaissance he took a cooking course, Don DeMarco remembered, "just to get away from the library." The chef, a fellow by the name of Jay Trubee, acquired an expertise in Northern Italian cooking, which in 1979, at least on Nantucket, was still considered exotic fare. As Don DeMarco once wrote, "On Nantucket, northern Italians were Italians from Vermont." The chef also had a sense of humor, though his bordered on the macabre. Once a month or so, wine salesmen would hold a tasting and a tutorial for the wait staff. The waiters would learn how to present and decant wine, among other things. One afternoon during a tasting, Trubee came running out of the kitchen holding a bloody napkin over his hand, screaming that he had just cut off two fingers in the Cuisinart. The wine salesman almost fainted. Trubee wasn't injured at all. A second chef had shaved one his knuckles slicing mushrooms. Though the wound was slight, it bled like heck.

The rest of the DeMarco staff was pretty interesting, too. Maybe Beth's closest friend at DeMarco was Paul Savage. Beth called him Paolo and Paul called Beth Bettina, so as to better fit into the restaurant's Italian theme. In 1979 Savage attended Haverford College, a Quaker school just outside of Philadelphia. Partly he came to Nantucket because he was assured a job at DeMarco: his older sister was the manager. Like Beth, Savage took to the restaurant business quickly, working his way up from dishwasher, to busboy, then waiter. He also served as something of a talent scout for DeMarco. He enticed other Haverford students to spend their summers working at the restaurant. One of the imports was an Irishman who was raised in Spain, Niall Burke. Savage and Burke were roommates all four years at college. With dirty blond hair and a classic, straight Irish nose, Burke's good looks were only exceeded by his natural athletic ability. He excelled in college soccer, basketball, and softball.

Beth and Niall hit it off right away. She was especially fond of his dry, almost arid, sense of humor, "an Irish Bob Newhart," as one of the DeMarco staff categorized him. But Niall was far from being just a straight man. After four years at Haverford, Niall obtained a dual postgraduate degree from Boston University in business and international relations.

The workday at DeMarco started about three or four in the afternoon. Around then, waiters, busboys, and runners would begin rolling in. There was setup work to do. Called "side work" in the restaurant business, the chores included polishing glasses, setting tables, and stocking stations with silverware and condiments. Far from the easy listening music that would soothe customers later in the evening, rock-and-roll blasted over the stereo as the staff set up the restaurant. There was a washer-dryer in the basement of the building, and some of the waiters would walk around half-dressed waiting for their uniforms to dry. Before hours, the restaurant had the feel of backstage at a Broadway musical.

The uniform for the wait staff was white shirt with black bow tie and black pants, except for Beth. As the only female waiter, she wore a rather dowdy black skirt that fell below her knees. Beth, whose pretty, athletic body was all but lost beneath the skirt, took ceaseless kidding from her fellow waiters.

A coworker recalled an evening when Beth came into the kitchen giggling and grinning, flanked by several of the waiters. "I wasn't sure why," remembered the coworker. "Then they turned and left the kitchen, exposing the fact that they had nothing on under their aprons."

Just before opening for business, the waiters would be given the dinner specials. Both the owners and the original staff of the restaurant learned the restaurant business together. Don DeMarco bought, for all employees, a copy of Waverley Root's *Food of Italy,* a classic on Italian food and culture. But Beth might have been the quickest study. She had an insatiable desire to learn the preparation of dishes. Had she not made so much money on the floor, she might have been just as happy working the line in the kitchen. But if she did work the back of the house, DeMarco would have lost out. Beth's personality was a perfect match for the restaurant business. At DeMarco, and for the rest of her life, she was the perfect host.

"If somebody ordered pinot grigio, Beth would know the six different vintages we had, and which wine goes with what food," said Don DeMarco. Years later, Beth went alone to Italy to tour wineries. During one side trip, there was confusion in transportation and she was left miles from a winery she was to visit. Beth walked the distance, some of it over rural, hilly terrain, asking directions along the way. She found the place in time to take the last tour of the evening. At the end of the tour, she engaged the winemaker in a long conversation. At one point, she mentioned she worked for DeMarco on Nantucket, and the man lit up with recognition.

DeMarco Restaurant was one of his best accounts in the United States.

Around six in the evening, customers would start coming in, and then the real fun started. "Every night was a show," said Don DeMarco. One of the most popular specials at DeMarco was salmon en cartouche, a salmon poached in parchment. The dish was served tableside, which meant spoon-serving the vegetables onto a plate, splitting open the parchment, then serving the fish. Part of the attraction of the dish was the waiter's performance. The parchment was opened directly in front of the customer, thereby delivering a waft of basil, beautiful salmon, and crème fraîche, a "little herbal facial," as Beth called it. The serving of the dish required close quarters with the customer. When a woman with a particularly low-cut dress would order the dish, the waiters would issue what they called "a salmoni alert." Even Beth was in on the code, and although none of those who worked with her would go on the record, at least one admitted that Beth would defer to a waiter when a salmoni alert was issued in her station.

DeMarco quickly began to cater to the top of the food chain on Nantucket, becoming an island version of New York City's Elaine's. Regulars included such VIPs as Jack Welch, Ted Kennedy, Nelson Doubleday, and Jackie O. Don DeMarco used to poke fun at the upper-crusty crowd. When a customer would ask for Perrier, Don would answer that the restaurant served Pellegrino, that the chef used Perrier to boil the pasta.

Beth's station was the first to fill, and would stay that way most of the evening. Customers requested her all the time. In his eulogy at Beth's memorial, Paul Savage, who knows the restaurant business as well as anyone, called Beth the best waiter he'd ever seen.

"She was the top tips earner nine out of ten nights, every summer," he said from the lectern in St. Bartholomew's Church in New York City. "She could remember more, deliver more, and clear more dishes than anybody. And she did it all with an alacrity that made her colleagues wonder. 'How does she do it?' and what motivated her to do it so well?"

Though her immediate motivation was to pay for college, Beth was dreaming bigger dreams. Throughout her childhood, Beth had seen plenty of people with money on Nantucket. Not until she worked DeMarco, however, had she experienced it with this kind of intimacy. She liked what she saw. She liked the lifestyle. She liked the elegance, the expensive clothing and shoes. She especially liked the shoes. During one of those busy nights at DeMarco, Beth decided that she wanted what her customers had. And, she was going to work as hard as she could to obtain it.

Beth saw each table as a step closer to her goal. Restaurant work is hard, and DeMarco was as busy as a restaurant can get. But Beth never lost her enthusiasm. She liked people, and liked making them feel wanted and comfortable. She was also a team player. DeMarco was a pool house, restaurant terminology for all tips going into a communal pot to be divvied up equally at the end of the night. Several times during her tenure at DeMarco, the subject came up of waiters keeping their individual earnings. Each time it did, Beth would shoot the idea down as counterproductive to good service. "This was like a politician refusing a huge infrastructure project in her own state, because it didn't make sense for the whole country," Savage said. "That's how unlikely Betty (Beth) was."

Not only did Beth learn everything she could about Italian food and wine, she also honed her skills as a salesperson. At one point Paul Savage bought an elementary Italian-language textbook at a hospital thrift shop a few doors up from DeMarco. Beth would look up the Italian words for dishes, then corrupt them a bit to make them sound as appetizing as they could. Savage remembered her Italian phrasing for blueberry pie: *Blubacca Cassis Timballo.* "You would be powerless not to order it," said Savage.

Beth also showed remarkable restraint with a very demanding clientele. More than once she smoothed over situations between customer and waiter that were headed toward confrontation. Beth could take things in stride that would send other waiters screaming into the night.

DeMarco had dining on two floors. On the first floor was the kitchen, with a back staircase to the upper dining room. One night, Beth had fixed a tray filled with espressos, cappuccinos, and coffee. It was a laborious task that took precious time during a busy rush. As she was walking down the back staircase with the tray, her brother, Tom, then a runner for the restaurant, charged up the stairs and clipped the edge of the tray. The coffees spilled all over Beth's chest. For a moment, Tommy thought he was in for it. But Beth burst out laughing. The rest of the night she wore a Cascade-white kitchen shirt.

After the last of the customers were fed and had paid their checks, someone would throw together a big salad, and the chef would cook pasta and fish or chicken, or whatever the kitchen had left over. Then the staff would sit for a sumptuous dinner, that is, except Niall, whose diet consisted of large amounts of white bread, Coca-Cola and Marlboro Reds. As the funny stories of the evening were told around the table, most often Niall would get the biggest laughs.

Beth's attraction to Niall was different from her first two boyfriends. By several accounts, Beth was into the relationship a little more than was Niall. At times he was aloof, almost as though he were playing hard-to-get. Unlike Tony or Matt, Niall seldom if ever went to the Lochtefeld gallery. In fact, except for Tommy, who worked for a while with him at DeMarco, the Lochtefeld family knew little about him.

There are conflicting accounts about Niall and Beth's relationship. At least one friend thought that Niall was the love of Beth's life. Others close to Beth thought that they were a mismatched pair from the start. One version has it that Niall was much too laid back for Beth.

"He was very mellow and relaxed," a close friend said. "Beth was active and wanting to get out and do things."

At some point, someone suggested that the staff meal be served before work, that the young bodies of the DeMarco waiters and kitchen help needed the fuel to work the busy shift. The DeMarco brothers agreed, and "family dinner" was moved to late afternoons. When that happened, the night became free for what Paul Savage called "the movable feast." The staff would go out en masse to places like the Rose and Crown, the Atlantic Café, or the Opera House. Fake IDs were flashed and accepted with a wink and a nod. Undoubtedly there were incidents of too much to drink (one night Paul Savage danced with an intoxicated Ted Kennedy); after all, Nantucket is synonymous with party. Everybody knew the crew from DeMarco, and many wanted to be a part of it. "People always asked me for a job," Dennis DeMarco recalled. Some nights, the crew would just head to the beach. There they would build a bonfire, bake clams, and drink beer.

It was perhaps on one of those nights on the beach when, illuminated by the licking flames, and under the usual brilliant canopy of stars, Beth, maybe for the first time, fell truly in love.

CHAPTER SIXTEEN

It was in his junior year at Xavier High School that Toolan, along with Lawrence Rivera and Steve Doran, studied in France. According to the school, participation in the exchange program is extended only to "academically qualified students." Toolan was in his third year of French Club, and his handle on the language was a work in progress. The trip included six weeks in Paris, living with a French family and studying at a Catholic secondary school. Toolan's host family lived in the wealthy Sixteenth Arrondissement. He attended Saint-Louis de Gonzague, a Jesuit school just a few hundred meters from the Eiffel Tower. The opportunity was unique: extraordinary immersion in a culture providing warm memories to last a lifetime. For most, that is. For Toolan the trip was little more than an extended drunken row that began on the Air France flight over the Atlantic. Lawrence Rivera remembered Toolan drinking on the plane. "They served him a few shots," Rivera understated. It was, perhaps, Toolan's first journey beyond his parents' reach. Along with underwear, socks, shirts, and trousers, he packed six or so stink bombs in his suitcase. "He was a prankster," Rivera said.

Toolan had a misplaced sense of humor. Things that he thought funny others found offensive and hurtful. But he didn't seem to care if others laughed. His pranks were worth it as long as he himself got a giggle out of them. In France, his pranks gained momentum. At first his conduct was relatively harmless. One afternoon Rivera accompanied Toolan to a Paris cinema. The Xavier junior had been drinking before the show and spent most of the film throwing popcorn at the people below him in the theater. "He was a joker like that," Rivera remembered. "I guess he was under the influence." Another time, Toolan's host family arranged for a trip to Normandy for him and the other American students. A man whom the students referred to as Uncle Pierre was the chaperone. One of the stops was the American Cemetery. As Uncle Pierre wandered through the rows of white crosses, Toolan jumped behind the wheel of his car. "He tried to steal the car for a joyride," Doran said. But Toolan couldn't figure out the stick shift and aborted the attempt. But as time went by in Paris, Toolan's attempts at humor were far more serious than popcorn tossing and joyrides.

Polite, well-behaved, and respectful, Lawrence Rivera was everything that Xavier hoped their students to be. In Paris his hosts were a wealthy Lebanese family. The father of the family was in the magazine publishing business. From very modest means, Rivera lived with his family in a tiny apartment on the Lower East Side of Manhattan. The joke was that, in Paris, Rivera had his own wing in the Lebanese family's apartment. (The following year, Ziad, the son in the Lebanese family, stayed with Rivera while he studied at Xavier.) A curfew was set for Rivera, to which he happily adhered. "I abided by their rules," he said. "I was home each night at nine, nine thirty." At that time, Toolan was just getting started. More than once he joked with Doran about the conservativeness of his hosts and how they disapproved of him staggering home in the early morning hours.

One night in Paris, near the Arc de Triomphe, a prostitute propositioned Toolan. A deal was struck, and Toolan followed the hooker to a parked Citroën. At some point, a young couple strolled by, interrupting the proceedings. When the hooker refused to resume, Toolan became incensed. Curses were hurled back and forth in English and French. Left with no recourse, Toolan slammed the car door and stormed off.

The following weekend Doran and Toolan were walking past the exact same location with the familiar Citroën parked in almost the same spot and the same hooker seated inside. "Watch this," Toolan whispered to Doran.

The prostitute, who either didn't remember him, or thought to let bygones be bygones, accepted Toolan's offer. Doran, who watched the proceedings some three hundred feet or so from the car, remembers seeing Toolan disappear into the passenger side. Just a few minutes later, heavy green smoke billowed from the windows of the car. The hooker jumped from the car screaming "Au feu! Au feu!" Toolan had set off one of his stink bombs. He climbed over to the driver's side and turned the key. There was one small problem with his plan. Like Uncle Pierre's car, the Citroën was a stick shift. As he tried to engage the clutch, it bucked and lurched, then slammed into one parked car, then another. The hooker stood on the sidewalk screaming. A door down the street opened, and several rough characters came running toward Toolan, who was still seated in the crumpled Citroën. Without question, Doran believed the men were associated with the prostitute, perhaps her pimps. They carried tire irons. Toolan bolted out of the car and down the street, with the posse of pimps in quick pursuit. Doran, who was starting to realize that hanging out with his pal Toolan could be dangerous, decided not to hang around to see how the situation was resolved. The next day, Toolan showed him the welts on his legs. He said that the French guys cornered him in an alley. He was able to escape only by climbing a spiked fence.

The episode did not frighten the teenage Toolan away from frequenting French prostitutes. According to Doran, Toolan thought the exchange rate of dollars to francs was favorable enough to support his growing hooker habit. But there was another element to the encounters that was even more disturbing than a seventeen-year-old having paid-for sex. Prostitutes in Paris then identified themselves by holding a set of keys. On the street, Toolan would approach a working girl with a smile and an easy manner, then scream as loud as he could: "Tu es sale!" (You're dirty). It seemed that the act of both frightening and humiliating them excited him. And calling prostitutes names was only the start. In Paris, Toolan began to show a pattern of the worst type of abuse against women.

One evening, Doran and Toolan decided to visit the Basilica of the Sacré Coeur, the church that overlooks Paris from the top of Montmartre. At the base of the famous hill there is plaza called Place du Tertre where Monet, Van Gogh, and Lautrec looked for inspiration. The plaza is also home to some of Paris's more unsavory characters. It is said that it's easier to get your pocket picked at Place du Tertre than anywhere else in the City of Light. There are also legitimate portrait sketchers who work the tourist crowd in the plaza. It was one of these artists, a young Frenchwoman, who, for no reason other than her vulnerability, became Toolan's target.

Doran admitted that he and Toolan had drunk quite a few beers during the afternoon and early evening. Doran's friendship with Toolan was based on two things: alcohol consumption and Toolan's entertainment value. Doran got a kick out of seeing just how crazy his friend would get. Though Doran didn't condone Toolan's actions, he didn't do much to actually stop them either. Back then, Doran's reaction to Toolan's behavior was a giggling seventeen-year-old boy's "Holy shit!" a sort of a Macaulay Culkin's *Home Alone* pose. In hindsight, though, Doran's voice shakes when he talks of Toolan's aberrance.

With the daylight almost spent, Toolan approached the young artist and began to chat her up. Though only three years removed from the freshman in the dance club whose words caught in his throat, Toolan now had no trouble approaching a girl. Usually they were happy to let him. His face had filled out; his hair was full and wavy. Although he still looked like a kid, it was obvious that he was not too far

away from being a handsome young man. And even in his
fledgling French, perhaps because of it, he already could be
charming. He talked the artist into moving her easel and
chair away from the crowd to a secluded spot. There, he
said, a certain angle of the church provided the best background. It was getting late. Business was almost finished for
the night. Toolan's smile was encouraging. The woman
agreed to move. He sat in the chair, straight-backed, as she
began to sketch. The artist's gaze alternated between her
subject and her pad. Toolan timed his move for when her attention was on her sketch. He jumped up and grabbed her by
her wrist. From his pocket he produced a pair of handcuffs.
The artist was frozen in terror as Toolan cuffed her wrist to
the door handle of a nearby parked car. Though the worst of
scenarios must have flashed through the artist's mind, it's
doubtful she could have imagined what Toolan was about to
do to her.

As the artist cowered before him, Toolan unzipped his
pants, pulled out his penis, and urinated on her. Finished, the
high school junior zipped up, unlocked the woman, and
walked away chuckling.

I n Paris, Toolan developed a ferocious appetite for alcohol. "He drank tremendous quantities of booze," Doran
remembered. "You name it. Beer, scotch, everything." In
the Parisian clubs that Toolan frequented, customers didn't
buy drinks by the glass; rather, they bought setups for the entire table, a liter of vodka or scotch, usually for about two
hundred dollars. "He'd buy one, then drink the whole bottle
by himself," said Doran. How he had the money to pay for
this type of partying is a mystery.

Doran was not just an innocent onlooker. On many of the
nights in Paris he went drink for drink with Toolan, and he
pulled his share of stunts. But none of them compared to
what his classmate did. What started as teenage oneupman-
ship, became, on Toolan's part, a twisted game of "Watch
this."

Toward the end of the stay in Paris, Toolan, Doran, and a

couple of French girls took a hot-air balloon ride. At five hundred feet up, Toolan decided to frighten one of the French students by threatening to push her over the side of the basket. "He had her by the legs, that's how far out she was hanging," Doran remembered. What was more frightening, at least to those safely inside the basket, was the look in Toolan's eyes. To Doran it seemed like he would really drop her. "It was scary," Doran said.

When Toolan returned to New York, he was a different person. Though chronologically still a child, in Paris he'd discovered the grown-up world of sex and booze, and he liked it. Back in Manhattan, each weekend found him in hangouts like the Palladium, Area, and Studio 54, then in its last throes. Sometimes Doran went along; sometimes Toolan did his drinking alone. It was during these solo crawls that Toolan picked up a habit that stayed with him into adulthood. "He would go to Greenwich Village, to restaurants on West Fourth Street and Bleecker Street," Doran remembered. "He would literally drink his face off, then run out on the check." With the number of bars and restaurants in Greenwich Village, Toolan could have pulled the act every night for a year and not hit the same place twice. According to Doran, Toolan "did it all the time."

The worst of Toolan's personality traits were amplified when he was drinking. One of them was a propensity for cruelty. Under the guise of doing it for laughs, he would surprise people on the street, sometimes elderly men and women, by sneaking up to them then pulling his arm back in a threatening way and hissing: "I should give you the back of my hand!"

By the time Toolan was a senior in high school, he had all the characteristics of an alcoholic. As soon as he picked up a drink, his life became unmanageable. Even in an atmosphere where beer drinking is expected, an all-boys high school, Toolan's alcohol habit stood out. Because of his drinking and acting out, his friendships at Xavier, few to begin with, were practically nonexistent by the time he graduated. Little is known of how his family handled this time of his life, whether his parents addressed their son's problems or whether they even knew of them. One thing is for certain, Toolan's problems with alcohol—and drugs—would get much worse.

I n Toolan's yearbook graduation picture, he looks debonair in a tuxedo jacket and formal white shirt with black studs and a black bow tie. His head is cocked slightly, his hair is full, wavy blond and brushed to one side. His smile is wide and shows a perfect set of teeth. The photograph looks something like a head shot for a soap opera actor—maybe the rich, love interest of the loose girl from the other side of the tracks.

There were times, of course, when Toolan acted just like the seventeen-year-old he was. As his high school days drew to a close, Toolan had some run-ins with his strict Jesuit teachers. According to Rivera, he was suspended from school several times in his senior year, but, as Rivera remembered it, for silly things like cutting up in class, and using bawdy language. Because they shared the trip to France, Toolan and Rivera remained distant friends in senior year. Once Toolan almost got Rivera in trouble when a Jesuit overheard him telling Rivera dirty jokes in the study lounge.

With his pal Mannix, Toolan would head to Shea Stadium and sit in a field box to watch the excitement build around the team from Queens. That version of the Mets, Darryl Strawberry, Dwight Gooden, and the rest, would go on to win the World Series against Boston the year after Toolan graduated from Xavier.

But there were also indications of a young man with developing taste and culture. He loved music, old-school rock: the haunting strains of the Moody Blues in "Days of Future Passed," James Taylor's "Walking Man," Neil Young, and even Billy Joel. He enjoyed some of the new albums, too, especially "Speaking in Tongues" by the Talking Heads. He was a voracious reader, a trait he no doubt inherited from his father, the English teacher. The classics that Xavier demanded resonated within him into his adulthood. Years later he would charm girlfriends, Beth included, with his knowledge of literature. Some of the works he especially liked were Twain's *Tragedy of Puddn'head Wilson*, Faulkner's *Sanctuary*, and, his favorites, as he told a girlfriend years later, *Tomorrow and Tomorrow and Tomorrow*, the collected essays of British novelist and critic Aldous Huxley, and Huxley's darkly comic novel *Time Must Have a Stop*. Perhaps inspired by such literary lights, Toolan nurtured his own creative yearnings. He worked for the school paper and wrote short stories and poetry, for which, according to several sources, he had an affinity. Years later, he met a girl at a bar in a restaurant near Lincoln Center. After chatting her up for a bit, he wrote her a poem on a bar napkin that won, at least temporarily, her heart.

CHAPTER SEVENTEEN

On the heels of his success on Nantucket, Don De-Marco opened a restaurant on Third Avenue on the Upper East Side of Manhattan. The New York version of DeMarco was an immediate success, gaining a coveted two-star review in *The New York Times*. To ensure a smooth opening, Don DeMarco had enlisted the help of the nucleus of the Nantucket restaurant, including Paul Savage, Rosanna Testino, who worked as the hostess, Niall, and Beth.

Don DeMarco is an interesting character. Although he bristles when you call him a Renaissance man, it is a fair characterization. For a while, he worked in politics, first for Nelson A. Rockefeller, then governor of New York State. He later played a small role in Mayor John V. Lindsay's administration in New York City. Then he worked for the National Urban League, where he became friendly with Ron Brown, President Bill Clinton's commerce secretary, who died in a plane crash. He also had a successful career in big business, working for Pfizer, and he is still a headhunter, placing executives in the highest corporate positions. But maybe Don's true love is his writing. He has written a novel, but has yet to find a publisher for it. He also writes songs.

By 1983 Don had completed a show, actually the score of a show, about his restaurant. That summer, his staff, including Beth, performed his musical in the dining room of a hotel DeMarco had rented on Nantucket. For the most part, the songs described the toil and trouble of opening and running a restaurant on a provincial island. Along with a singing chef and a bartender, there are several Nantucket selectmen who perform as a kind of Greek chorus. Beth's role in the show is quite haunting, even given Don DeMarco's denial that the lyrics are in any way connected with her. The character played by Beth is a waitress who receives a Dear John letter from her investment banker boyfriend. The torch song is titled "Don't Save Me a Glass of Wine." Though it does have a few funny lines, it's a sad song, which, according to DeMarco, Beth "sold" in her performance. "It was random casting," DeMarco said. "There was no one else on staff that looked good and could sing."

Manhattan in 1983 was a whole lot of fun. The New York island was electric, fueled by a surging stock market. It was the time of Jay McInerney's *Bright Lights, Big City*, when nightlife was dominated by red-velvet-rope places like the Odeon, Red Parrot, and Area. Tenements that were once home to immigrants now housed yuppies or young people, sometimes two and three in a studio apartment. Beth roomed with Rosanna in a walk-up on the East Side. Niall and Paul were roomies. Beth, especially, took to New York. She had an insatiable desire to explore new things. She loved music, and took in concerts in Central Park as well as places like the Bottom Line and the Lone Star Café. In Manhattan, it seemed every other door was the entrance to another restaurant with every conceivable kind of cuisine. There were the museums, one after the other, on Fifth Avenue's Museum Mile. Beth loved the neighborhoods of Manhattan: Little Italy, Chinatown, and especially Greenwich Village.

The DeMarco staff had just as many giggles in Manhattan as they had on Nantucket. Celebrities like Robert Redford, Ernest Borgnine, Barbara Feldon, Stockard Channing, and Jerry Stiller and Ann Meara were regulars. A scene from the first of the FX movies was shot in the restaurant. One Halloween, Beth dressed up as a bumblebee, an appropriate costume given her energy, and worked the whole night wearing it. One of the customers that night was Joseph Verner Reed, a lifelong diplomat and then U.S. ambassador to Morocco. Reed was instantly fond of Beth and insisted on having a picture taken with her.

The New York DeMarco was fun, and Beth was still an enthusiastic waitress, but she knew she wasn't going to be waiting tables forever. In a conversation with her dad, he expressed his concern for the way she was using her Notre Dame degree. Not that he was pressuring his daughter. All of the Lochtefeld children were encouraged to go to liberal arts colleges, and all took quite different career paths.

Oldest brother Jim went to Colgate for his undergraduate studies. After graduation he spent six months staying with an uncle in Idaho figuring out what he wanted to do with his future. He then went on to study religion at Harvard Divinity School, where he received his master's. Brother Peter, two years Beth's senior, wanted an art career of his own. He became an artist and potter, but with marriage and family he had to make more money than his art was generating. Always a talented carpenter, he went into the contracting business and ultimately built several houses, two of them on Nantucket. Younger sister Cathy worked as an environmental advocate, taught school, and was employed by the United Nations translating French. For a while she studied design and fabric in France. Most recently, Cathy again teaches French, now in Buffalo. Of all the Lochtefeld children, Tommy was the one who took the most traditional path. Though he dabbled for a while in retail, he has spent most of his adult working life in banking and finance. Ultimately, John and Judy wanted for Beth whatever career made her happy. And though there might have been a conversation or two in which John suggested to his daughter that she wasn't getting a full return on her American studies, Beth didn't need much prodding from Dad. She was far too smart, had far too much enthusiasm, to get stuck in the restaurant business for any length of time. Beth knew better than anyone, her nights of slinging hash were almost over.

But there was another reason Beth's days at DeMarco

Even into adulthood, Beth often told her family that catching this bluefish off Nantucket was one of her proudest moments.
Courtesy Tom Lochtefeld

Beth and her brother, Tom. Nantucket's Old North Wharf is in the background. *Courtesy Tom Lochtefeld*

Beth working at the Nantucket Bake Shop. *Courtesy Tom Lochtefeld*

Beth receiving First Class
Girl Scout award.
Courtesy Tom Lochtefeld

Beth and Tony dressed for their senior prom.
Courtesy Tom Lochtefeld

Beth and the DeMarco gang getting ready for work.
Courtesy Tom Lochtefeld

Beth made many of her own outfits. This one was for a friend's wedding.
Courtesy Tom Lochtefeld

With the World Trade Center in the background, Beth posed
for this photograph during her fortieth birthday celebration.
Courtesy Tom Lochtefeld

Beth painting cabinets at
22 Grove Street, her new
apartment. *Courtesy Tom
Lochtefeld*

Beth in Chambord. *Courtesy Tom Lochtefeld*

Tom Toolan soon after his arrest for the murder of Beth Lochtefeld. *Courtesy Associated Press*

Tom Toolan at his arraignment. *Courtesy Associated Press*

Beth's headstone on Nantucket. *Courtesy Tom Lochtefeld*

Ship's Officers

Follow your heart, follow your soul, but also follow your conscience and do what is right and fair. Be thoughtful and intentional, and aware of what is prudent and imprudent behavior. Nightmares are possible when dreaming. Don't fall overboard or do something that will get you thrown in the brig. Take responsibility for your actions.

John Lochtefeld's "Ship's Officers," from *Tell Me About Your Dreams . . .* , John and Beth Lochtefeld's self-published book.
Courtesy Tom Lochtefeld

Even into adulthood, Beth often told her family that catching
this bluefish off Nantucket was one of her proudest moments.
Courtesy Tom Lochtefeld

Beth and her brother, Tom. Nantucket's Old North Wharf is in the background. *Courtesy Tom Lochtefeld*

Beth working at the Nantucket Bake Shop. *Courtesy Tom Lochtefeld*

Beth receiving First Class
Girl Scout award.
Courtesy Tom Lochtefeld

Beth and Tony dressed for their senior prom.
Courtesy Tom Lochtefeld

Beth and the DeMarco gang getting ready for work.
Courtesy Tom Lochtefeld

Beth made many of her own outfits. This one was for a friend's wedding.
Courtesy Tom Lochtefeld

With the World Trade Center in the background, Beth posed for this photograph during her fortieth birthday celebration. *Courtesy Tom Lochtefeld*

Beth painting cabinets at 22 Grove Street, her new apartment. *Courtesy Tom Lochtefeld*

Beth in Chambord. *Courtesy Tom Lochtefeld*

Tom Toolan soon after his arrest for the murder of Beth Lochtefeld. *Courtesy Associated Press*

Tom Toolan at his arraignment. *Courtesy Associated Press*

Beth's headstone on Nantucket. *Courtesy Tom Lochtefeld*

Ship's Officers

Follow your heart, follow your soul, but also follow your conscience and do what is right and fair. Be thoughtful and intentional, and aware of what is prudent and imprudent behavior. Nightmares are possible when dreaming. Don't fall overboard or do something that will get you thrown in the brig. Take responsibility for your actions.

John Lochtefeld's "Ship's Officers," from
Tell Me About Your Dreams . . . , John and
Beth Lochtefeld's self-published book.
Courtesy Tom Lochtefeld

Manhattan were numbered. The passing of twenty years makes the sequence of events hazy and conflicted in people's accounts, but the fact remains that at some point Niall began to date Beth's roommate. Naturally, there were hard feelings. Beth moved out of the East Side apartment she shared with Rosanna and into a tiny place on Bedford Street in Greenwich Village. One person close to Beth called the situation a "serious conflict." But another friend said Beth was already tiring of Niall. Time after time, Beth asked Niall to come along with her as she ventured out into New York City. Time after time, Niall refused. To her brother Tom, Beth quoted Niall as saying: "Beth, go out and do your thing. I'll be here when you get back." But Beth didn't want Niall waiting for her, she wanted him to do things with her. According to a DeMarco friend, however, Beth tried to conform to Niall's wishes. Whatever the circumstance, Beth had to feel betrayed, and by two people: her boyfriend and her roommate.

Perhaps it was just a coincidence, but around the same time Beth seemed to focus on a career and success. A Freudian therapist might call it sublimation, a defense mechanism that keeps uncomfortable feelings at bay through a drive to succeed. It's not the worst defense mechanism to have.

Beth's first job in Manhattan outside of the restaurant business was a company that did multimedia presentations for business meetings. Paul Savage remembered the job as "grueling" for Beth. The company squeezed from her as much value as they could. Beth thought the firm was run in a rather slipshod manner. She told her brother Tom that the people she worked with "would goof around the week before, then pull an all-nighter and put out a half-assed product." As organized and motivated as Beth was, that kind of environment must have been hard to endure. Plus, she still had to wait tables because the pay wasn't nearly enough to live in Manhattan. She was only making about twelve dollars an hour.

Beth was at a crossroads. Around that time, on a Thanksgiving Eve, a friend took Beth to Central Park West and Seventy-seventh Street. There they watched as the Macy's Parade floats, Goofy, Popeye and the lot, were inflated to their larger-than-life expanse by machined air. Beth identified. "I felt like a puddle of material on the ground," Beth once said of that time of her life.

Years later, in front of classroom filled with college kids, Beth reflected on that Thanksgiving Eve: "You have no idea what the balloon is going to be until it's time to blow it up," she said. "I was going to find out what shape I was going to be, I was going to find out what my limits are. I'm going to figure out who I am."

As it happened, Beth was just then on the verge of finding out who she was. And, that answer would come in the most unlikely of places.

CHAPTER EIGHTEEN

In June 1985 Toolan, along with around three hundred other young men, graduated from Xavier High School. The commencement was held at St. Patrick's Cathedral. No doubt his father and mother, like the hundreds of other parents, sat in the pews to watch their sons walk into manhood dressed in cap and gown. The school motto is "Men for Others," and with the trappings of the cathedral, the stirring music, and the pomp, the day is filled with emotion. According to Doran, Toolan drank heavily before the ceremony and was drunk when he received his diploma. "It was a running joke," Doran said.

There is little information about what Toolan did that summer after high school. For the sake of context, let us point out that it wasn't the most exhilarating time in America. It was the year that actor Frankie Muniz was born, *Back to the Future* was the highest grossing movie, Rock Hudson told the world he had AIDS, and Ronald Reagan's supply-side economics was tripling the national debt, widening the gap between rich and poor, and yet lowering unemployment. In the poor neighborhoods of New York City, crack cocaine ravaged the streets and drove the murder rate to unprecedented highs. The following year, 1986, there were almost sixteen hundred murders in the city; many of the dead black and Hispanic teenage boys who died within a few miles' radius of Park Slope. But the neighborhood in which Tom Toolan lived only became more affluent. A *New York Times* real estate article deemed it "the hottest" neighborhood in the city. As the demographic of the young and the privileged swelled, there was less and less to hold their interest. Even an American Express card and BWM 535i lose their luster after a while. Meanwhile, the temptations of Manhattan, drugs, and sex called.

That September Toolan began classes at Colby College in Waterville, Maine. According to Colby's Web site, the school is a "highly selective liberal arts college." Chartered back in 1813, Colby calls itself the "twelfth-oldest independent liberal arts college in the nation." In 1871 it became the first previously all-male college to admit women.

Though Colby offered a first-rate education within the trappings of a small New England college, Toolan's experience there would be limited to one semester. At Colby, or perhaps the summer before, Toolan stepped up his substance abuse to include LSD. He rarely went to class; instead, his time in Maine was like a continuation of Paris—even to the point of exhibiting some of the same sickening behavior.

According to one story that filtered back to Park Slope, during his first and only semester, Toolan took a road trip to Bowdoin College, another prestigious private school about an hour's ride south of Colby. There he attended a party thrown by a Bowdoin fraternity. At some point he climbed onto a piano, unzipped his fly, pulled out his penis, and urinated on a horrified female student.

Colby might be selective about admission, but when Toolan decided to leave, the school gladly opened the door. According to Colby records, Toolan withdrew from every class in which he was enrolled that first semester. On his departure from school, he was given no grades, received no college credit, and never returned.

By Christmas break he was back at 35 Prospect Park West looking nothing like the young man in the Xavier crimson blazer. His hair was unkempt and down to his shoulders; he had a full, scraggly beard. Though he was trying hard to affect a Grateful Deadhead look, he managed to hold on to some of Park Slope's pretensions. He smoked Dunhill English cigarettes, and had a penchant, according to Doran, for blowing smoke in your face when he talked to you. His parents, lifelong educators, couldn't have been happy with their son's aborted college career. There must have been a great deal of tension in the Toolan home that Christmas. By then, Toolan had tasted freedom twice: in Paris and at Colby. He had seen and experienced too much to play the role of dutiful son if, in fact, he'd ever played that role. His Christmas stay at his parents' home would be short, and his exit would be talked about for years afterward.

According to two people close to Toolan then, the story goes something like this: On the evening of the day after Christmas 1985, Toolan ran into Jim Mannix in the elevator of 35 Prospect Park West. The two childhood friends hadn't seen each other since the fall, when they both left for school. After they traded college stories, Mannix mentioned that his father had given him a brand-new red station wagon for Christmas. He asked Toolan if he wanted to take a ride. When they returned to their building, Toolan told his friend that he had forgotten to buy cigarettes. He asked to borrow the car to go pick some up. Mannix was leery, but Toolan could be very persuasive. Mannix gave in to the request; after all, they had been best friends all their lives.

As Mannix watched Toolan drive off down Prospect Park West that evening, he saw the last of his Christmas present. In fact, it was the last anyone from Park Slope would see of Toolan for quite some time. According to most accounts, weeks became months, and Toolan made no attempt to contact his mother and father. According to Doran, Toolan's parents didn't know if their son was dead or alive.

There is no record of the car being reported stolen to the police. Mr. Mannix had far too much class and money to embarrass his good friends and downstairs neighbors. And though the story hit the Park Slope rumor mill—in fact, twenty years later it is still told—in the world of social climbing the rumor mill is not nearly as damaging as newsprint or police reports. But inaction by friends and family may have damaged Toolan more than if charges had been pressed. Though surrounded by academics his whole life,

Toolan never learned the basic lesson that his actions had consequences.

I f you remove the fact that Toolan stole his best friend's car, there is a certain free-spirited innocence to following the Grateful Dead: jester hats, save the trees, and the odd tab of acid. By 1986 the Dead had, literally, a new generation of fans. Toolan, at nineteen, fell squarely in the middle of that demographic. It was a year of crisis for the Dead, as Jerry Garcia's continued drug use caused a near-fatal diabetic coma. Garcia recovered and the band played on. As always, the Dead sold venues out across the country. Huge gatherings for concerts were like carnivals, with tie-dye as far as the eye could see. But there was an unseemly underside to the new version of "tour heads," as they were called. In 1995 Carolyn Ruff, then a news aide for *The Washington Post*, wrote about her experiences following the Dead:

"In my seven years as a devoted Deadhead—including two spent touring the country—I came to take for granted that people would steal from a friend's backpack and rationalize their actions. I saw friends sleep with other friends' partners. I saw young women sexually assaulted after being unwittingly dosed with acid. I saw someone give a friend's dog acid just to watch it lose its mind. . . ."

The new generation of Deadheads was not nearly as innocent as their predecessors. By 1986 crack cocaine had its claws deep into the Dead's following. Although Deadheads will assure you that they were the targets of Gestapo police, by the early 1990s there were over two thousand Deadheads serving long-term drug sentences in prisons across the country. Acid-propelled suicides were commonplace. And there was an army of parents left wondering whether their sons and daughters were dead in some seedy motel room or in a shallow desert grave.

In all, Toolan was gone for seven months. Steve Doran said that it was common knowledge in Xavier circles that Toolan did "heavy" amounts of acid while following the band. He made and sold bracelets, a commodity on the

Dead's tours. Eventually, the station wagon was found with a broken axle, abandoned somewhere in the Southwest, perhaps New Mexico.

After Toolan returned to Park Slope, his parents lived in constant fear that he would disappear again. "They were afraid he'd go underground," said the father of one of Toolan's classmates. "They were scared he'd just take off." But the fear didn't keep them from trying to control his life, at least according to Toolan. Years later a friend who was in a therapeutic situation with Toolan said that he often lamented his life choices, that he wanted to write and act, while his parents demanded he prepare for a career in something more substantial, like finance.

Somehow Toolan pulled his act together and enrolled in Columbia University. Private universities like Columbia are notoriously tight-lipped when it comes to divulging student information. Toolan's name is not listed as a graduate in any yearbook, nor does he show up in any clubs or fraternities. Columbia does, however, confirm that Toolan graduated in 1991 from their school of General Studies with a major in English literature.

It was after graduating from Columbia that Toolan first traveled to Nantucket. There he worked as an intern for the Actors Theatre of Nantucket. He even had a small role in a one-act thriller, *Specter*. The founding director of the theater company, Richard Cary, told the Nantucket *Inquirer and Mirror* that Toolan was a "serious guy," but he couldn't clearly remember Toolan's stage talent. "I think he was a good actor," Cary said.

One of the first friends Toolan made on Nantucket was Will Berry, who worked as an artist and set designer with the theater company. Toolan and Berry would remain friends for years, though to other friends their relationship was something of mystery. Toolan had several of Berry's paintings in his apartment on West End Avenue. One longtime girlfriend of Toolan's remembered him talking about Berry often, and in devoted terms. But in the year and a half the girlfriend and Toolan were together, only once did they visit the artist at his studio near Union Square in Manhattan.

If Toolan kept his partying under control long enough to get through Columbia, in Nantucket the restraints came off. A woman who gave an interview to *The Inquirer and Mirror* knew Toolan from those days. She described him as having a drinking problem and, when he was drunk, habitually asking her to marry him. "There were times I was tempted," the woman, who asked not to be identified, said about Toolan's marriage talk. "He and I were a perfect match because he was a lot of fun. But this was before I would see him waking and drinking. . . . Later on in our friendship-relationship, I saw him wake up and drink and throw up and continue to drink rather that eat." The woman said that Toolan drank liters of booze in a day. "I really mean liters," she said. "He put away a lot of alcohol."

As the years passed, the deleterious effect of Toolan's alcohol consumption would grow greater. Rapaciously, it ripped at his life, and the lives of those close to him.

CHAPTER NINETEEN

Beth had no idea of the depth of the shark pool into which she was about to swim. She learned of the job through Paul Savage in 1986. He had answered a job listing in *The New York Times* for a position at an architectural firm. Savage told Beth that he had liked the people he met with, but he didn't think the job was for him. He then handed the firm's business card to Beth. For a while at Notre Dame, Beth had worked in the architecture library. It just might be a good fit, she thought. She took the card from Savage and, later, called the number.

For years, all you had to do to become a building code expeditor in New York City was to call yourself one. Only recently was any kind of certification required. Hired by architects, building owners, or contractors, an expeditor essentially obtains the appropriate building permits from New York City's Department of Buildings. Perhaps the first time anyone used the term "expeditor" was in 1931. A man by the name of William Finn was testifying in court in a case of graft during the construction of a Broadway theater. Finn told the judge that he was employed by a group of builders; his job was to "expedite" the necessary building permits from the city. He insisted that his dealings with the city were honorable. According to the *Times*, "Finn declared he never gave even a cigar to advance projects in which his clients were interested." If Finn was telling the truth, which is debatable, he might have been one of the few honest expeditors. That is, until Beth.

Though becoming an expeditor is easy, being an expeditor is anything but. The Department of Buildings in New York City has an encyclopedic collection of rules and regulations. There is the old building code (prior to 1968), the new building code, multiple-dwelling laws, and asbestos-removal laws. There are zoning ordinances, fire-safety codes, housing maintenance codes, and that's just to scratch the surface. In all, the building codes of New York City comprise a volume that is three thousand pages thick. Each year the DOB handles forty thousand applications for building permits. When Beth started expediting, she had to know by heart more than fifty different standard forms. But perhaps even harder than learning the codes and the forms is dealing with the people who inhabit the industry.

There has been graft and corruption in the construction business in New York City since the Dutch swindled the Indians out of Manhattan. One of the first major recorded scandals was in the nineteenth century and revolved around William M. "Boss" Tweed. The undisputed heavyweight of the crooked political machine Tammany Hall, Tweed was convicted of accepting bribes from municipal contractors. The amounts were staggering, enough to make Tweed in the 1860s the largest single property owner in New York City.

Throughout the late 1800s into the 1900s, as the city continued to grow, so did opportunities for construction kickbacks and graft. A good portion of it was conducted with impertinence. An investigation into the Bureau of Public Buildings in 1907 uncovered bank deposits in a public building official's account that exactly matched the amounts of a series of government contracts. The official defense was that it was just a "strange coincidence."

In 1930 the resignation of New York City Mayor James J. "Jimmy" Walker came about partly as a result of an investigation into the city's Bureau of Buildings, the predecessor of the DOB. Famed jurist Samuel Seabury led the investigation of Walker, who was, as one *New York Times* writer recently called him, "complaisant, casually corrupt." One of Walker's underlings was Rollin C. Bastress, a crooked chief inspector in the Bureau of Buildings. In front of the Seabury Commission, Bastress denied any knowledge of graft in his bureau. When Seabury offered a mountain of evidence to the contrary, Bastress backpedaled a bit. He said he had "from time to time" heard "rumors" of graft. Jimmy Walker would hightail it out of New York and sail to Europe, in part, because of those "rumors."

In 1972 a *New York Times* exposé estimated the construction industry paid twenty-five million dollars a year in bribes, mostly to building inspectors and other city officials. "Hardly a skyscraper is built, scarcely a change is made in the world's most celebrated skyline, hardly a brownstone is renovated or a restaurant expanded without the illegal payoffs," the article stated. One expediter tried to bribe an undercover police officer involved in a sting operation. The expediter would later testify in front of a grand jury that he bribed about a hundred people in the DOB and other agencies. Most of the bribes were in the form of cash, though there were also theater tickets and dinners. The amounts ranged from as little as two dollars to as much as fifteen hundred. He told the jury that he had bribed "everyone from clerks to planning examiners, chief planning examiners, building inspectors, their supervisors, a deputy borough superintendent, the borough superintendent—just about everybody in the line." According to one commissioner of the NYC Department of Investigations, corruption in the DOB was "systematic, widespread, high-dollar and driven by supervisors."

Beth felt a bit out of place when she first walked into the DOB. In describing those days to a class of college students, Beth said, "There were old guys with toupees and pinky rings chomping on their cigars, and the woman had really high heels, really big low cleavage."

Expeditors sometimes called themselves "fixers," as in "we can fix any problem for a price." Sometimes that "price" was paid directly to officials at the Department of Buildings. Beth often told friends and family about the building inspector who called himself "the Doctor." Under his desk, the doctor kept a coffee can, and if you paid your insurance, "you'd get the cure." There were certain expediting companies who told their female employees "to wear spandex" when an important permit or approval was needed. Beth would never rely on spandex. Instead, she approached her new job with a terrific memory for details, and the saccharine attitude of a new intern.

Paul Savage once said that Beth could take a dessert order for a table of eight, complete with espressos, cappuccinos, and after-dinner drinks, without writing it down. Relying on that ability, Beth committed much of the often-used rules and regulations of building permits to memory. The ones she didn't know right off, she knew where to find. Although she wasn't a city kid, Beth had some street smarts, perhaps learned in her nights in the restaurant business. She was savvy enough to learn quickly the procedures at the DOB. In very simple terms, the whole point of expediting is to get to see a building inspector as quickly as possible. During Beth's time, when the DOB was headquartered at 60 Hudson Street in lower Manhattan, there were only twenty-two inspectors in the building, and sometimes as many as three hundred expeditors.

In 1991 an article by Sarah Bartlett in *The New York Times* explained a trick of the expeditor trade: "On many a weekday morning at, say, 5:30 or 6, a visitor to the New York City Department of Buildings will step out of an elevator into a series of empty corridors and stumble upon briefcases, standing in lines like toy soldiers, with their owners nowhere in sight." The briefcases were there to save spots, and Beth's was always one of the first in line. According to a friend, Beth was quoted in the article, though she refused to give her name for fear of reprisal from the city agency. "I get up at 5:30, throw a coat on over my pajamas, hop in a taxi, and go down to the Buildings Department. Then I go home and go back to bed," Beth presumably said.

In the beginning, income from expediting wasn't great. Beth was paid twelve or thirteen dollars an hour, about what she had made at the multimedia company. But she learned at every step, and right away the clients liked her. She also quickly realized that she was being woefully underpaid. The company she was working for was billing her out to other firms for as much as sixty dollars an hour. An idea began to form. If she could work freelance for her employers, why couldn't she work freelance for herself? But it was the slimy side of the expediting business, rather than the amount Beth was being paid, that finally convinced her to go out on her own. "I loved the industry," Beth once said. "But I had a little problem with their ethics."

Several years after Beth started expediting, fourteen inspectors in the Department of Buildings were arrested in a sting operation. One expeditor who testified for the prosecution said that an inspector had a series of simple hand signals that he worked out with expeditors. If he put two fingers on his cheek, he expected a payoff of two grand, four fingers, four grand, and so on. There is one expediter who goes by the name "Fat Nate," whom at least one building executive calls a "made guy," in the development mafia. Beth called the shadowy figures in her industry "the cement shoes people." Years later she said, "I was working with the Sopranos ten years before I even knew about the Sopranos."

One day Beth's employer asked her to drop a briefcase off at a work site. When she asked the contents, she was told it didn't concern her. Beth remembered the conversation to a college class: Just drop it off in the bathroom of the site, they said. "I'm not doing that," Beth answered. Come on, her boss said in a cajoling way. You don't have to unzip the briefcase, you don't have to know what's in it, you don't even have to pay attention to it. Just put it on the job site; that's all you have to do. Again, Beth said no. "I was ready to give notice and leave that very day," she said. Instead, that night she had a talk with her dad.

"I wish I could just quit and go off on my own," Beth told her father. "Well, why don't you?" John answered. Beth began to whine about the startup costs: the expensive code books she'd have to buy, the copy machine she'd need, and a couple of months rent she had to have just in case.

"How much do you need?" her father asked.

Beth quit the architectural consulting firm and on April 1, 1987, eight days before her twenty-seventh birthday—when she was "still twenty-six," as she liked to say—Beth, all by herself, opened Beth Lochtefeld, Code Consultant/Expediter, Inc.

Certainly, there were conveniences in working out of her apartment. She was her own boss. There was no office politics. The commute was short enough. But there were also drawbacks. First of all, the apartment was tiny and dark. Two bedrooms, but one was only seven feet by seven feet, and the other wasn't much bigger. As Beth did at Notre Dame, she stayed up all hours figuring out codes for jobs she had procured. Now, instead of textbooks and term papers spread across her bed, it was the thick code manuals of DOB. As in her college days, she wouldn't go to sleep until the bed was cleared of work. The work was tedious, and went late into the night. But maybe her biggest problem was her neighbor.

Narrow and crooked Bedford Street is one of the more colorful in Greenwich Village. The entrance to Beth's apartment building was just a few steps away from Carmine Street where a Mafia don named Chin Giganti for years fooled the FBI into thinking he was mentally unstable by walking around in his bathrobe. A few blocks beyond stands a bar called Chumley's. Once a speakeasy, Chumley's operates without any sign and with a secret entrance through an arched doorway. Like most New York City apartments, though, the walls in Beth's place offered practically no sound insulation. Some nights, Beth could swear the woman in the next apartment was standing in the same room with her. To make matters worse, the woman had a very active gay social life, often coming home late with prospective lovers whom she had met during her nocturnal sorties. There were times Beth was downright embarrassed by the passion loudly playing out next door. To drown out the bawdy talk and moans, Beth would turn on her television or put on headphones. But that only proved a bigger distraction. For Beth, the colorful Village was turning into a nightmare.

One night, curiosity took over. Beth told friends and family that she overheard the conversation next door.

"There's a first time for everyone," Beth heard her neighbor reason.

"I want to, but I don't know if I should," the prospect quavered.

"It's really not so bad," the neighbor soothed.

"I think I'm attracted to you," said the new friend, her defenses slipping.

"You won't regret it," said the woman.

Beth couldn't keep quiet. She stood sock-footed on her couch and began banging the wall. "Don't do it!" she screamed. "Don't do it."

The neighbor's apartment fell silent, and then there was the sound of a door slamming and footfalls down the hallway. Beth heard nothing else coming from the apartment the rest of that evening, and, for that matter, all the evenings that followed. It took awhile for Beth to get back to normal, though. For about a week's worth of nights, she found herself listening for developments.

Though Beth loved the Village, it was a place that never really felt safe. Some of that fear was well founded. Lower Manhattan in the late eighties and early nineties still had its share of crime. It was just good sense for a single woman to keep alert. But some of Beth's fear stemmed from a less tangible source.

At some point during Beth's life, she had had her astrological chart read. At least one friend of the family remembers it being at a fair during her high school days. Someone else said it was done on Nantucket. Wherever the chart was read, it had an enormous effect on Beth. Among astrologers, it is considered verboten to reveal a horrible or violent ending to someone's life. For one thing, any astrologer worth their tarot cards knows that the future is fluid, that the events that form it can and do change all the time. Whoever read Beth's chart didn't know the rules.

At one point, Beth gave her sister, Cathy, a key to the Bedford Street apartment in case she ever needed a place to stay in the city. One night, Cathy was on a date in Manhattan that went later than planned. While Beth slept in the bedroom, Cathy let herself in. Cathy tiptoed into the bedroom and gently nudged her sister. Beth bolted awake and screamed in sheer terror. When she finally realized it was Cathy, she began to sob uncontrollably. That night she confided to Cathy that, since the reading of her chart, her worst fear was of being attacked when she was alone. Next door to her apartment was a gypsy palm reader. Beth walked past her several times a day, and her heart would quicken each time she did. No one, friend or family, could talk Beth into going into the place.

Out in the real world Beth had enormous courage and confidence. Filled with the toupee-wearing cigar chompers, the DOB was something of a bullpen, a men's locker room populated with ex-plumbers and electricians, the same guys who'd wolf-whistle at a girl going by at lunchtime. Beth quickly figured out how to use the testosterone-driven atmosphere to her advantage. She was no longer the jeans and T-shirt college girl. Having now worked for years in upscale restaurants on the islands of Nantucket and Manhattan, Beth had acquired cosmopolitan tastes and a wardrobe to match. She could even produce a "salmoni alert" of her own. Bob Burke, a contractor who dated Beth briefly, observed Beth at work in the DOB. "Here was this stunning redhead, tall, great body, then she comes in and dazzles them with her knowledge of the code," Burke said. By all accounts, Beth used the advantages she could.

Her company appealed to the upscale architects who didn't want to deal with the dirty-fingernail crowd of expediters. At first the denizens of the DOB saw Beth as an amusing curiosity, a sort of Girl Scout in stockings. "They laughed at her," said her brother Tom. But the laughter subsided as more and more business went Beth's way. She came up with a price chart, a menu of sorts, and a practice unheard-of at the DOB. She quickly built a reputation for sticking to the price she quoted—no matter if the job took one day or six months. According to Beth, her company was the only one in the industry that had standardized contracts, whereas others charged what the market would bear. "A lot of other people in the industry would determine just how desperate the guy needs his permit," she once said. Not only did Beth have to make enough to live and to keep the business going, she had the pressure of her clients, which could be extreme. If, say, an expeditor got the wrong permits for a restaurant under renovation, the restaurant might remain closed for weeks longer than it had to and cost the owners tens of thousands in lost business. Maybe it was all those slamming nights at DeMarco that readied her for the DOB pressure. Maybe it was her organizational skills, the homemaker's tools she had learned from Judy Lochtefeld. Whatever it was, Beth showed remarkable cool for her situation.

In no time, the business phone in the office was ringing steadily. She hired an expeditor named Wafa. Most days were spent in the halls of the DOB. Work went late every night. Her social life suffered. She ordered in a lot of takeout food and gained some weight. Off and on during her life she struggled with an acne problem that was a result of stress and poor diet. But she knew she was on to something. Although she wouldn't go so far as saying she had a good chance of becoming rich, the money was coming in steadily. And the future looked pretty good.

CHAPTER TWENTY

By 1988, after only one year, Beth's business had grown enough for her to buy a small one-bedroom apartment at 22 Grove Street, a postcard block. With five- and six-story buildings with red doors and fronted by high steps, Grove Street is the quintessential Greenwich Village street, and a realized dream for Beth. Her first night in the new apartment, Beth and a friend drank Veuve Clicquot champagne and did ballerina twirls through the rooms. They were a good match, Beth and the Village. The neighborhood spoke to her heart. For as much as Beth was her mother's daughter, with her A-personality organization, she had much of her father's artist soul. In the late eighties, Greenwich Village was both as dynamic as anytime in its rich history and also one of the saddest, most affecting places on the planet. The stock market plunge of 1987 had driven the new Wall Street money from its crooked blocks. This was a good thing. Back was the creative spirit of artists and students that had always characterized the Village. But it was also ground zero of the AIDS plague. There weren't enough flowers, quilts, or tears to pay appropriate homage to the dead. Memorials ran one into another until they became part of the routine, an unpleasant chore. But somehow fun was still had. And Beth knew how to have it.

Maybe the largest party New York City throws, outside of New Year's Eve, is the Halloween Parade in the Village. It started in 1973 when a puppeteer and mask maker walked with his wares from home to home in his Greenwich Village neighborhood. In its beginning, the parade wound through the West Village streets, just steps from Beth's Bedford Street apartment. The parade grew quickly, though, and was moved in 1985 to Sixth Avenue and West Fourth Street. Even with the pallor of AIDS hanging over the Village, the parade was the one night when partying was most appropriate. And Beth never met a party she didn't like. Somehow, in the midst of running her own business, Beth had time to make her own costume for the parade. Under Judy's tutelage, all of the Lochtefeld children had learned how to sew. The boys mended sports gear and trouser cuffs; the girls altered Scout uniforms and party dresses. After making the dress she wore to her senior prom, a Halloween costume was kid stuff. One of the more memorable of her getups was a pair of lips surrounded by tubes of lipstick.

But the main reason Beth had fun in the Village was Kevin Yoder.

Though it had been four years, the instant Beth saw Kevin it was the first six weeks of Notre Dame all over again. Kevin had moved from California and lived just blocks from Beth. "By then I could run with Beth," Kevin said in his eulogy. "And run we did." Each Christmas Beth and Kevin would host a party they dubbed "Bacchanalia." They had matching aprons made emblazoned with the head of Bacchus, the Roman god of wine. "When I was most under fire," Kevin told those gathered at St. Bartholomew's, "she would sneak into my apartment to work alchemy in the kitchen, with recipes cribbed from her years at DeMarco." Beth's philosophy when it came to cooking was the same as hers in life, Kevin said. When possible, double all the interesting ingredients. "Bourbon balls became lethal asteroids of cocoa and whiskey, soups an indulgent savory bath of flavor."

Beth had more than a bit of Martha Stewart about her. She began a ritual she called "pancake Sundays," a brunch that she prepared for friends that went on for years. Several Christmases were spent at the home of her brother Peter and his first wife, Angela, in New Hampshire, a spot the family called Midnight Farm. Beth left this note one Christmas morning for her hosts:

12/25/93

   Dream of Christmas—the holly and ivy, the delicately decorated pine boughs of the tree, the crackling fire the nectar sweet clementines, the salty Christmas ham, the snow on Christmas morning, the pots of good coffee and the mounds of gifts. The parade of family and the continuously growing piles of paper torn from packages swept to the side. The row of nut crackers, the bowl of citrus fruit, the new toys with lots of pieces, the shrinking woodpile, the effervescent champagne, the rolled up rugs for the dance party, the glorious black goblets filled with Kendall Jackson nature's reserve chardonnay, the urns filled with cut boughs.

   Christmas traditions are started with the first Christmas at home and as such a basis to grow from! I will be part of your recipe anytime!

   XO love, Beth

By most accounts, Beth's dating during the early years of her business was sporadic. There is little doubt that her business took priority in her life. It had also taken some time for her to get over Niall. At least one friend said that Beth's heart hurt over Niall for years. Yet when opportunity and appeal presented themselves, Beth took the chance. None of her liaisons worked out in the long term. Of Beth, Vickie Taveras, one of her longest-term employees, said that she wished she could find a guy like her brothers: Jim's intelligence, Peter's creativity, Tom's responsibility. It was a tall order to fill, and perhaps a clue to why she stayed single: She set the bar impossibly high.

One of the guys whom Beth dated briefly was contractor Bob Burke. Beth and Burke met in a businesslike setting: at a building on the Upper West Side owned by a mutual friend. Burke remembered the moment: "She wore charcoal slacks, a black blazer." Burke was impressed by Beth's business acumen. "She had a knowing smile that said: 'I know the game, and I know I'm good at it.'"

Their first date was at an outdoor opera concert in Central Park. The weather cooperated; it was a warm summer night. Beth, in full Martha Stewart mode, showed up with a picnic basket filled with dessert cheeses, strawberries with powdered sugar. She remembered that Burke had told her he didn't drink alcohol, so she brought a bottle of sparkling cider for him and a half bottle of wine for herself. "At night she was so much softer, more feminine, not that she could be unfeminine," Burke said.

In addition to the construction business, they had Catholic colleges in common. During breaks in the music, they compared his years at Boston College with hers at Notre Dame. By appearances, they looked a good fit. Though perhaps ten years older than Beth, Burke was athletic and handsome. He had had a fairly successful acting career and had had a substantial role in the singles-bar nightmare movie *Looking for Mr. Goodbar.*

Beth and Burke went to a tiny, romantic restaurant in the Village on their second date. "She wore a blouse with a high collar, Victorian lace, a fall of strawberry blond hair," Burke remembered. Over dinner they chatted about Beth's growing business. Burke remembered clearly that Beth was excited and confident. At some point during the evening, they both realized that their relationship was not meant for the long term. Burke's acting career had ended when he was married and had a child. His daughter was then three years old. Though Burke was then divorced, Beth wasn't in the market for an instant family. "I got this sense that in ten years this woman would be fully established and then she would have a family," Burke remembered thinking. "This is a woman way out of my sphere," Burke thought. "I was working as a carpenter just at sixes and sevens; she was a woman with a purpose."

That night, Beth invited Burke up to her apartment. He

remembered it as being warmly lit, with soft yellow walls hung with sketches and paintings. Her comforter was the color of eggplant. Beth told him she drank buttermilk before she went to bed, and she offered him a glass.

CHAPTER
TWENTY-ONE

By 1990, the downstairs neighbors in the Grove Street apartment house were complaining about Beth's chair rolling on the wood floor at all hours of the night. Beth had carpets installed, but that only slightly muffled the sound. She had hired Vickie Tavares as a secretary. Vickie sat behind a mountain of paperwork at a desk in Beth's dining-living room. The phone rang all day, the doorbell, too. Sometimes there were as many as twenty or thirty UPS pickups and deliveries a day. The apartment became so crowded that Beth moved the fax machine and file cabinets out into the hallway.

With a mortgage on the apartment, and the business still new, Beth was under a considerable amount of stress. Though she never showed anger, she became frustrated quickly, especially when her workers made lazy mistakes. She rented a piano, and would make sure she took an hour each day to practice. Some years later, her dad would pick up the same habit; in Nantucket he would play the piano for an hour at noon to help him settle his thoughts. She also joined a stretch class that, no matter how busy she was, she faithfully attended. Beth told her family she felt "like Jell-O" after the class. But maybe it was the long hours on the phone talking to her brother Jim, who is, according to one family member, the best listener of the Lochtefelds, that helped Beth handle the stress best.

Though Beth was organized to a fault, the tedium of

billing clients, paying insurance, investing, and doing pay-roll for herself and Vickie was not how she wanted to spend her time. She'd much rather be out in the field, so to speak, generating business and taking care of customers. Beth was a natural salesman. Just as in DeMarco when she offered the blueberry dessert, clients found it hard to say no to her. She'd make time for lunches with clients. She'd remember birthdays and anniversaries of clients and send flowers or homemade cards. On her business checks she'd draw a little smiley face or personalize it with a note. She was even mindful of competitors. When one rival expeditor was given a promotion by his firm, Beth sent him a congratulatory card. When business overflowed, Beth sent clients to rivals, a practice unheard-of in the contentious world of expediting.

But the business of doing business was wearing on her. Too much of her time was spent preparing her clients' bills and paying her own. Each morning she was at the DOB be-fore sunrise, her briefcase holding her spot. Beth needed to hire someone, this she knew. But there was a trust issue at work. To bring a stranger in and to give him the keys to the company safe, so to speak, wasn't something Beth was ready to do. So, as she would do all of her life when she was in a tight spot, Beth went to her family for help.

Younger brother Tom had graduated from Harvard a few years before and was working at Republic National Bank. He lived in Brooklyn and his commute home from work brought him right by Beth's apartment. Once every week or so, Tom spent four or five hours in the evening going over Beth's billable hours and expenditures. For a while Tom's help was enough. But soon Beth needed more than just a sec-retary and a part-time bookkeeper. She asked Tom to come work with her full-time.

Tom left his job with Republic National Bank in May 1990. His first assignment at his new job was to find office space for Beth's company, which now numbered four em-ployees. The best estimate is that the company was then grossing about a half million dollars a year. The company moved into an office at 536 Broadway.

Despite Wall Street's difficulties in the late eighties, Manhattan's real estate market was gaining momentum. With a considerable mortgage, Beth paid $175,000 for the 22 Grove Street apartment. Moving her business out of her apartment was important to Beth for a couple of reasons. The move was a direct result of the business's growth. In her eyes, an office made her company more official. Plus, the move gave Beth part of her life back, made her apartment more of a home. There was a big problem with the picture, though. She didn't get a good deal on the apartment. She had paid more than market value.

What's more, the apartment received very little sunlight, which would be a plaintive wail of Beth's for some time. "If I could just get an apartment with more light, I'd be so much happier," she often said. If that wasn't bad enough, it turned out that the building had serious financial problems. Light or no light, Beth didn't want to lose her apartment or her money. She came close to losing both.

The co-op market in Manhattan is like no other business in the world. The practice of co-oping apartment buildings actually began in the 1880s. Then building co-ops were formed for the express purpose of excluding people. Even today, a co-op board answers to practically no regulatory body. Co-op boards can turn down applications for apartments for almost any reason they want. Though some upscale buildings still adhered to the narrow-mindedness of that practice, co-oping by the 1980s was all about money. Owners converted their buildings for instant cash payouts. Even longtime renters were beneficiaries. To be a tenant in a building going co-op was tantamount to hitting the lottery. Owners standing to earn huge sums bought out tenants' leases or offered them an insider's price for the apartment. The tenants could then buy their own apartment for sometimes as low as half the market value. If they turned around and sold it right away, they made a hundred percent profit. If they held the apartment for a couple of years, they could often triple their investment.

Even banks fell under the intoxicating spell of the co-op market, often lending money to building owners with less than reputable histories.

To fully explain the situation of Beth's building would be a tedious affair. Simply put, however, like any business, a co-op has to at least break even in order to survive. Each apartment in the building has to pull its own financial weight. Twenty-two Grove Street was not breaking even. One of the reasons was there were tenants who had lived in the building for years and paid only minuscule rents. With nowhere else to go, these tenants wanted neither to buy their apartments nor accept the cash buyout. It was a lose-lose situation for some: The building owner couldn't sell the apartments, and the co-op, the owners of the other apartments, had to assume the maintenance cost of the rental apartments. It was not a hopeful situation. To make matters worse, the owner of the building had a myriad of business problems, not the least of which being that the building was broke. The building owner had obtained a "wraparound loan," which essentially was a refinancing of the building. Such loans are supposed to be presented in full view of the co-op board. But banks, looking to cash in on the fat market, sometimes cut corners. It wasn't a sound business move on the bank's part. Worst still, the building's owner was in default and nowhere to be found.

Not long after, Beth came home and found an official-looking paper that had been slid under the apartment house front door. It was a notice from the bank that the refinancing of the building was in default. There was a very good chance that Beth was going to lose her apartment. She went looking for a lawyer.

Stuart Saft is often referred to as the "dean of co-op law." As a longtime officer in the Council of New York Cooperatives, Mr. Saft is often called on to lend his experience and opinions to *The New York Times*. Most of Saft's clients own big buildings and deal in lots of money. An architect friend introduced Beth to Saft. At first, Saft only agreed to find Beth someone better suited to represent her. He met with the co-op board of 22 Grove in Beth's apartment. Since it was Beth who had found the notice, the ad-hoc co-op committee appointed her to be their spokesperson.

A week later, at Stuart Saft's office, Beth met with the banker who held the note on her building. A surly man, with the manners of a loan shark, the banker lit right into Beth. "Beth was just a kid then," remembered Saft. "And the gorilla starts to yell at her. He says: 'You're not an officer, you're not a director. What are you doing here?'"

Beth was completely taken by surprise. At one point Saft noticed tears welling in Beth's eyes. In that moment, the dean of co-op law decided that 22 Grove was plenty big enough for him to represent.

Beth didn't stay the weeping victim for long. The first thing she did was to ingratiate herself with the co-op board, and she quickly became the board president. Up to that point she hadn't the time, or the inclination, for building politics. But now it was her home that was at stake. The next thing she did was to call everyone she knew in the real estate business, a considerable list. She asked advice from building owners and plumbing inspectors, from real estate sales people and architects.

Meanwhile, Saft rattled his sword. He threatened to take the case to the state attorney general's office. Through tedious petitioning and litigation he was able to have those apartments whose titles were still held by the building owner seized. Most of the apartments weren't pulling their own weight financially. They either housed elderly or illegal tenants, people using the apartments as a secondary residence—a direct violation of rent-control laws. The ownership of those apartments was transferred to the co-op board, a substantial financial burden. Several of the co-op members had the wherewithal and the foresight to see the potential in the apartments. One member, a well-to-do stockbroker, bought two or three of the available apartments at auction prices. The only other person to buy multiple apartments was Beth.

As mentioned, this is a very rudimentary telling of the story. Beth and Saft returned to the angry banker. At that meeting, and at subsequent meetings, Beth was a completely different person from the one who quailed before him. She was now an officer of the building, knew what she was talking about, and did so with authority. Ultimately, Saft and Beth convinced the banker to allow them to refinance the building, easing some of the pressure. "She knew nothing about it when she started," Saft said of Beth's knowledge of co-op law. "She made herself into an expert. She was running a multimillion-dollar real estate business."

In many ways, Beth lived a charmed life. But it seemed the harder she worked, the luckier she got. The apartments Beth bought, 6E and 6F, were on the top floor of the building. Elderly women paying about two hundred a month in rent occupied both apartments. When Beth restructured the loan on the building with the bank, one of the consequences was that the maintenance on every apartment rose to eight hundred dollars. That meant Beth had to pay the six-hundred-dollar difference between the rent, which was now paid to her as owner of the apartments, and the maintenance. It was a gamble. Beth had to keep paying it as long as the women lived in the apartments. It was also a gamble because the sale of the apartments had to be public, an auction. Beth filed all the appropriate paperwork and was ultimately the highest bidder: seven thousand dollars for each apartment, a total of fourteen grand.

Within a year, both tenants died. One of the women had no family or close friends. Beth contacted a nearby church and put together a memorial. She spread the word around the building, and many of the neighbors came to pay their respects. Brian Porzak, one of those neighbors, talked about Beth to *People*: "There were pictures from throughout the woman's life that Elizabeth had collected from her apartment. It was very fulfilling and it was all Elizabeth who had done it."

Beth hired a contractor who broke through the wall separating the apartments and began renovations in late summer of 2001. From her living room and bedroom, she had a terrific view of the Twin Towers of the World Trade Center. In the weeks following 9/11, the construction crew loaded lumber onto wheelbarrows and pushed them across the Brooklyn Bridge because trucks were forbidden in lower Manhattan. Beth used only the best materials. She had marble floors installed in the kitchen and bath, and top-of-the-line marble countertops. She had central air-conditioning installed. The two apartments that cost her fourteen grand were turned into one apartment worth well over a half million dollars. But perhaps even sweeter than the profit were the skylights she had cut into the roof. Beth wouldn't live in a dark New York City apartment ever again. She told her brother Tommy the apartment extended her stay in Manhattan for two or three years.

CHAPTER
TWENTY-TWO

Along with spending several summers on Nantucket, Toolan moved around in the early nineties. Records show that for a little over a year he lived in Santa Fe. Those same records have him living at two different addresses on Santa Fe Avenue. According to a rental agent who handled one of the properties, Toolan was not on the lease of the apartment she represented. The house, she said, was officially occupied by three single guys who were in the bar and restaurant business. But there was a lot of coming and going by other lodgers. When contacted, two of the guys who lived at the address said they have no recollection of Toolan. What's more, the other address in Santa Fe does not exist. He even had one address in Roswell, New Mexico, the Bethlehem of extraterrestrial hysteria. It is known that Toolan spent some time in the Southwest when he was following the Grateful Dead in '85. He also talked often to friends about a girlfriend he had in Santa Fe.

At least one friend of Toolan's said that he followed the Santa Fe girlfriend to Atlanta. At one point, either in Santa Fe or Atlanta, he worked as a car salesman. Years later he confessed to friends that he would often get drunk with a buddy or girlfriend and, late at night, go to the car lot. There he would help himself to a set of keys and take a car out on a joyride. At least once, according to these sources, he was in an accident and left the scene. He came into work the next day as if nothing had happened.

It would be soon after he moved to Atlanta that he began his career in finance. How Toolan obtained the job for the Smith Barney branch in Atlanta is not clear. But records show that a relative of Toolan's named Jack Toolan held a high position with Smith Barney in New York.

Toolan's first job for Smith Barney in Atlanta was as a broker. After a salaried period of training and getting established, brokers work on straight commission. Even a bad broker can make eighty or ninety thousand dollars a year. Though available records are unclear as to how long Toolan worked for the brokerage in Atlanta, he would leave his position there in something of a hurry—and take a huge pay cut in doing so. In all, Toolan lived in Atlanta for five years. During that time he had at least two major relationships. One was a girl with whom he was said to have been engaged. A friend of Toolan's said that the girl had been in a serious car accident. Toolan supposedly stayed with her throughout her convalescence, and then moved on when she recovered. It's not known what prompted the breakup. One of the problems in trying to assemble Toolan's past was because of the way he compartmentalized his life. No matter how close a person was to him, he never heard the whole story. Toolan could seem brutally honest, but that honesty was always accompanied by omissions.

By 2000, Toolan was back in New York. Records show that he received mail at 35 Prospect Park West, but whether in fact he moved back in with his parents for any length of time is not known. Not too long after his return to New York, he moved into an apartment on West End Avenue, the same address where he was living when he met Beth. In New York, he was still working for Smith Barney, but now on the brokerage firm's unit funds desk. His job was to answer questions the brokers selling the funds might have. Simply put, he was a glorified librarian. His salary was something in the range of thirty thousand dollars. He reported directly to Jack Toolan. It appears that Tom Toolan was on a short leash.

Years later, Toolan told Beth that he had been in three alcoholic treatment centers, one of which was Hazelden, a factory of a rehab with facilities in Minnesota and South Florida. Another of those rehab stints could have come during his time in Atlanta. Years later, in group therapy, Toolan admitted that one night in Atlanta, after heavy drinking and drug use, he shot off a handgun in front of his girlfriend to frighten her. The only record the Atlanta Police Department has on Tom Toolan is a minor traffic accident, so the incident was apparently not reported to police. But one friend of Toolan's said that the girlfriend was so "freaked out" that she was afraid to go to police for fear of reprisal by him. The relationship was, obviously, volatile. According to friends, Toolan was engaged to the woman at one point and took the breakup extremely hard. Maybe his move to New York was just to leave the bad memories of the two major relationships in Atlanta behind. More likely, though, his drinking was causing his life to spiral out of control.

I f his family was trying to fix Toolan, it didn't work. Just two weeks after he took the position in New York, Smith Barney fired him for acting inappropriately at a company function. He had attended an after-work cigar and single-malt scotch party that was also attended by Smith Barney executives and top personnel from other brokerages like Merrill Lynch. According to a source quoted in *The Inquirer and Mirror*, Toolan drank too much and "engaged in near-physical altercations with higher-ranking executives." Toolan's association with Smith Barney, however, wouldn't end there.

He rebounded nicely, landing a job with a business that sold stock plans for companies to offer their employees. The company was called AST, and for a while it was a hot idea. A dynamic salesman named Uri Kaufthal ran the company. At its zenith, AST had over five hundred corporate clients. Smith Barney took notice of the growth, and in August of 2000 began the acquisition. All one hundred of AST's employees were part of the deal, including Toolan. When a

Smith Barney computer matched Toolan's social security number with one belonging to a former employee, a red flag shot up. With his brawl at the scotch and cigar night still fresh in their memory, Smith Barney didn't want any part of Tom Toolan. But Uri Kaufthal was an extremely loyal boss. He demanded that every single one of his employees be included in the deal. Smith Barney blinked, and Toolan was back on the Smith Barney payroll.

Though Toolan had bar pals believing that he was making upward of a quarter of a million dollars a year, his salary was actually eighty thousand. He was a vice president, but a VP in a corporation like Smith Barney, though not an entry-level position, is not a big deal. But you have to give Toolan credit. He went from being fired as a glorified secretary for Smith Barney making thirty grand a year to eighty grand and a VP title, all for the same company. Not bad.

His job was to train financial consultants in the stock plan offerings. His territory was the metropolitan area of New York City. In front of a room filled with finance guys, with a PowerPoint illuminating a screen behind him, Toolan exuded confidence. He dressed like the quarter-of-a-million-a-year employee he thought he was. His wore his hair slicked back, à la Gordon Gekko. The skin on his face was as smooth and soft as buckskin from the steams at the New York Athletic Club. His nails were manicured. But the neon harp over the entrance to Dublin House called to him each night after work. It was only a matter of time before his second term of employment with Smith Barney would end. His final departure from the company would be quite dramatic.

CHAPTER
TWENTY-THREE

By 1993 business at Beth Lochtefeld's company "blew out," as one former employee described the growth spurt. Beth's knowledge of building codes distinguished her from her competitors. Though she always stayed within the law, she knew the law's limits and got every inch she could. When a Manhattan restaurant named Verbena wanted to use their backyard space as an outdoor dining area, which in most cases is against ordinance, Beth found a way to make it happen within regulations. One architect came to Beth with a construction problem in a Versace store on Madison Avenue. The architect wanted to build an open staircase from the ground floor to the second floor. The idea was against building code. Beth found a way to have the ground floor of the store classified an atrium, and the staircase was allowed. She was also a grinder. Each day was brand-new, and each day was another opportunity.

In no time, the company outgrew 536 Broadway and moved to 435 Hudson Street. By then Beth had hired three more expeditors. Now she had nine people working for her. The office was on the sixth floor, and looked west. When a particularly nice sunset occurred, Beth would herd everyone over to the window to watch.

Working for Beth could be difficult only because the boss worked sixty hours a week. Though Beth didn't expect her employees to work as many hours as she did, she did expect to get what she was paying them for. But, in a volatile business, Beth remained remarkably even-tempered. "I never once heard her raise her voice in seven years," said Helen Golduber, who worked as an expeditor for Beth. But that didn't mean Beth was a pushover. When Beth got angry, "There was something in her tone," said Golduber.

Beth told Golduber that she hated to fire people. When she did, she did so quickly and cleanly. Golduber once recommended a friend for a job with Beth. He turned out to be habitually late for work. Beth gave him a couple of chances, then called him into the conference room. "Sorry," Beth said simply, sitting at the oval table. "We're going to have to part ways." And that was the extent of it.

The only situation that would stir anger in Beth was when someone put her reputation at risk. According to Golduber, one of Beth's expeditors had offered an inspector a twenty-dollar bribe. Supposedly, the offering was only a joke. But Beth wasn't laughing. "She was so freakin' clean," said Golduber. In speaking to a class of college students years later, Beth put it this way: "I worked in an industry that was the unions and the Mafia. And my group, we were the Girl Scouts in the middle of all of this. We were reliable. We were honest, trustworthy. We did what we said we were going to do."

Because of the camaraderie Beth enjoyed with the crew at DeMarco, Beth knew that an enjoyable workplace made for more productive workers. She went to great lengths to make her employees happy. "She was a mother and a friend that was always willing to lend you her ear," wrote Robert Locadi on a Web site dedicated to Beth. Locadi remembered that Beth's apple pies and artichoke Parmesan dip "could cure all the woes in the world." Beth always remembered her employees' birthdays, and would bring in a homemade pie or dessert for the celebrant. Each employee's anniversary at the firm was celebrated by a lunch at the restaurant of their choice. Beth took time to give one employee, Yee Yip, driving lessons for an upcoming driver's test. Every Christmas Beth took the whole staff out to lunch at a German restaurant called Rolf's. Beth thought eating under the decorations in the restaurant was like "sitting in a Christmas tree." On each employee's plate Beth placed a present, and an envelope with a bonus. The meal was sumptuous: veal, potato pancakes, schnitzel, and applesauce. When Rolf's changed hands, Beth had the Christmas party in the Hudson Street office. She hired the best caterers in Manhattan, and a deejay who played tunes that Beth helped pick out. One year she had the party at the Greatest Bar on Earth, a lounge at the top of the World Trade Center. She closed the office Christmas through New Year's and paid her employees for the time. Beth's generosity and loyalty to her staff were overwhelming.

Helen Golduber left the company when she married a navy man stationed in Newport News, Virginia. The marriage lasted only three months. When Golduber called Beth to ask for her job back, Beth said sure. "Come on back, I'll give you a raise." During her divorce, Golduber leaned on Beth for support and advice. "She told me men can't make me happy unless I'm happy with myself," Golduber said. "She was the only woman role model I've ever had."

If you were honest with Beth, she would accommodate you in any way she could. Once, Beth was interviewing a woman for a job in the office. During the interview, the woman confessed that she was in early pregnancy. Beth hired her with the proviso that after she gave birth she would come back to work for the company, which is what she did, working for Beth for four years.

I n 1993, her brother decided to leave the company. Two years earlier, Tom had started an MBA program at NYU part-time. Tom told his sister that he wanted to finish up school quickly so he could get a job in the financial industry. Beth and Tom were decidedly different people, at least in the world of business. "I liked being in business with my sister," Tom said. "I just didn't like the business we were in." Where Beth wouldn't take the pettiness of building inspectors personally, Tom did. "The inspectors would come in and say: 'Well, the knob wasn't installed on the bottom of the handrail so I can't approve the job.' I felt like pounding them." Solidly built, no doubt Tom could've prompted some sweaty collars at the DOB. But Beth handled building inspectors and clients like they were customers at DeMarco. In his eulogy, Paul Savage remembered Beth telling her secret to soothing the rough edges of her business. "Ya know, Paulo," she said of the people in the building permit process, "they're just like grumpy diners waiting for their appetizers. If you convince them it's coming, and you're in control, and you make them comfortable while they wait, they can feel better right away." Helen Golduber watched Beth work her soothing magic over and over again. "She'd explain to a client, and by the time she was done, the client wasn't upset anymore," Golduber said. On the Web site dedicated to Beth's memory, a friend wrote: "I can't remember Beth angry or pissed off—ever. And when you are working in a restaurant, that's remarkable. I can remember everyone else getting short at one time or the other, but not her. . . . Damn. . . ."

Tom handled a lot of what he called "the back of the house" at Beth's company. Essentially, he ran the business end of Beth's business. By leaving the firm he was, in his own words, "leaving Beth in the lurch." But Tom said Beth never complained. "Go get your dream," Tom remembered his sister telling him. She only asked that he "tie things up" before he left. "On top of that, she basically paid for my school," Tom remembered.

I n 1996 the company moved again, this time to 40 Worth Street. By then, Beth's reputation in the industry was as considerable as it was unimpeachable. She worked with the top architects, and directly with their clients, a list that read like an award show's: Robert Redford, Sarah Jessica Parker, Mathew Broderick, and Liv Tyler, to name a few. Business clients included the likes of Dolce and Gabanna, Gianni Versace, and TAG Heuer. She also donated time and expertise to the ASPCA, and the Fresh Air Fund, an organization that provides free summer vacations for inner-city kids.

When brother Tommy left in 1993, Beth's workload increased. The staff had increased to fourteen, and accounting for payroll and insurance alone was time-consuming. She needed to bring someone in to help. This time she went out of family.

It's a fair assumption that Beth, after the way her romance with Niall ended, had at least some issues with trusting men. She was also extremely protective of her company, which she had built, nearly all by herself, into a very successful concern. Therefore, bringing on a guy she knew from Notre Dame to fill the void of Tom Lochtefeld's departure showed a great deal of trust on Beth's part.

Tim Westbrook would have a dramatic effect on Beth's business life.

Westbrook began working for Beth around 1994, first on a part-time basis. But the two old classmate's business relationship evolved quickly. An architect, Westbrook's knowledge of design and construction was a huge asset. He also had experience as an office manager. His part-time status with Beth lasted only about six months. Though the details and exact timing of the deal are not known, soon after Westbrook started working for Beth fulltime she offered him a partner's share of her company. Beth put any personal issues of trust aside taking on Westbrook. She had evolved, business-wise at least, to a place where she knew that growth meant taking calculated risks. Her gamble with taking on a partner paid immediate dividends. Business was never better, and the future never looked friendlier.

In 1997, Beth celebrated her tenth anniversary in business. That year she changed the name of her company from Code Consultant Expeditor, Inc., to CODE, Inc. Along with Westbrook she started to formulize a plan that would ultimately lead to the sale of the business. The plan began with the hiring of what they called "project managers," each for the healthy starting salary of seventy thousand dollars a year. The idea was to create three such positions, thoroughly train these associates in the business, and then sell them CODE.

By 2000, CODE was grossing, conservatively, about $1.3 million annually. Beth had fifteen employees. By then, her business had completed some ten thousand contracts. Even as optimistic as Beth was, her company had grown beyond her wildest dreams. But Beth had grown weary. All those mornings at the DOB, all those sixty-hour weeks, all the pressure of running the business had begun to seriously erode her enthusiasm. Years later Beth said she had "had it up to here" with the business by then. It was time to start the process of divesting.

Beth and Tim came up with what they called "the five-seven plan." Tim took off from January to May, Beth took off from July to November. Only in June and December did they work together in the office. When Beth was off, the associates were learning under Tim's tutelage; Beth taught them her side when Tim was gone.

Beth made the most of her five months off. In the early nineties she briefly dated a man in Greenwich Village. At some point during their relationship, the man came out to Beth: He was gay. For Beth, the end of the romance wasn't that big a loss. Besides, the upside was she gained a perfect friend. He knew art and music, loved to travel. Just after he gave Beth the news, he moved to Paris and lived in a tiny *chambre de bonne* apartment. Beth went to visit and instantly became a Francophile. For one of the five-month stretches that she was away from CODE, Beth lived in France. She'd swapped her apartment with a French couple and lived in theirs in a town outside of Paris. Each day she'd take the B commuter rail line into the city. In the city she'd do tourist things like museums and historic places, but she tried hard to live the life of a Frenchwoman shopping in the local markets and such.

• • •

I n 2000 Beth turned forty. She was still single, and without any real prospects for marriage. But her life was anything but small. She planned and executed an incredible bash for her birthday to which she invited scores and scores of family and friends. The movable feast would stretch over four days and include twenty-one events. Of course, she made the invitations herself, cards with a sparkly Statue of Liberty under a big red "I Love New York" apple.

The first night the party was held at Beth's apartment. She served chilled champagne, asparagus and prosciutto with hot artichoke dip, salami, olives, cheeses, and dried apricots. Some of the revelers, a group her brother Peter called "the advance guard," then went to a nearby theater to watch *Fully Committed,* an off-Broadway play that mocks a chic restaurant. No doubt Beth picked the play because of her time at DeMarco. After the show the evening continued with dinner at the Odeon, the club-restaurant made famous by Jay McInerney's *Bright Lights, Big City*. The following day, groggy but willing, the gang took a Circle Line cruise around Manhattan. In a photograph from the cruise, Beth wears a foam rubber Statue of Liberty crown and holds a plastic torch as she stands above the gang. Later that evening they gathered at the Metronome, a well-known watering hole, for "Emergency Cocktails," as Beth called what was a regular Friday night get-together. Throughout the party, folks wore name tags, like in a Shriner's convention. After Emergency Cocktails, it was on to Thai food at the Bangkok Café, where Hilary, Beth's pal from the China trip, presented Beth an "Oscar" as the best friend in a supporting role. The following night was for family and special friends. At dinner, Eric Lochtefeld, Beth's California cousin, gave Beth a Rolex watch. She treasured the gift and wore it for the rest of her life.

A picture taken from the second night of the party shows Beth with the men in her life: brothers, cousin, and friends. The guys are all dressed in black leather jackets. Wearing a flowered print dress, Beth sits on the lap of one of the guys. Another fellow leans in for a kiss.

After a third-night "town-house" party at Beth's, the last day of the celebration included lunch at a chic French restaurant, a snack at Ruby Foo's, the hip sushi place, the movie *Fantasia* at the IMAX theater, and, finally, cocktails at a wine bar called Merlot.

Exhausted, family and friends caught flights home the next morning, which was April 8. Beth boarded a plane, too, that day, for a sea-kayaking trip in Baja California. She went alone, and would spend her actual birthday, April 9, with strangers. There are several pictures of that trip posted on Beth's Web site. In one, Beth is kneeling on the beach at night holding a platter with two yellow and white birthday cakes. She is surrounded by fellow kayakers. When she returned home, she sent a thank-you note to the kayaking company:

> It's Elizabeth, the rookie kayaker from New York City, the one who was full of curious questions just six short weeks ago.
>
> Let me tell you, I did indeed have the time of my life. It was fantastic—I expected the scenery and the physical activity to be extraordinary, but I failed to suspect that the company would be so great.
>
> Please tell Grant and Janice that the guides were A+ tops #1. I felt that they were both totally competent, which made me relax and trust them immediately. They were also both so friendly, and fun. Their cooking was amazing, as was their knowledge of the fish, the birds and the stars in the sky.
>
> The week was amazing . . . It was wonderful to be in a place of no electricity, no phones, no clocks and no money. Hurray!
>
> Beth Lochtefeld, New York NY

Around the time of her birthday—maybe because of it—Beth began to seriously plan out her life after CODE. In the early nineties, Beth had lent financial support to an idea her cousin Eric had for starting a concert tour that would play across the country, like dozens of mini-Woodstocks. For the most part, the tour featured underground punk rock groups. But as the tour gained popularity, the acts got bigger. Though Eric's idea was a huge success, he and Beth perhaps sold the concept a little too early and a little too cheaply. Vans Warped Tour is the biggest concert tour in the world. A few years back, Eminem played the New York version of the tour.

In 2000 Eric approached Beth again. This time his idea was matching college students with their dream internships. He called his inspiration "the University of Dreams."

It was an ambitious plan. Eric saw the growth potential of the company on a global scale. In this venture, Beth wanted to be more than just an investor. In the first few years of operation, Beth gave lectures. In front of classrooms filled with wide-eyed college seniors, Beth told about her nights at DeMarco and sitting cross-legged on her bunk at Notre Dame. With rapt attention, the students followed Beth as she rode the Trans-Siberian railroad. As Beth talked about starting her business, they hung on every word. They loved her stories of big hair and toupees, of mob guys and the Girl Scout who took them on. Beth was perfect in the role of role model, especially for the girls. She was just like them, she said, only farther along on life's journey. And the students believed her. They believed their dreams could come true. One of the University of Dreams students, Lindsey Kane, posted this on her memorial Web site:

It's taken me a long time to figure out just what to say, but I think I am finally ready: Every time I think of Beth, it still brings tears to my eyes. I met Beth during the summer of 2003 through the University of Dreams NYC program. Beth was such a special part of my summer there. Her dedication, constant interest, and amazing attributes were things that I was in awe of and will miss greatly. She was ab-

solutely one of the most amazing and inspirational people I have ever met! I will never forget the legacy she has left behind, not only in the program, but in the lives of everyone she touched.

CHAPTER
TWENTY-FOUR

In January 2001 Toolan was arrested for trying to steal a marble bust of a Roman aristocrat from an art and antique show at the Seventh Regiment Armory on Park Avenue. He tried to hide the sixty-pound sculpture under his jacket and walk out the door. A security guard stopped him and called the police. Toolan told the detectives that he was only pulling a "prank." The cops didn't see the humor.

Bad luck for Toolan. That Saturday happened to be a slow news day. A reporter for the New York *Daily News* saw the arrest on the police blotter and decided to write the story. Toolan's unlucky streak continued when his immediate boss the next morning picked up a copy of the *News* to read over a muffin and coffee.

This time Smith Barney had had enough. They wanted out of their relationship with Tom Toolan, and right away. But the company was in a rather sensitive situation. First off, Toolan had been charged but not convicted. Smith Barney didn't want to play judge and jury. Secondly, Toolan admitted to the court he had a problem with drinking. In the corporate world, alcoholism is considered a disease and not, on its own, a fireable offense. For all intents and purposes, Smith Barney told Toolan he was done, but they made it easy for him by giving him a small severance package.

Toolan eventually pleaded down from grand larceny to disorderly conduct and was sentenced to community service. He was also either remanded by the court, or decided on his own, to attend group therapy to address his admitted drinking problem.

He might have addressed the problem, but he didn't stop drinking.

By early 2003 the source of Toolan's income was a mystery. After being fired from Smith Barney, he worked for a period of time for Mellon Bank. At some point, he left Mellon and took a job with UBS, another international bank. That job would only last two weeks. Though he passed the screening process for the position, someone, either at the bank or a customer he dealt with, knew the story of the stolen bust. Word got back to Toolan's boss, and he was quickly dismissed.

On the outside, Toolan gave no indication of the downward spiral of his financial situation. According to neighbors and bar buddies, he was always just about to make the big deal.

Darlene Young is a dog walker whom Toolan approached about one of those deals. "He talked about a doggy day-care place," she said. Young was wary of Toolan right off and remembers him as always being on the phone. "I can spot a bullshitter a mile away," she said. "Quite frankly, he was looking for someone with money."

One time, Toolan was at Young's apartment to drop off a friend's dog. That night, Young's best girlfriend happened to be visiting. After Toolan left, the girlfriend remarked that Toolan was her type. "Something about him rubs me the wrong way," Young told her girlfriend. "He reminds me of a used-car salesman."

Along with being a good storyteller, one of the big reasons Toolan was able to convince people his life was in order was because of his Park Slope foundation. Though he seemed to contribute very little to it, the world in which Tom Toolan operated was firmly set in blocks of granite and marble. One of those firm foundations was on the corner of Seventh Avenue and Central Park South.

From the day it opened in January 1929, just ten months

before "Black Monday" and the stock market crash, the New York Athletic Club was an essential membership for bankers and stockbrokers (if you were a man and Christian, that is). Though women were finally allowed to join the club in 1989, the club still remains a business phallic symbol. In the twenty-four story clubhouse at 180 Central Park South, deals are made in the wood-paneled taproom and on the squash courts. There are forty-two "intra clubs" within the New York AC, including boxing, rugby, and basketball. The handball club is called "the Killers Club." Toolan was a member of a badminton team. He also belonged to the Mercury Society, which held social events for members under forty. He attended the singles dances the society held, and the popular "scotch and cigar" night. But mostly Toolan used the AC to impress dates.

According to the pool attendant, the girls Toolan brought to the club, and there were a few, were young and pretty. "They were all hot," the attendant said. One of his regular dates was tall and blond and "had been a model of some type," according to the attendant. But even when he was with his regular girl, other girls would call him on the phone in the room where the pool is located. On those occasions Toolan would signal to the attendant to tell them he wasn't there.

Despite the steamy temperature, he would often wear a double-breasted blue blazer in the pool room, sometimes even an ascot. Though he looked like a million, there were indications that Toolan was starting to feel the heat of limited finances. According to the pool room attendant, Toolan had a strange relationship with an older, gay member of the AC. Toolan would flirt with the man in the pool room, but would then come back and laugh with the attendant about his leading the man on. The attendant was under the impression that Toolan was using the man simply to get a cab ride home, but Toolan was always trying to sell his next big idea, and the man could very well have been a target for Toolan's pitch. And the question of who paid his bills lingers. Toolan had little if any income throughout 2002 and 2003. He told one girlfriend that he had "considerable savings." But Toolan had a significant gambling habit. A gambler with a savings account is rare indeed. The savings certainly didn't come from any of the five jobs he had held most recently. At the club Toolan spent little of his own money. The club's policy is to add a fifteen percent gratuity to the bill, but most members give the staff a little extra in cash and usually a Christmas bonus. Toolan did neither. He'd sit at one of the round pool room tables, drink Heineken or Beck's for hours, and not leave a dime.

At the club Toolan was reticent about his employment. Telling big money tales at the Dublin House was one thing, but trying to pass himself off as a financial wonder boy in a dormitory of wonder boys at the AC was something else. The Finance Channel plays constantly on the television in the pool room. Only when there is a big game on is it tuned to another station. According to the attendant, members sit for hours, drink beer or iced tea, and watch the stock streamer at the bottom of the screen. But not Toolan. He never gave it a glance.

But the high wire Toolan was on was getting shaky. Sooner or later, the money that paid his bills was going to dry up. Sooner or later, his drinking was going to land him in trouble again. Sooner or later, people would see through his act.

CHAPTER
TWENTY-FIVE

In July 2001 Beth high-fived Tim Westbrook and walked out of the office door to begin her five-month sojourn. The plan was almost complete. By the time she returned in November, the process of the transferring the company to the associates would begin. It was a time for her to both reflect and look forward.

She would walk away from her company a rich woman. Though she was very involved with the University of Dreams, its demands didn't nearly approach the time she spent with CODE. She had a dream of her own: She was in the midst of writing a novel, and she wanted to publish a book of her father's artwork.

By this point of her life, Beth had friends on three continents. She could pick up and go just about anywhere in the world and feel welcome.

For fifteen years New York City had been her home, the place where she filled and floated the Macy's Parade balloon of her life. But Beth was tiring of New York, too. The city had offered up a lot, but came up short in one very important way. Beth wanted someone to share her time with. For fifteen years New York hadn't come through.

Late that summer of 2001, Beth headed to San Francisco to help with the inaugural program of the University of Dreams. Early September found her visiting Kevin Yoder and his partner, Jeff, in Los Angeles. Beth's friendship with Kevin had survived his move back to California. He and

Beth signed a "contract" that they would visit each other at least four times a year, two on each coast. Yoder talked about the contract in his eulogy to Beth: "And being Beth, we crafted in some exigencies. In the event the party of the first part decided she wanted to compel her visit someplace else and the party of the second part agreed, that was fine." Among other jaunts, Yoder and Beth spent more than one weekend together in London and three trips to France, one of which included a long weekend in Normandy and a visit to Omaha Beach. They once went to Hawaii to watch Mars align with the earth and sun. The went hiking in Bryce Canyon, a trip that in a letter to Stuart Saft Beth said she felt like "eight-years-old all over again."

In Los Angeles Beth had what Yoder called a "typical" southern California week. They took in a movie premier, experienced a small earthquake, and were entertained by some of Yoder's "fabulous" friends. All was great fun—until they awoke the morning of September 11.

Beth's faith in her younger brother had paid off. Tommy graduated from business school, got a job in finance, began a family, and moved to Connecticut. He took a job with a Japanese bank. His office was in the World Trade Center on the eightieth floor of the South Tower. It was just after five A.M. California time when the planes hit. By the time Beth awakened and heard the news, the towers had already fallen. She had no idea whether her brother was dead or alive.

In his office, Tommy was checking e-mails and drinking coffee at his desk when he heard what he described as a "thunderclap." As he looked around, the faces of his coworkers mirrored his puzzlement. How could there be thunder on such a beautiful morning? His desk was about thirty feet from the window that looked out on to the North Tower. Debris, papers, and smoke flew past. Along with the other traders and office workers, Tom ran to the window for a better look.

In the middle of all the commotion, four of the bank executives, Japanese who were in New York on a rotational basis, ran into the office and ordered everyone to leave. Tom ran for the exit, then went back to his desk twice, once for a "grab and go" bag, a kit with flashlight, smoke mask, and other survival gear, and once for his cell phone. On his second trip back, the CEO, one of the rotational execs, screamed at him to get out of the office at once. In that moment, Tom said he was more afraid of being fired for insubordination than anything else.

The staff of Tom's bank began a hurried descent down the Trade Tower staircase. When they came to the fifty-second floor, they heard an announcement over the loudspeaker saying the building was secure, that it was safe to return to the office. There were so many people squeezed onto the staircase and landing, it took several minutes for the crowd to get redirected for the march back upstairs. In those moments, there was an explosion above, and the whole building rocked. In that instant, Tom had the distinct feeling that someone was trying to kill him. At first, there was pushing and shoving. But then, miraculously, the crowd resumed a fairly orderly descent. When Tom got to the fifteenth floor a group of firefighters rushed past him and up the stairs. Later, when the buildings fell, Tom cried at the realization that all of those firemen must have died.

The fuselage of the second jet smashed through the eightieth floor of Tower Two, through the same window Tom had looked out of less than thirty minutes before. All four Japanese executives, including the CEO who had yelled at Tom, were killed instantly in the fireball.

John Lochtefeld was on the golf course that morning. As he watched the towers collapse on a TV in the clubhouse, he accepted that his youngest son was dead. When he found out he was wrong, he spent the rest of the day in the Church of St. Mary, Our Lady of the Isle, praying.

In the utter chaos, a reporter for NBC approached Tom. That night, the interview ran on *Dateline*. Beth cried when she saw her little brother Tommy on TV.

• • •

After Beth found out that Tommy was alive, she thought about her company and employees. She knew that two of her staff took the PATH train each morning, the line that ran directly below the World Trade Center. Both employees had taken early trains to be at work for a staff meeting. Beth never bought shades for the office windows because CODE was literally in the shadow of the towers, only eight blocks away. Yet no one on her staff was hurt in the attacks.

When she finally was able to get a call in to the office, she told one of the associates that she was heading back "if I have to drive across the country." As it turned out, there was no need for Beth to hurry. Downtown Manhattan was virtually shut down tight. CODE's office would be closed for four weeks. A fine dust from the collapse was ankle deep in the streets. Vickie Taveras remembers that, for months, the smell of the fire at Ground Zero was overwhelming in the office.

For months after the attack lower Manhattan was a gaping wound. For those months, any business problems were small. But Beth's plans were about to be considerably altered. One of the associates whom Beth and Tim had spent so much time and money training, changed his mind about the deal. As many people did after the terrorist attack, he rethought his life. He married his high school sweetheart and moved to Connecticut to help run his father's construction company. Without him, however, the sale of the business couldn't proceed as planned. According to one person close to the situation, Tim had made business or real estate investments in Argentina, where his future lay. But the Argentinean economy took a severe downturn. Tim pressed Beth to go through with the sale to the remaining associates. It would mean settling for two-thirds of what they originally had planned to get. Certainly, there was much contention, and strained relationships. On top of everything, some of the co-op board at 22 Grove brought suit against Beth, contend-

ing that she hadn't acquired her apartment legally. Beth
again developed a stress-related medical condition, a facial
rash and a severe allergy to certain foods. She went to a series of doctors for help, including an acupuncturist. One
friend of Beth's remembered that the relationship between
Beth and Tim was severely damaged. At least one employee
said that Beth felt short-changed in the deal she would eventually accept.

Ultimately, Beth did accept the reorganized deal. And, after fifteen years, Beth stepped cleanly away from the seamy
world of the expediting business. She was excited with the
prospect of the University of Dreams. She began to plan a
move to Nantucket. She wanted to spend time with her
nieces and nephews.

B oth the memorial Web site and family interviews
document a titanic love Beth had for her brothers'
families. She would send her nieces and nephews,
ten of them by the end of her life, cards on all the holidays
and birthdays. For Valentine's Day, she would cut tiny hearts
out of red and white construction paper and fill handmade
cards with them. When the eager child ripped open the envelope, the hearts would spray like confetti. There is a picture
on the Web site of Beth tenderly holding Tom's oldest,
William, when he was just one year old. Tom recalled that
when Beth visited she would stop by a favorite bakery in the
Village and pick up cakes and pastries for the children. One
time she brought chocolate éclairs, and William loved them.
From then on, each time Beth visited, she'd make sure she
brought a couple of éclairs.

Only once did she forget the birthday of another of Tom's
children. Beth called Tom nearly in a panic when she realized the oversight. Her brother reassured her a belated card
would rectify things. In the summer of 2002, Beth flew to
Wisconsin to visit her eldest brother, Jim, and his family.
The trips came in the midst of the upheaval at CODE, yet
Beth's family ties took precedent. "She was the doting aunt,"

Jim wrote on the Web site of those trips. Beth and Zuzu, the daughter of brother Peter and his wife, Santje, had a special relationship. Zuzu's first-grade teacher remembered on the Web site Beth's picking her niece up from school and how Zuzu would run to Beth and hug her. On the Web site, there is another picture of just Beth and Zuzu playing dress-up. Loving aunt and niece both wear the same satisfied expression, but only Zuzu wears the fashionable hat.

On her memorial Web site, there is picture of Beth a few days after the last CODE party. In the photograph, she sits on the carousel in Central Park with her nephew Sam. Beth's face is sunny and a direct contrast to the dark, ominous clouds that gather in the background. The day was unusually warm for April, Peter remembered. They made a run for the subway, but the rain clouds didn't wait. They were soaked to the skin.

And then there is a picture of Beth in the home of her brother Peter on Nantucket, taken just two days before she was murdered. In the photograph Beth sits on a red flowered love seat reading a children's book to her Nantucket nieces and nephews, who are squeezed in next to her. It's hard to judge someone's mood from a captured moment, but it's one of a few pictures of Beth in which she isn't smiling. It almost looks like she's worried. In regard to the picture, Peter wrote that the children had her read the same story three times in a row. The last family members to see Beth alive were Peter's children. The day Beth was murdered, she dropped Zuzu and Sam off at school. Just after Beth died, Zuzu drew a card with stick figures of herself and Beth. On it she wrote: "When I think about Beth I cry."

In April 2003 Beth threw the last of her CODE parties, this one to celebrate the completed sale of her business to the associates. She rented a flower shop for the day. The weather was extremely warm after three days straight of ninety-degree temperatures. As the party wound down, she and Peter and several of her longtime employees and other friends strolled down the street to a local bar. Beth bought a round. With eyes that glistened with tears, Beth raised a glass of cabernet and toasted the end of her business. The sixteen years had flashed past like lightning in a summer sky. But she had no regrets. And Beth was not one to dwell on the past. The tears in her eyes would not last long. Some might think that, at forty-three, the best of Beth's life was over. Some might, but not Beth. According to her plan, her life was just beginning.

Back in 1988 Niall had married Rosanna. There must have been quiet moments then, perhaps late at night in the cramped Bedford Street apartment, when Beth allowed herself a good cry over him and things that might have been. If Niall was the love of Beth's life, then his choosing Rosanna had to have had an enormous effect on Beth. At the time, Beth was working incredibly long hours getting her business started. Maybe Beth's singleness of purpose in business was to not feel the hurt.

Beth would cry again over Niall. In 2001, he died of stomach cancer. But this time Beth's tears didn't come from the hurt in her heart, but because Niall was a father and husband dead far too soon. Beth attended the funeral, as did most of the old gang from DeMarco.

Maybe it was Niall, this time in death, who gave focus to Beth's life once again. Beth loved her nieces and nephews with all of her strength. But she wanted a child of her own. Though her worst fear might have been to die violently, she also feared dying alone.

Maybe it was Niall who made Beth see the missing pieces of her life.

CHAPTER
TWENTY-SIX

Even in her forty-third year, even in pseudoretirement, Beth's life was still a race. It was as though, somewhere deep inside, she knew time was running out.

Part of Beth's last chapter in life she was to write herself. For much of her time in Manhattan she was far too busy to take a class in writing, which had always been a passion. Beth found her writing voice on birthday cards and thank-you letters. Never one to rely on Hallmark to express her sentiments, she sent out handmade cards by the hundreds. Her Christmas card list alone was voluminous, the addresses as far-flung as Toronto, Paris, London, and Amsterdam. It also spanned decades of her life and included friends with whom she had grown up and gone to grammar school, Notre Dame pals, DeMarco buddies, and people she knew through business. The cards would often include notes that ran several pages, bringing her friends up to date on her life and remembering family additions and important events in the lives of others. And then there was e-mail, for which Beth was famously prolific. On Beth's memorial Web site, a classmate from Notre Dame remembered that Beth sent him a handmade card each holiday season even though they hadn't seen each other for twenty years.

Each day Beth would pass, on the corner of her block in the Village, a yellow newspaper box with GOTHAM WRITERS' WORKSHOP written in black letters on the side. It was not exactly serendipitous, the box's being there.

There are similar boxes on just about every street corner of Manhattan. Still, taking a course catalogue from one in the winter of 2003 was something of a fateful act. For around four hundred bucks, she could take a twelve-week course in anything from children's book writing to science fiction, business writing, and even stand-up comedy. Partly, the writing school is in the business of dream fulfillment; it attracts the thirty-something computer geek who is halfway through the next *Matrix* screenplay, and middle-aged men and women who believe their lives are at least as deserving of a memoir as Mary Karr's or Frank McCourt's. Most of the students who take Gotham's classes are a bit more realistic, however. Some are happy just to have their writing read in class and to talk about it afterward over a glass of wine.

Beth was somewhere in between. She loved the camaraderie of the class. She befriended several of the students, and she did have drinks after class with them. But she was also serious about her writing.

Fiction 1 met every Tuesday morning for ten weeks at eleven in the morning. It was held in an office building on West Sixtieth Street in Manhattan between Broadway and Columbus Avenue. With Lincoln Center only a few blocks to the north, and the heart of the theater district only twelve or so blocks south, and dance schools on either side, Beth must have appreciated the neighborhood's pulsing creativity. Though Beth could be a pragmatist and have the work ethic of a Quaker, she was drawn and moved by ethereal forces. On her memorial Web site, a friend of Beth's wrote that she once discussed with him her theory that meredians of energy intersected under Manhattan's bedrock. If you were receptive to the energy, Beth thought, you would thrive there.

Though the energy beneath Manhattan may be bountiful, the living and working spaces aboveground are usually small and stuffy. Beth and eleven of her classmates sat cramped around a white Formica table in a room on a floor mostly occupied by psychotherapists. There were some uncomfortable elevator rides with weeping patients.

The chemistry of a writing class, especially an adult education class like Gotham's, is not always perfect. Personalities grate. Teacher-student relationships get off to a bad start and don't recover. Life issues invade. Focus is lost. Beth had one such experience in another writing class. She and the teacher just didn't hit it off.

But sometimes the mix is magical. Beth's first teacher was Susan Breen. Petite, with short blond hair, wearing glasses, Susan looked more like she belonged behind the wheel of a minivan with four kids and a house in suburban Westchester. That image of Susan is not far off the mark. In her previous life Susan had a career as a reporter for *Fortune* and an editor for the Foreign Policy Association. But fiction writing is her enduring love. Her short fiction has been published in, among other places, *American Literary Review*. Susan's classes fill quickly, which, by most writing-school barometers, is a sign of a fine teacher.

If there is one thing that sets apart writing classes in New York City from those anywhere else in the world, it's the diversity of the students. In Beth's class there was a man who worked for CBS News. As U.S. forces were then gearing up for the invasion into Iraq, breaking news pulled the man from class often, but provided plenty of insider stories when he did attend. There was a woman who had once been a professional ballet dancer. At the time, the movie *The Pianist* was in theaters, and the woman gave the class an extended tutorial on the inconsistencies in the movie's details. Another student, a safari guide in Tanzania, was writing a hallucinogenic novel that, though beautifully written, was impossible to follow. One student was writing a murder mystery, another an autobiographical novel of her travels around the world. And then there was Beth.

"When I see her in my head," Susan Breen remembered. "I see her with a silk scarf around her neck. She always had beautifully cut hair. And whatever makeup she wore, and she didn't wear much, it looked good." The teacher bumped into Beth at a party Gotham throws a few times a year. "She had found just the perfect party dress, a little bit elegant," remembered Susan. But the way Beth saw the world through her writing is just as vivid a memory in Susan's mind.

The class's first homework assignment was to pick a person from history and describe him or her having a meal. Susan encouraged the students to bring the character to life through details: what they imagined they would eat, with whom they would dine, what they talked about, and so on. Along with sharpening some writing skills, the homework, read in class, gave the students some insight into one another. "It's a nice way to bring the class together," Susan said. For the most part, according to Susan, students picked well-known historical figures—Hitler, Picasso, Joan of Arc, Cleopatra. One of Susan's students described Marie Antoinette having lunch. Beth chose to write about the Widow Clicquot. The Widow Clicquot? That is exactly what Susan and the rest of the class wondered.

The story goes something like this: Married to a winemaker named Clicquot, Nicole Barbe Ponsardin was widowed in 1805. Left with a young daughter, and no knowledge of the wine business, Madame Clicquot Ponsardin unsteadily took the reins of the family concern. In a Europe torn by the Napoleonic wars, she established shipping lines to Russia and other important courts on the Continent and in England. She bought the most fertile lands and cultivated the best vineyards. By the time she died, in 1866, the family champagne business was an empire, and the orange label of Veuve Clicquot-Ponsardin ubiquitous around the world. "Veuve" is French for widow. In tribute to her, contemporaries called her "La Grande Dame de la Champagne," and the best of Clicquot's champagne is called "La Grande Dame" after her.*

*The class loved the story of the widow. Emboldened by their support, Beth looked up the Veuve Clicquot Web site and e-mailed the company a copy of the story. Several months later, after Susan's writing class had concluded, Beth received in the mail a leather-bound biography of the Widow Clicquot and a letter of thanks from the champagne maker. In an e-mail to Susan, Beth wrote: "It was a thrill. It is my first tangible reward for something I have written."

• • •

On one level, Beth's choice of the widow is somewhat perplexing, like choosing to write about Johnny Walker. Most people close to Beth deny she ever had a problem with alcohol. But wine is a constant theme in her life. She knew restaurant wine lists by heart. In his memorial remarks, Jim Lochtefeld said this about his sister: "Beth was no Mother Teresa."

Some of Beth's high living was a mask she wore. "Beth always put on a happy face but did not always feel that way inside," Jim continued. "Perhaps because I listened so much to her, I saw the sadness seeping through the cracks."

Beth did try to outrun her feelings. She thought if she worked hard enough, played hard enough, traveled far enough, she could keep the emptiness in her life a few lengths behind. In another writing, Beth's description of a main character could have been a description of herself: "She had been involved in many affairs, many relationships, but had never lived with a man, never been married. She had felt like a stone skipping the surface of the pond, and ached to settle in." For Beth, happiness was just around the next corner, and she was always running to get there.

Besides the obvious identification with the Widow Clicquot, both of them resourceful and successful women in industries dominated by men (though Beth didn't trade with Russia, she certainly created new ways of conducting business at the Department of Buildings), there was also something about the widow's loneliness that drew Beth to her story.

One of the reasons Beth had taken Susan's class was because she had an idea for a novel. If the homework assignment gave the class a hint of Beth's loneliness, the novel idea shouted it to them.

The story was about a shoe designer named Spike, a woman whose creations are whimsical, with long stiletto heels. For the most part, the tale takes place on Nantucket and was perhaps inspired, at least the shoe-designing lead character, by Vanessa Noel, the bridal shoe designer who

owns a boutique and a small, posh hotel on Nantucket. For
Beth, the idea was a perfect fit. Her love of shoe shopping
was legendary.

In the love story, Spike once lived in Italy under the
tutelage—and the suggestion of something more—of an older
Italian man. But her heart belonged to a young man for whom
she pines and with whom she planned to spend her days. In a
scene read in Susan's class, Spike finally sees her young love
on Nantucket, seated on a bench in front of her store. But as
she begins to run to him, another young man comes into view.
In that moment, she realizes her true love is gay.

Despondent, Spike seeks the comfort of the owner of a
nearby coffee shop. All is not lost, the woman says comfort-
ingly. Spike could always live her years away with her one
true love and his boyfriend.

Susan Breen remembered Beth's descriptions of the
island as engaging. "We all wanted to move there,"
she said. And the class loved the story and thought it
had good, commercial appeal, a literary *Will and Grace*.
But, for Susan, the biggest selling point was Beth's passion.
"She could tell a story . . . and [had] a narrator that was sympathetic." No wonder. Beth opened her lonely heart and let it
bleed over the page.

In real life, Beth wasn't giving up, wasn't about to live out
her days with a gay couple. She had her antenna up for
single—straight—guys. Though it was not her primary purpose in taking a writing class, she did hope to meet someone. Beth was then trying Internet dating, with limited
success. At one point she briefly dated a guy she'd met in
Michael Jordan's restaurant in Grand Central Terminal.
Beth's lawyer, Heidi Rigney, wrote on the memorial Web
site about having dinner with her during this time. "She was
wearing a beautiful black dress and every guy in the place
noticed her. She was hoping to meet Mr. Right and get married, but it was tough because she was successful and very
sophisticated. You would think it would make it easier for

her, but I think it made it harder for her to find guys that weren't intimidated by her."

In November 2002, a Spaniard she'd met in New York City invited Beth to Madrid. In a diary entry Beth called the man "beautiful," but wrote little else about him except to say, in hindsight, she needed "a man with English." But Beth did just fine in Spain by herself. She wrote about a small hotel in which she stayed for just two nights. It was on Arcos de la Frontera with a view. "The cliff fell away, and there was a river in the valley, winding curvaceously," she wrote. "There were hillocks and orchards, golden fields of some kind of grain." There were birds actually flying below where she stood on the cliffs, and several hang gliders, suspended in updrafts. She had arrived at the hotel just before sunset, and found a viewing spot. She described the moment:

"The sunset was a spectacular palette of reds and oranges, fading to navy. The sky was so huge, and the air was fresh. It was one of those times when you can feel the beat of time, and wish to be vividly present in every moment as it is so glorious, impossible to photograph, impossible to repeat, and must be savored so it can be replayed in the mind's eye another time. . . . It is the reason to be alive, to tender and shelter and replay when times are more ho-hum, more tedious . . . it was a moment of pure joy."

For Beth, the hotel was right out of a dream. There was a small library with overstuffed chairs and volumes in many languages. Opera music played on the stereo. Local port was served in crystal.

The second evening there, she ventured into the small mountain village. Alone in a local tavern she drank a few beers. There had been a raging storm the night before, and it began to rain again. She thought she'd better make it back to her hotel before the weather turned any worse. "I opened my Totes and ducked under it, holding it with two hands against the wind," she wrote. "Around the corner and down the block, suddenly two young boys, shorter than my chin, dashed across the street and without a greeting, beyond irrepressible laughter, joined me under my umbrella." The unlikely threesome walked down the block that way. "I was happy to share my umbrella for their trust and laughing eyes," she wrote.

B eth found companionship in her travels, and they came in all shapes, sizes, and ages. When in London, Beth would visit Kevin Yoder's friend Durell. When Durell's father died, Beth wrote this:

> It was at Foxleigh House that I first raised a toast to absent friends. It was the tail end of 1990, and Durell had invited me to celebrate the New Year with his family. The days seemed to revolve around a dinner party that started in the later part of the afternoon with tea in the drawing room, which segued on to cocktails, and then moved to the dining room, to an enormous table with an impressive array of forks. Several courses later came the port and the cheese. To my amazement, the port was passed to the left and the earnest toast was made to absent friends.
>
> The house was a boisterous place with family portraits barely keeping their secrets to themselves, chiming clocks and scintillating conversation. It was a raucous rollicking good time ringing with laughter. It was a world that I had dreamed of that somehow was congruous with feather boas, champagne flutes and Baked Alaska. It was glamorous, intelligent and witty. It was grand and larger than life, but it was also very kind and loving and at times very silly. The first time I went to visit Foxleigh House, I felt like I had come home.
>
> I was often seated next to Ted, who was never at a loss for words. He had an endless supply of stories, and a steady stream of compliments. I was charmed not only by his words, but by his accent, and his eyebrows, which had a language all their own. I was enraptured by this witty raconteur, this worldly Brit, this classy older gent. I could

tell he enjoyed my company and, to reference Austin Powers, he made me feel like an International Woman.

Ted was the incarnation of my romanticized version of a dramatically gracious man, a generous host, and an interesting interested whimsical man. He fulfilled my wildest dreams of a fabulous weekend in a country house. He was the Lord of the Manor.

I will miss Ted. I will miss his lead. I will miss his élan and his joie de vivre. I pulled out my albums last week and lined up all my photos of Ted on the windowsill. In almost every last one of them, he is wearing a bow tie and a big smile. And in most of the shots he is holding a glass of champagne.

So to that end I raise my glass and say, "Ted, here's to you." Thank you for the warm welcome to your magical world at Foxleigh House. Thank you for your love and acceptance. Thank you for making me feel so good about myself when I was around you.

To close, although I generally always prefer champagne, in this particular circumstance I would like to defer to port. Ted, although you were at first my friend Durell's father, you became my friend, too. I will miss you, but I thank you and will always remember you for showing me such a good time, although these days you are absent.

Beth's life would change remarkably in writing class. But, as it happened, writing had little to do with the change. The new path that Beth was to walk the rest of her time on earth, the path that in some way would lead her to Tom Toolan, began as a simple homework assignment.

A boat sinks during a storm and only ten of its passengers make it on to the lifeboat. One by one the survivors are knocked off, until, after a month at sea, only two survivors are left. There is not enough food for both of them, and one of them is going to have to get rid of the other. One of them is a teenage girl who is very strong for her age, but she is blind. The other is a musician from a very successful boys' band. He is 26 years old and smaller than the girl. Who will survive? Show me the final scene.

Beth's class returned with their completed assignments the following week. The boy band member drew little sympathy from the students. Almost to a person, Susan remembered, her class had the teenage girl survive. Some of them killed off the boy band member in the most lurid fashions, in bloody detailed fights. One student had the teenage girl trick him into sex and then stab him in the back.

Beth's homework stood out because of how nonconfrontational it was. Instead of creating conflict, Beth had the boy band member sing one last song before he threw himself overboard. Her story took a fair amount of constructive criticism from her fellow students and Susan. Writing is one of the most personal endeavors, and many writing students' fragile egos are irrevocably wounded from criticism. But Beth had experienced too much in life to cower from a writing critique. Instead, she gave considerable thought to the suggestions of her classmates and teacher.

During the next class session, Beth told Susan that her problem with conflict was not confined to her writing, that a fear of confrontation pervaded her life.

"It's something I have to address," Beth said.

CHAPTER
TWENTY-SEVEN

In the winter of 2003, Tom Toolan started dating Jessica Northrup,* a sales representative for a large clothing manufacturer. They met at a crowded Café Luxembourg, an upscale restaurant a few blocks from Lincoln Center. Jessica had just finished dinner with her parents and sisters, while Toolan was with two friends waiting for a table. Tall, pretty with her wheat-colored hair, Jessica, who bore a resemblance to Beth, had Toolan's attention right off.

As she walked passed him, Toolan caught Jessica's eye.

"Table for two?" he said, with a maitre d' gallantry.

"Actually it was for six," Jessica replied with a sweet giggle.

Dressed in sports jacket, with white silk scarf, Toolan looked confident and was talkative. He said he was from Brooklyn, which Jessica thought was cute. Her sister, however, thought his manner of speech a bit too lock-jawed for that borough, and she also thought the scarf a bit much.

Toolan handed Jessica his business card and a few days later she e-mailed him.

The romance lasted about a year and a half, though Jessica spent long stretches of that time traveling for business. But when they were together they liked each other's company. They would take long walks through Central Park. There Toolan would show off his local knowl-

*"Jessica Northrup" is a name change.

edge. They'd sit in Strawberry Fields, just across from the Dakota where John Lennon lived and was murdered. While dragonflies hovered over nearby Turtle Pond, they'd hold hands in the shadow of Belvedere Castle that overlooks the Park and the outdoor Delacorte Theater. On the steps of Bethesda Terrace, they'd chat while being sprayed by the Angel of the Waters Fountain. Toolan's education at St. Saviour, Xavier and Columbia University stood him in good stead. He could recite Aldous Huxley, discuss Faulkner's *Sanctuary*, and giggle at J. P. Donleavy. They both loved music: Dylan, Clapton, Coldplay, and Bruce Springsteen. And, Jessica had an immediate and positive effect on Toolan. When she first walked into his apartment she was aghast at its condition. Toolan had tapestries and posters over the windows to block out the light. A pack rat, he had piles of CDs, vinyl albums, books, and magazines. His closets were a catastrophe of clothing, shoes, and tennis racquets. By the next time she came over, however, he'd hung shades and curtains, and also cleaned and organized. On Sunday mornings then, from Toolan's apartment, they would order in breakfast—bagel and egg sandwiches—from the New Wave Cafe, a diner on Broadway two blocks from his apartment. Toolan knew the workers at the restaurant so well, he would only have to identify himself as "Tommy," and the food would seem to magically appear. Comfortable in each other's silence, they would read the *New York Times,* the "Arts and Leisure" section of much more interest to Toolan than the financial page. He also read the *New York Observer,* a salmon-colored broadsheet that contains high-tone gossip and a Brahmin view on politics. Toolan staunchly defended the Catholic Church, even during the worst of the recent sex scandal. Like most New Yorkers, 9/11 had had a major impact on him, and the threat of terrorism was always a topic of conversation. In a less somber atmosphere, they played board games together, though Jessica stopped playing Monopoly with Toolan because he took the game too seriously, bought too many hotels, and was ruthless in trying to bankrupt her. But she'd hug him tightly when, spontaneously, he'd compose a poem for her, or do, what she called "his little jig."

But there were also early indications that Toolan had serious flaws. Although, at times, he was disarmingly honest, he was also secretive. He talked lovingly about his parents and sister, but spent very little time with them. (Northrup does remember him rushing up to Westchester to see his sister's new baby.) He was nostalgic about his past, but there were large holes in his chronology. In the shower, he had some kind of religious medal hanging on a chain. When Jessica asked about it, he said it belonged to a friend in Atlanta who had either drowned or died suddenly some other way. But he would never elaborate on the subject. He talked about traveling with a friend to Istanbul to buy rugs, but Jessica always had the feeling Toolan was either making up the whole thing or leaving parts of the story out. He would tell the truth, but never the whole truth. And then there was the way he drank.

The block on which the Dublin House sits has the antiquated look of a black-and-white photograph. Once grand residences, the five-story brownstones there have stoops that lead to second-floor entrances and Corinthian columns. Bay windows bulge toward the street. But where once the buildings were home to wealthy families and, perhaps, a noted Broadway actress or two, they now house dental co-ops, a tarot card reader, video and liquor stores. Above the door to the Dublin, and the height of a full story, a neon harp glows a steady green until closing time. Below and to one side of the giant instrument the words "tap room" and "bar" blink in red neon. The harp emits a buzzing sound like a swarm of yellow jackets, or a bug zapper in a Texas truck stop. It's been hanging over the entrance to the Dublin for seventy-five years. It's the first thing subway commuters see when they climb the stairs from the Seventy-ninth Street subway station. The harp is impossible to miss even by the most preoccupied passerby. For someone with a drinking problem, the harp has the magnetic pull of the North Pole.

The Dublin is a two-fisted joint. It accepts no credit cards, doesn't serve food, and doesn't even have a blender. You want a frozen margarita or an apple martini, one bartender said, you go over to Columbus Avenue. The daytime crowd at the Dublin looks as though it sprang from the imagination of Eugene O'Neill or Damon Runyon. Most of the customers are older fellows who spread fannies wide on their bar stools and drink with a quiet desperation. They pass the time by watching the ball games on the tube, doing the "Jumble" in the *Daily News* or doping the horses in the *Daily Racing Form*. In the Dublin you can bet on anything from video bowling to the Super Bowl, and everything in between. There is even a rumor that one could get into a rather high-stakes card game on any given afternoon. One of the regulars known to book action was a fellow named Louis Lump-Lump. Two Lumps gained a measure of fame when he shot and killed a patron at Rao's, an East Harlem restaurant and celebrity and gangster hangout. John Gotti had his own table at Rao's; Martin Scorsese cast some of the regulars in Rao's bar in *GoodFellas,* including a guy named Johnny Roastbeef.

Toolan liked to bet, thought himself something of a riverboat gambler. But one bartender confided that Toolan would never be allowed in the card game. Bruce Kelly, a financial reporter and Dublin patron, remembered that Toolan at least talked a big game when it came to betting.

Both Kelly and Toolan followed the New York Mets. In the beginning of the 2002 season Kelly proposed a twenty-dollar bet that Mets pitcher Tom Glavin would win fifteen games that year. Toolan took the bet that Glavin wouldn't, but with a caveat: "Let's make it for real money," Toolan told Kelly. "How about a hundred? Or five?"

Kelly laughed off the increases, reminding Toolan that he was an "underpaid reporter."

"I can barely afford to come in here," Kelly had said.

There were times when even Kelly, who is imbued with a reporter's natural cynicism, found himself thoroughly enjoying Toolan's company. Toolan would tell stories of childhood afternoons spent at Shea Stadium watching the Mets play. He told Kelly that his family was friendly with the Paysons, the original owners of Mets, and that he'd sit in the Payson field box. For a diehard Mets fan like Kelly, no story could keep him more entertained. It wasn't the Payson box in which Toolan sat, however. Jim Mannix's father had a field box on the third-base side. Mr. Mannix often took his son and Toolan to the games.

Though Toolan always talked a good game, whether it was his high-roller bets, or six-figure salaries, at least one bar patron at the Dublin remembered him a bit frayed at the edges. The cuffs and collars on his Oxford shirts were worn; his Brooks Brothers suits had a sheen and were threadbare in spots. Even his aftershave had a cheap scent.

Though Toolan loved to bet, he didn't particularly like to pay up. If he lost a hundred dollars, he'd pay it off in twenty-dollar increments. In fact, being slow in paying was a running theme in Toolan's life, a shortcoming that didn't endear him to a drinking crowd like the one that frequents the Dublin. Toolan had a habit of paying his tab, then hanging around in hopes of a buy back from the bartender. And the Dublin wasn't the only bar Toolan tried to beat. In this way, his adult drinking was just like high school all over again. "He looked like he made a good living—he was always well dressed," Patty McGreevey, the part owner of a West Side saloon named Blondie's told *People*. "But he was always walking out without paying his tab." At the Dublin, more than once he had arguments with bartenders over whether or not he had paid up. Though no one remembered any of the bartenders falling for the ruse, they do remember Toolan trying to get away with it on several occasions.

But Kelly remembered one day when Toolan's luck was running hot. The reporter arrived at the bar late one Sunday afternoon. Toolan's face was bathed in the broadcast light of the TV, a small tight smile on his face. "I'm running the table," he told Kelly as the Jets scored. He also got lucky betting basketball one year. A friend remembered Toolan's life was small when he gambled. "He'd work, go home, isolate with the dog, and watch ESPN," she said. "I remember him rushing home to get the score of an NBA playoff game. He won big."

Another gambling friendship Toolan made at the Dublin was with George Gross. They met at the bar in June 2002. That night they had struck up a conversation about the upcoming heavyweight championship fight between Lennox Lewis and Mike Tyson. Toolan proposed a wager of fifty dollars on the fight. He liked Lennox Lewis. Gross wasn't exactly enamored with the bet; he wasn't the biggest of Tyson fans. But Gross had purchased the fight on HBO Pay-Per-View and thought the bet would make the viewing more interesting. He invited Toolan over to his apartment to watch the fight, but Toolan declined the offer. A few nights later, after Lewis won, Gross was in the Dublin looking for Toolan. "I asked the bartender what kind of a guy he was, if I should pay him," Gross said. The bartender assured Gross that Toolan paid his bets.

Eventually Gross and Toolan became friends. "One of the funny parts about hanging out with him was he'd hype things up more than the reality," Gross remembered. The bar crowd at the Dublin is by no means naive. You might be able to fool them once, but twice? Not likely. Toolan's propensity to embellish quickly became a running joke. He would tell Gross that he had been off working on certain banking deals. "I'm not even sure he was working at the time," Gross remembered thinking. He once told Gross that he was "making a name for himself in the banking industry." Yeah, by stealing the bust out of the armory, Gross reminded him. One of the bartenders remembered Toolan coming in one weekday afternoon and, with a sweeping gesture, asking the owner how much would he sell the bar for. "It was two thirty on a Tuesday, and he's acting like he's going to buy the place," said the bartender with a smirk. Toolan once explained a short absence from the bar by saying that he'd been in Zurich on business. But he quickly recanted the story when one of the bartenders announced that he saw Toolan on Seventy-ninth Street when he was supposedly in Switzerland.

During their first few weeks of dating, Toolan took Jessica Northrup to the Dublin often. Unpretentious, Jessica liked the saloon and the guys who inhabited it, but she didn't particularly want to be there every night—especially as Toolan seemed to get drunk and boorish each time. After one bad night, Jessica threatened to call the relationship quits. But Toolan apologized profusely; and promised to amend his behavior, which he did for a short period of time.

In February 2004, about a year into their relationship, the couple took a trip to upstate New York. There, one of Jessica's sisters was having a baby shower. With the whole of Northrup family gathered, Toolan took that opportunity to ask Jessica to marry him. As he would with Beth months later, Toolan first went to Jessica's parents for their approval. In hindsight it seems an affected move. On the surface traditional and courteous, but rather antiquated and, given the circumstance of the baby shower, spotlight-grabbing. Still everyone was happy, especially Jessica who made a mistake made by many—thinking that she would be able to change someone's addictive behavior. It was a mistake that almost cost Jessica her life.

When Toolan was drinking, a myriad of character defects surfaced. Among the worst of these was his paranoid jealousy. With increasing frequency, Jessica was awakened in the middle of the night by her phone ringing. When she'd answer, there would be no one on the line and the Caller ID would be blocked. She didn't want to believe it was her fiancée, but she came to the realization it couldn't be anyone but. When she confronted him he denied any part of it. At one point, Toolan had a set of keys to Jessica's apartment.

She was going to be away on business for a few days, and she asked if he would look after her dog. When she came back from the short trip, she noticed that several photographs in an album, photographs of her and an old boyfriend, were missing. When she asked about them, he adamantly denied that he had touched the pictures. No one else had access to the apartment. No one else had a motive.

Tension between them was building. Jessica began wondering just how well she knew her boyfriend. Though the thought fell short of frightening her, it was disconcerting nonetheless.

Then it became really scary.

They had returned to Toolan's apartment after having dinner in a restaurant one evening. Toolan had been on his best behavior, he had just one beer with the meal. In the apartment, they had amiable conversation and listened to music. The last thing Jessica Northrup remembered was drifting off to sleep, Toolan next to her. Sometime in middle of the night, Jessica blinked open her eyes in horror. It was like some kind of a nightmare: the pitch-blackness of the apartment, the several seconds before she realized it was him, then the murderous look in his eyes when she did. She couldn't scream, his hands vice-like around her neck. Frozen in fear, she could barely breathe. In that moment, Jessica wondered if he was going to let her live.

In the middle of the night, Toolan awakened and decided to go through Jessica's wallet. There he found a business card of one of her previous boyfriends. He left the apartment in a rage and stormed the few blocks to the Dublin where he drank ferociously for a few hours. By the time he returned he was angry enough to kill.

Jessica knew she couldn't fight him off. Instead, she went limp. As she did, his grip loosened slightly. Enough for her to plead for her life. Slowly, he took his hands away, but the fury in his face remained.

As Beth would do a few months later, Jessica sat and talked to him, biding her time until he passed out. She waiting until the sun came up to pack the few things she had in his place. As she did, Toolan awoke. In an innocence that mystified her, he asked where she was going.

"You're not serious?" Jessica replied.

As he would with Beth, later that morning Toolan began a barrage of phone calls. For days he kept calling, begging Jessica to forgive him.

As it happened, Jessica was scheduled for a business trip to Europe. It gave her time to think. But Toolan's e-mails and phone calls followed her. Each missive was more remorseful, more repentant than the last. Each of them was a declaration of love and a promise to change. He was wearing her down. When Jessica returned home, her mother came into New York for a visit. One night, they had reservations at Café des Artistes, a fancy restaurant on Central Park West. Somehow Toolan found out and called the place and gave them his American Express Card number to pay for the meal.

It seems unreasonable that she gave him another chance. In looking back on those days, Jessica doesn't want to be perceived as naïve or needy. She says that at that point of her relationship with Toolan, she tried to concentrate on his good points, of which there were many. When sober, Toolan seemed the perfect boyfriend—attentive, endearing, and impulsive. She thought, rightly so, that he was an alcoholic. And, she believed that divorced from that addiction he was basically a good person. She set up a meeting with him, and then set down the guidelines. He would have to either give up drinking or the thought of being with her. Toolan readily agreed to every condition, and it was after this that Toolan put together his longest period of sobriety.

The red door on the west side of Lexington Avenue on the Upper East Side leads to a church basement. At specific times of the day, in the early morning and early evening, a small tin sign is hung from the door handle. At those prescribed hours the door is opened often—mostly by young people mostly in their twenties and early thirties. Down a couple of steps is a Formica-tiled room bathed in fluorescent light. Plastic chairs are arranged in a circle. If an observer didn't know what the gathering was, it would be hard to guess. Some in the room brandish Mohawk haircuts and boast tattoos. Others wear hip-hugging jeans showing tight, bare tummies. There are Ashworth golf shirts in spring and summer and Helly Hansen jackets when the ski slopes are open. And there are a few—just a few—hunched shoulders slung with knapsacks that carry all the person's worldly belongings. Altogether, at the beginners' meeting on Wednesday night, there are a hundred and fifty, maybe more, attending. The noise is a din, until a bell is rung and the room falls suddenly quiet. Someone, picked arbitrarily, then begins to read the preamble from a plastic-covered sheet of paper: "Alcoholics Anonymous is a fellowship of men and women . . ."

For six months Toolan dutifully attended AA meetings. At first he seemed willing to commit to the rigors of getting sober. It is strongly suggested that someone trying to get sober attend ninety meetings in ninety days, and work AA's Twelve Steps with a sponsor. It's also strongly suggested that he make daily phone calls to other recovering alcoholics. Toolan went to meetings all over the city, and, for a while, had an AA sponsor. Northrup remembered seeing him with AA literature and Pete Hamill's getting-dry memoir, *A Drinking Life*. He even found ways of having fun without booze. He took tango lessons, and tried them out at AA dances. Physically, the change in him was remarkable. Quickly, he lost the bloat he'd accumulated from drinking beer. When Toolan and Northrup first began to date, she was flabbergasted that he didn't own a pair of blue jeans. After he had lost some weight, she insisted they go to a Levi Strauss store to buy some, which they did. But Toolan never took the tags off of the pants, and returned them soon after.

His personality changed, too. He became friendly with some of the other members of his group therapy, going out for dinner or coffee afterward. It was in this group where he confided that he always wanted to be a writer, that his career in finance was all his parents' idea. To friends and group members, Toolan confessed he was never able to live up to his father's high literary standards. He had completed several stories and, according to one friend, a movie script. For the most part, he kept his writing to himself. Because of his literary bent, a group member urged him to get a job in a library so he would be surrounded by books. But maybe the biggest addition Toolan made to his life at this time was a live-in companion.

One night in the winter of 2003 Eddie Lama was driving his green Subaru through a snowstorm. He was headed from New York City to his animal sanctuary in Sullivan County in upstate New York. He had traveled as far as Yonkers when he decided to turn around. The storm was too dangerous. As the Subaru crawled through the snow-covered streets of the Bronx, the headlights reflected off something that ran across the car's path. "It blended in with the ambience," Eddie said. He slammed on the brakes and jumped from the car. "I thought he was gray, he was so filthy," Eddie remembered. Eddie knew right away it was an unusual dog: a white shepherd purebred. Eddie opened a can of dog food, and the dog happily crawled up into the backseat. Eddie would call him "Yeti," after the Abominable Snowman.

Toolan knew Eddie Lama. He would often walk by this veterinarian's office just a few doors down from the Dublin House. Pictures of dogs and cats up for adoption hang in the window, some of them from Eddie Lama's sanctuary. A few months before, Toolan had seen a picture of a mixed Labrador in the window. But "Twisla," whom Eddie described as a "hip-hop dog" was a bit too energetic for Toolan. All adoptions from the sanctuary are preceded by a one-week trial, which Lama call a "fostering" period. Toolan and Twisla were just not meant for each other.

It wasn't that Toolan was bad with pets. Quite the opposite, he loved dogs. He had had a St. Bernard for several years. When the dog died unexpectedly, a weeping Toolan called a friend and asked what he should do. The friend spent an hour consoling him and then suggested he call New York City Sanitation. He did. When he was told to wrap the carcass up and leave it on the street to be picked up during the regular garbage collection, he slammed down the phone. Instead, he swaddled the dog's body in a blanket and laid it on the floor of his apartment. Most of that night he spent drinking and crying over his lost pet. It took a few months for Toolan to get over his grief. When he did, he went in search of another dog.

Meanwhile, Eddie was having a hard time finding a home for Yeti. Though beautiful, Yeti had dental problems and the temperament of a dog that had been abused. The dog needed an inordinate amount of attention and love, something that was hard to find in the overdrive atmosphere of Manhattan. Plus, Yeti was big, nearly a hundred pounds. Sometime around May 2004, Toolan walked back into the vet's office and saw the picture of a striking white German shepherd on the wall. He gave Eddie a call.

Toolan liked the shepherd right off. "Yeti was more docile," Eddie remembered. "More responsive to orders." But finding a dog that was right for Toolan wasn't enough for Eddie. Toolan had to be right for the dog: "We decide whether it's good for all parties involved." The sanctuary does a cursory background check on people interested in adopting. "If something came up, we would never have given the dog to him." A Brooklyn guy, who describes himself as having "grown up on the streets," Eddie also relies on his own instincts. He gave Toolan high marks. "He was very polite, considerate, like a good Catholic schoolboy," Eddie said. "He just didn't come off like a creep. I'm not a psychologist, but you can usually spot one." Toolan took Yeti home and renamed him "Jack." He had his hands full with the animal. According to several accounts, the dog was antisocial both to other dogs and people. Still, those same sources say that Toolan's fondness for Jack was evident, as was Jack's for Toolan.

◆ ◆ ◆

I n ways, sobriety brought out the best in Toolan. He talked to Jessica once a day, either by phone or e-mail, even when she was in Europe on business. He brought her flowers and, once, a gift of diamond earrings. Together, they did engagement things like hunting for co-ops, even though Toolan was out of work and it was unlikely he could afford to buy one anytime soon. On Jessica's part, she tried hard to forget that night she'd awakened in such terror. But the truth was she never would forget. What's more, she began to see that Toolan's problems went deeper than alcohol. One time, Toolan agreed to watch after her puppy while she was away on a week-long business trip. She had her suspicions that he wasn't following through on his promise. She called a friend of her sister's and asked him to stop by her place. When he did, he found the dog hadn't been walked in a couple of days and had relieved himself in the apartment. But even more than the dog incident, it was Toolan's secretiveness that bothered her most. When she'd ponder the stories that he told her she'd wonder where the truth ended and fantasy began. Once when they were walking near his apartment, he pointed out a diesel Mercedes station wagon parked on the side street and told her he had just bought it. But a week later when they took a trip out to Long Island, they rented a car. When Jessica asked after the Mercedes, Toolan at first seemed unaware of what she talking about. Then quickly he made up a story about the car being at the mechanic's.

Coincidentally, Jessica and Toolan's relationship ended where it started. But this time at the Café Luxembourg there was no breezy flirting on Toolan's part. Instead, he was especially dour. After several callback interviews, he had lost out on yet another bank job. Financially, his life continued to unravel. At dinner that night he seemed to take it out on Jessica. He called her a variety of nasty names, including "asshole." When he uttered that particular word, she stood and walked out of the restaurant. Sometime later, Toolan was in the lobby of Jessica's building, a landmark hotel converted to residences. From there he called her, once again begging for forgiveness. But this time she was having none of it. After Jessica told him to stay out of her life for good, she rang the front desk to make sure they didn't let Toolan get to the elevator. According to one source, Toolan had a brief confrontation with one of the doormen. Apparently, the doorman remembered Toolan from a previous drunken episode in the lobby and relished the opportunity to enforce Jessica's request. Still, the very next day, Jessica had the locks changed on her apartment just in case.

CHAPTER
TWENTY-EIGHT

Beth addressed her problem with conflict in the most unlikely way. It was so improbable that Beth would find her path in martial arts that friends and relatives really didn't know how to respond. Yet she spent the last year of her life crisscrossing the globe studying the discipline. In the spring of 2004 Beth wrote a letter of introduction to Louis Guarnaccia, an aikido teacher on Nantucket. In it she described how she came to study martial arts:

"The key to good fiction is conflict" was my fiction writing instructor's mantra. Every fiction writer builds architecture for characters to inhabit while creating conflicts, making sparks fly and providing resolution. It is the flying sparks that seem to fascinate the reader most. She said my characters were too nice, that there was not nearly enough conflict in my work and sent me home with special homework: to watch WWF on television.

A friend suggested I take up martial arts instead, but being a woman in my midforties who had never been athletic, I couldn't imagine myself in such a physical, seemingly violent environment. A few days later, I was walking down the street in a snowstorm, when for no apparent reason, I looked up to see the banner for the New York Aikikai, and to my left, a sign on the door that said "visitors welcome." I climbed the stairs and as I got closer to the top could hear the crash of break falls in an otherwise silent setting. That evening I bowed onto the mat for the first time.*

Beth wasn't exactly a natural. The classes were hard and had her "weeping through the entire hour," as she wrote to the sensei. Three times each week she'd trudge up the stairs at the New York Aikikai. And after each class she hobbled back down. There were plenty of moments when she thought herself crazy. But she wouldn't quit.

The New York Aikikai is a part of the following of Morihei Ueshiba, or O Sensei (Great Teacher). Ueshiba was the founder of the Japanese martial art called aikido. According to the New York Aikikai, aikido means to harmonize with the life force of the universe. It has also been called, according to the New York Aikikai, "the Way to Spiritual Harmony."

Though it espouses nonviolence, the art contains a study of physical defense and responses to different types of attacks, including knife attack. Beth learned throws, holds, joint locks, pins, and disarming techniques. Though undoubtedly Beth was attracted to the discipline's spiritual component, it was also the promise of physical safety that appealed to her.

"I had lived in NY for twenty years," Beth wrote to the sensei, "and although I had never been mugged or otherwise attacked, there was always a vivid fear I carried with me."

In the letter, she told the sensei about a "strike," or attack, that she feared for most of her adult life. "I had no idea how much it cost me to carry that fear around," Beth wrote. "Although I'm not so sure that aikido techniques will prove effective if I ever am attacked, what I do know is that the fear of being attacked, and the accompanying emotional undertow, is no longer part of my shadow."

---

*Though Susan Breen remembers the series of those events slightly differently—"I wouldn't suggest anybody watch wrestling"—she said Beth had captured the spirit of the conversation correctly.

Beth settled into a regimen of two or three aikido classes a week, or when she was "not too black and blue to roll." She called her dojo a "very yang place," with its eighty percent male membership. "It scared the wits out of me," she said of fighting the men. But she would say a prayer before bowing onto the mat and, as the weeks went by, she became less intimidated. "I learned how to take better *ukemi*," she said of the art of breaking the fall and rolling. But mostly she learned how to get up again.

After only a few months of classes Beth had lost twenty pounds. She was amazed at her body's pliability and resiliency. She radically changed her diet, cutting out wheat, vinegar, and alcohol. She drank only springwater and ate fresh fruit and vegetables. She felt better physically and mentally than she had in years.

The following summer Beth traveled to San Francisco. There she attended aikido classes and studied aikido philosophy, which is influenced by the ancient Japanese religions of Shinto and Buddhism. Of the teachings, Beth said: "I had spent my whole life looking for this philosophy; it was as if it was written just for me, or for that matter, I had written it myself."

Robert Nadeau taught one of the classes Beth attended in California. A former police officer, Nadeau was a seventh *dan* (black belt) and had studied under aikido founder Ueshiba. Nadeau sometimes used Fred Astaire and Ginger Rogers as an example of how to blend with the motion of attack. Though Beth understood the concept, she had trouble assimilating the technique. "I couldn't feel the energy," she said. But then Beth heard Nadeau tell a struggling student, "If you don't know where you are, you can't know where you're going."

"My ears grew about three inches," Beth wrote to the sensei. "I suddenly realized that the practice of aikido was not a sport at all, but the practice of life. It was redolent with metaphor, with lessons, with guidance if I chose to listen."

At the end of the summer, Beth came back to New York and stepped up her study. She had a goal in mind, a fifth *kyu*, an important beginner's level and two rungs beneath a brown belt (if there was such a thing as a brown belt in the aikido discipline she was studying). She searched out a sensei by the name of Yamada. When Beth introduced herself, Yamada replied: "I know who you are, you're the Crying Girl." Though Beth was embarrassed, the moment made her appreciate how far she had progressed in seven months of aikido. "It takes seven years to get a black belt," Beth once said. "Seven years with nothing in between. I love the idea if I stick with it. I don't know whether I will or not, the idea that there's so much to learn it takes seven years."

Along with aikido, Beth regularly meditated and saw spiritual healers. She took an "Astrology Journey" in Half Moon Bay, California. Run by the Animas Valley Institute, the journey is a five-day trek into the wilderness, where one aligns the soul with nature. On the journey, she met Dabney Oliver. On Beth's memorial Web site, Oliver wrote that Beth had told him that she was an Aries, and as such often felt great fear and that so much of her life was spent in reclaiming her own courage. "She was exploring the boundaries of her own courage," Oliver wrote. "Beth was at a crossroad," Oliver later wrote in an e-mail. "She was looking at her life and deciding where to go next. She seemed to get a great deal out of the retreat and left more peaceful than when she arrived."

Family members remember Beth's confidence in those days soaring. Anything foretold in a birth chart no longer frightened her.

By Christmas of '03 aikido was perhaps the biggest part of Beth's life. She took pictures of the New York Aikikai Christmas party and mugged for the camera herself. In one picture, she has her cheek pushed up against the sensei, both of them grinning eagerly. Beth didn't give up writing, however. She kept Susan apprised on her progress in both aikido and her literary endeavors. One note read:

Dear Susan,
Warmest wishes for the holidays and the New Year to come.
I'm indebted to you for pointing out that there was not

enough conflict in my work, which led me to begin training
in aikido, the Japanese martial art. I earned my first belt in
September and love love love the art and the community . . .
    All the best,
    Beth

At the end of her letter to the Nantucket sensei, Beth again wrote of her experience in Susan's class. "Last year, I wasn't very good about writing about conflict," she said. "I was too afraid of it, worried about how many ways I could get hurt, so preferred to avoid discord at all costs." But through aikido, she wrote, she was able to stand in the face of conflict. "I've learned to transform the attack in a nonviolent way without escalating the situation."

In January 2004 Beth left a cold and dark New York and headed to Guam. Over the Christmas holiday Beth had finally come to a decision about leaving Manhattan for good and moving to Nantucket. Since the day she sold CODE, she'd flirted with the idea. Now she'd made up her mind. "Five weeks in Guam was to be a physical and spiritual retreat in preparation for breaking my bonds with Manhattan," she wrote.

Along with the island's beauty, and the balmy change from New York City's winter, one of the reasons Beth chose Guam was because of a woman aikido teacher that ran a dojo there. Mutsuko Minegishi Sensei is a sixth-degree Japanese lady black belt (*rokudan*), the highest rank a woman has achieved in the art. Beth thought that the feminine influence would be a softer, kinder form of aikido than the ones she was used to in New York and California. Nothing could be farther from the truth.

"Minegishi Sensei is a force of nature, and out to prove that she is not a little old lady," Beth wrote. "She thought nothing of yelling through most of the class, mostly in Japanese, although her English was impeccable." Beth called her experience training with Minegishi "harrowing," with nights after classes spent in baths of Epsom salts and with self-administered rubs of Tiger Balm. Yoko Pipes, a fellow aikido student in Guam, remembers that, despite being discouraged, Beth "always kept a positive attitude." As usual, Beth wouldn't quit. She saw Minegishi six days a week, sometimes as many as three classes a day. "It looked like she was getting to realize the true depth of the art," Yoko Pipes remembered. Beth's persistence paid off. "During the fourth week I had a major breakthrough, which resonated not just in my aikido, but also in my life," she wrote. "It was as if I finally lost all fear of being annihilated and if I were to be annihilated, then so be it."

When Beth returned to New York, she literally embodied her aikido training. "I know what it feels like to listen with my skin, through my touch," she wrote. "And it was healing, cleansing, energizing. I felt plugged in to the energy of the universe. I felt I was in the right place and the right time. . . ."

Beth had fixed a date in the spring for her move to Nantucket. Her letter to the sensei on the island was not only an introduction; it was also a Dear John letter of sorts addressed to New York.

New York City meant a great deal to Beth. In many ways, the city was her lover. It was there she had made her fortune, where she had made many of her friends. She had built, with amazing energy and creativity, the apartment of her dreams. It was in the pulsating world of New York business, the sultry clubs and chic restaurants, that Beth had found and embraced her power as a woman. But New York had also been the biggest of disappointments. The shimmer and style of the city had promised love but hadn't delivered. It had been twenty years since she moved there as a spunky twenty-three-year-old. She had truly given the city her best years.

CHAPTER
TWENTY-NINE

On her last night as a New Yorker, Beth dressed in a beautiful gold brocade jacket and silk slacks and, all by herself, headed to the Metropolitan Opera to watch a performance of Rossini's *L'Italiana in Algeri*. Because it was a spur-of-the-moment decision, Beth settled for a ticket in the Family Circle, the cheap seats in the upper reaches of the theater. There she sat next a fellow opera buff named Liz Mackey. That afternoon Beth had bought a cellular phone, one of the then new models that doubled as a camera. With the enthusiasm of a tourist, she showed Liz Mackey the pictures she had taken. One was of a subway station, Mackey remembered, another of Carnegie Hall, the rags-to-riches juxtaposition of the pictures standing as a metaphor for Beth's own New York journey.

By the time the curtain rose, Beth and Mackey were fast friends. Beth seemed thrilled to have a companion with whom to share the evening. She told Liz how she fell in love with opera at a performance of *La Traviata* that featured the American soprano Renée Fleming. Beth talked about a trip she had recently taken to the Santa Fe Opera, and also about a wonderful performance of *Salome* she saw at the Glimmerglass Opera near Cooperstown, New York. She explained how much she loved Verdi and Puccini, but didn't much care for Handel and other Baroque composers. Liz Mackey is used to letting people talk. A journalist, she writes for a museum magazine. But listening to Beth was infinitely more enjoyable than any interview. "It was a time of my life when I wasn't quite sure there were people like her out there," Mackey remembered thinking. "She was so full of life, so attractive. I could see her being a senator, president."

After the performance, the two women descended the stairs to the bowels of the theater and boarded a subway car. Beth had already sublet her apartment and was staying with friends in the Village. Liz Mackey was heading home to Brighton Beach, Brooklyn. Bathed in the garish subway light, Beth told Mackey that she was moving the following day to Nantucket. She was gushing about a painting she had bought for her cottage. But Mackey also noticed sadness in her new friend. Beth told Mackey about a man, a sculptor, she knew. "There was definitely a shadow," Mackey says, "a level of disappointment that the relationship didn't go farther."

About a year before, Beth had attended an art opening on Nantucket. A loud, rather overbearing man approached her. Beth was polite, but wanted to get out of the conversation as soon as she could. Just as she was making an excuse to leave, a fellow whom Beth later described to friends as "beautiful," with dark, brown hair and a stoneworker's body, walked over to the man to whom Beth was talking. "I want you to meet my younger brother," the man said.

Beth's heart quickened.

As a sculptor, Patrick Beaugard worked in large dimensions. Beth would buy an eighteen-hundred-pound Buddha from him. He had spent time in Asia, and he followed Eastern teachings and religion. He also loved to cook and invited Beth over to his house for dinner on several occasions. Beth fell hard.

Among friends and family, it was thought that Beth's decision to move to Nantucket was at least partly due to a desire to be closer to Patrick. But what at first seemed serendipitous with a future was neither.

By this point Beth had made up her mind that she was going to find someone who wanted to be her partner. At forty-three, she knew that realistically her window for motherhood was closing quickly. Patrick had never been married and was not interested in anything more than what he and Beth already shared.

There was no acrimony involved in their decision to go in different directions romantically. Patrick even helped Beth move into the cottage on Hawthorne Lane. Beth promised Patrick that she would help him with the business side of his art career.

Though Beth put on a brave face, her heart was wounded. Rarely, maybe not since Niall, had she opened herself to someone as she did with Patrick. But this time Beth wasn't going to insulate her feelings with twelve-hour workdays. She wasn't about to retreat anymore. Aikido had not only helped Beth allay her fear of being attacked, it had given her a confidence that she'd never really owned. There was someone else out there for her. This she fervently believed.

On the subway, Beth's smile returned when Mackey suggested that love awaited on Nantucket. "Maybe you'll meet a Dutchman," she mused.

It was a romantic idea, a writer's cottage on Nantucket. Even the name of the road, Hawthorne Lane, brought images of *The Scarlet Letter* and Nathaniel Hawthorne's friendship with Herman Melville. Kathy Legge, the president of the Artists' Association of Nantucket, told reporters that Beth was headed to Nantucket to regroup. "Sometimes people, especially in their forties, try to recapture their personal time," she said. And, certainly, Beth wanted to be close to family, especially Peter's children.

But Beth really never really understood the concept of slowing down. She jumped into island life, as she told a friend, "whole hog." In a late April e-mail to Liz Mackey, Beth wrote: "My *Opera News*es as are stacked up along with *Saveur* and *The New Yorker*. I just haven't had a chance to catch up on my magazines. . . . I have not been working a job, but still settling into my new life here in a small town, on a small island. I am loving it, much to my surprise. It was a real leap of faith to get up here, but I really feel like this is a great decision."

Beth planted a garden of arugola, radishes, mint, chives, and onions just steps from the cottage. A quarter of a mile away, in the communal garden, she grew tomatoes, ancho chilies, cucumbers, herbs, and kale. In her e-mail to Mackey, she wrote that the forsythia and daffodils on the island were in full bloom. She described the characters on Nantucket as "odd bits that swirl in eddies alongside the big river." Beth wrote that the locals had already warned her that she wouldn't last a year before the island became too small for her. Locals say it "closes in" on off-islanders. "We will just see what we will see," Beth wrote. "I am rather enjoying it at the moment."

Helping Patrick was the beginning of a service Beth was putting together that was the perfect marriage of her business sense and knowledge of the artist community on the island. The enterprise was so new, she really hadn't settled on a name for it. At first she wanted to call the business "The Left Side of the Brain," but one newspaper reported that it was called "Venus Rules." Regardless of the name, the cornerstone of the project was to publish a book of her father's artwork. Nothing would have made her happier. Along with her brothers and sister, Beth believed (many collectors agree) that as an artist their father was underappreciated. Though John Lochtefeld has a steady and faithful clientele on Nantucket, in art circles of Boston and New York he's gone largely unnoticed. According to one Nantucket gallery listing, John's "work with elements of fantasy and fairy tale has quietly captured the imagination of his collectors for over thirty years here on Nantucket." Beth and her siblings believed that their father's dedication to them came at the expense of his career.

The quick story of John Lochtefeld's decision to favor family over art begins with his mother. Dorothy Champe was a West Virginian, from English, Welsh, Scots, and Irish extraction, and scandalously (at least to the

Maria Stein Lochtefelds) Protestant. Vernon Carlin Champe, Dorothy's father, performed in a minstrel show in New York City in the early 1900s. A Renaissance man, Vernon Champe had earned his law degree when he was only nineteen. He would eventually practice law in West Virginia, and was later a judge there. He kept his contacts with the theatre, however. Vernon wrote the will for the stage actress Maude Adams. According to Lochtefeld family lore, he also represented Lionel Barrymore and, perhaps, John Philip Sousa, in legal matters.

Soon after Vernon dropped dead of a heart attack at fifty-three, Dorothy met Charles Lochtefeld on a blind date in West Virginia. Charles, who worked for the Ford Motor Company, picked her up in his automobile. A rapier wit, Dorothy often said that Charles asked her to stand in the headlights so he could see what she looked like. Dorothy and Charles went on one date a month for six months. Apparently that was enough of a courtship. They were married in Maria Stein. Charles's brother, Mel Lochtefeld, performed the ceremony. It was his first duty as a Catholic priest. For Dorothy, the marriage was the culmination of a quiet sacrifice. When Dorothy was a young woman, she'd studied to be an opera singer. When her father died, so did her dream.

Like his mom, at one point in his youth, John flirted with the idea of a singular life as an artist. After graduating from Notre Dame, he applied to the Ringling School of Art and Design, a rather forward-thinking art school in Florida. That summer, however, he happened to be in Boston, where he met a waitress in one of the big wharf restaurants that lined the North Shore. Judy was about to enter her senior year at Michigan State. According to one family member, John then looked something like a young Paul Newman, though his eyes were light green and not Newman's china blue. Judy, it is said, fell "head over heels." Pretty and outgoing, Judy brought her own charms to the equation. As they did in the 1950s, things would progress very quickly. First, the navy drafted John in 1955, but the last thing he wanted was to spend any time on a boat. Instead, he enlisted in the army. Though Uncle Sam had John's immediate future mapped out, he took his distant fate into his own hands. He and Judy were married in 1956 in a small ceremony in New Jersey. Afterward, they went on a short, three-day honeymoon on the Jersey Shore. When John finished basic training at Fort Bragg, he was sent to Honolulu. Soon after he settled in there, he sent for his new wife.

After his army service, John and Judy stayed on in Hawaii. There Judy gave birth to a baby boy, Beth's oldest brother, James, and John got a master's degree and taught art in a local high school. He also sent out résumés. His first college job was at Mercyhurst in Erie, Pennsylvania, where he taught for five years. During that period, Judy gave birth, in rapid succession, to four more children, Peter, Beth, Cathy, and Tom.

There is a photograph from those days that dispels any notion of regret in John's choice of life paths. In the picture, Beth is just one. She wears a frilly dress, white baby shoes, with hair combed and cut, and she sits on her dad's lap. He smokes a pipe and wears a grin.

The way John lived his life as a husband, father, and teacher indicates he never looked back. It would not be until his children were grown with lives of their own that he finally dedicated himself fully to his heart's desire. By that time, much of his opportunity to be recognized as an artist had passed him by. The book was Beth's way of giving her father a final shot at a lost chance.

Appropriately, the theme of the book was to be about the positive interpretation of dreams. Beth still kept in touch with Susan via e-mail. In one message, she asked her former writing teacher for advice on how to get her father's book published. Beth had sent it to the publisher without representation. It was rejected. "I told her rejection is part of the business, and I told her she should keep on sending it out," Susan said. At some point, Beth made up her mind that she was going to see the book in print if she had to publish it herself.*

The last weekend in April on Nantucket is called Daffodil Weekend, an event that celebrates the million or so daffodils that the Nantucket Garden Club planted on the island. Main Street is closed to traffic, and vintage cars are parked on lawns along the thoroughfare. That Daffodil Saturday, Gene Mahon was walking along Main Street when he saw Peter Lochtefeld with his wife, Santjes, and another woman he didn't know. He thought the woman he didn't know was pretty and barely realized she was carrying one of Santjes and Peter's children on her shoulders. It was Beth who drew Mahon's attention.

Mahon caught up to the Lochtefelds and engaged Beth in a short conversation. She reminded him that they had met when she was working at DeMarco. Mahon made a mental note to call Santjes for Beth's number. He wouldn't have to. Several nights later, Mahon was at an organ recital produced by the Nantucket Arts Council, of which he is a member. At intermission, Beth walked up the aisle smiling broadly. "She lifted your spirits when she smiled," Mahon said.

After the recital, Beth accompanied Mahon to the American Seasons, an intimate restaurant only a hundred yards or so from the church where the recital was held. There, Mahon told Beth his story.

For two years, 1978–80, Mahon ran a jazz club on the island called Roadhouse. One of his partners in the place was writer Frank Conroy. In his memoir of Nantucket, *Time and Tide*, Conroy describes the Roadhouse at length, though he veils Mahon's identity by calling him "partner b." Trading

*Tell Me About Your Dreams . . . was published by the Lochtefeld family with money that largely came from Beth's estate. Proceeds from the book go to the University of Dreams Foundation. It is available in bookstores on Nantucket and at the Lochtefeld Gallery on Fair Street or from Beth's memorial Web site at www.bethlochtefeld.org.

on cold beer, good jazz, and a bit of Conroy's notoriety (Conroy wrote *Stop-Time*, still considered by many as the standard in memoirs), the Roadhouse was a legend in the making. Mahon confided to Beth that he was looking to recapture some of those heady days with a new club on the island. Beth was always quick to assume the role of benefactor; she told Mahon that she was interested in his idea. "The theme of her life was to fulfill people's dreams," Mahon said. As they chatted, the thought came to Mahon that he would like to spend time with Beth Lochtefeld.

He wouldn't have the chance.

On Memorial Day, Beth sent another e-mail to Liz Mackey describing the kickoff of the summer season. "Saturday afternoon until Monday the fleet of the Figawi Race arrives," she wrote. "I understand it is about 100 sailboats in a race from Hyannis with the most badly behaved group of drunken sailors you could every [*sic*] imagine. The race got its name from sailors, alcohol and fog and the constant comment of 'where the figawi???' "

The last summer of Beth's life started in Paris. After a weekend there, she traveled to the Loire Valley, where she explored castles and attended the wedding of a close girlfriend. In Nantucket she had boned up on her cursory knowledge of French. She ordered language lesson CDs and met once a week with French speakers on Nantucket. Beth also talked to her sister, Cathy, once a week. Cathy teaches French. "What good is a wedding if you can't flirt?" Beth wrote to Liz Mackey. The European vacation was supposed to continue with a trip to Seville, Spain, for an outdoor performance of the opera *Carmen*. Beth had sent an enthusiastic group e-mail to her opera pals looking to round up people to go: "Acts 1 & 2 are held in the Plaza de Espana, Act 2 is held in Park Maria Luisa, and act three is in the Plaza de Toros—the bull ring. There are a few houses between acts, and you physically move from place to place, stopping for tapas and sherry along the way perhaps? Taking a horse-drawn buggy perhaps?" Alas, there were problems with the production, and Beth had to put off the side trip to Spain.

Beth was back on Nantucket by July 4. Her garden was producing almost more than she could handle. "I feel like a sorcerer's apprentice," she wrote to Liz Mackey. "A few small seeds makes a bunch of plants makes A LOT of produce! There is something fun about knocking on a friend's door with a bunch of radishes and scallions." The island also proved neighborly to Beth. She told Liz Mackey that a neighbor had left a pot of fresh-dug clams simmering in broth and butter outside her front door. There was only one thing missing from Beth's fabulous life—someone to share it with. By summer's end, she thought she'd met that someone.

CHAPTER THIRTY

A long-ago August rushed through Matt Bresnahan's memories as the summer wind blew against his face. His rental bicycle bounced over the cobblestones, and each sight brought back another vignette from his past. He was with his wife and family on the island where he once spent the last part of a summer with his college sweetheart. His memories were warm, and a lot of them were about Beth.

Judy Lochtefeld knew it was Matt right off. Having spent many years in front of classrooms, Judy was used to recognizing faces from long-ago moments. "Oh, you're the fellow who got into the hot water with David," she said with a smile. In the summer of 1981, Nantucket police had escorted Matt and Beth's cousin, David Joy, home for hot-rodding on mopeds after the two threw back a few cold beers. Matt hadn't thought of that incident for years. "I couldn't even keep the moped upright," Matt remembered later. David got the worst of the incident, however. He was scraped from head to toe.

This summer of 2004 Matt had awakened early and rented a bicycle. He stopped at the counter at Congdon's and got a coffee and a muffin, sat on a bench, and watched the town stretch itself awake. The first of the smiling day-trippers walked up Main Street from the Fast Ferry. Other early risers ambled into the Hub for the morning papers. Several young Irish lasses, with bleary eyes, hurried into the Even Keel a bit late for their breakfast shift. Judy had walked out of the Nantucket pharmacy. She explained that John was suffering from sciatica. Matt asked after Beth's brothers and sister and was assured that everyone was fine. Matt said that he saw Tommy Lochtefeld interviewed on TV after he'd escaped from the World Trade Center. Judy answered that all of the Lochtefeld family was eternally grateful for that. The conversation, as conversations with grandmothers invariably do, wound around to the topic of grandchildren. Matt asked if any belonged to Beth. Beth was never married, Judy Lochtefeld replied.

"We're still hoping the right guy comes along for her," she added.

Matt handed Judy Lochtefeld one of his business cards and asked that she pass it along to Beth. Maybe they could catch up via e-mail, he said. His behavior was almost shy, as though he was afraid Beth wouldn't remember him. Matt climbed on his bike and began to peddle back toward the hotel.

Halfway across the island, Beth hung up her phone after a short conversation with her mom. *Matt Bresnahan,* she mused, a smile coming to her lips. A vision of his boyish looks undoubtedly formed in Beth's mind. She wasn't about to let him off the island without seeing how he had turned out. When Matt returned to his room, a message from Beth was waiting.

Sometime later that day, Matt, along with his wife and four children, sat in a booth in a restaurant on Main Street. It was a beautiful early July afternoon. The sidewalks of Main Street were filled with folk holding ice cream cones and frozen frappacinos and peering into the windows of the shops and galleries. But the restaurant in which Matt and his family sat was nearly empty. The lunch crowd had moved on to shopping or to the beach.

Beth walked into the place wearing a huge smile. Her teeth were perfectly straight and white. On her memorial Web site, Beth's dentist wrote about her dentist phobia, but how she had summoned the courage for regular work and polishing. Her blond hair was short and pulled back behind her ears. She wore a floral-print dress and a stretchy leotard blue top. "She looked great," Matt remembered. The way she looked made it even more surprising to him that she was still single. During the course of their conversation, Beth mentioned a few of her past relationships, but seemed to shrug off her marital status. "Nothing has worked out," she told Matt at one point.

Outwardly, at least, Beth gave no indication of being sorry about her life choices. "She had three or four projects she was gearing up for," Matt remembered about that conversation. "She said she had put the troubles with her business behind her."

Beth was then very involved with the Nantucket Arts Council. In an e-mail to Liz Mackey, she told about a concert she had attended that was produced by the council. The featured performer was Greta Feeney, a soprano with the San Francisco Opera and stepdaughter of Beth's friend Bernadette Feeney. The following day, Beth was invited to be on the board. She was under the impression that a faction of the Arts Council was desperately looking for new blood. "There are about a dozen or fifteen people on the board, three of whom are as old as Methuselah and knew me when I was five year [*sic*] old," she wrote. "There is a young guard trying to liven things up, and the three old farts who are a reactionary as you can imagine."

Beth regaled the Bresnahans with stories of her travels to Paris and the Loire Valley. She talked at length about the book of her father's artwork. She told them about the University of Dreams. Throughout her soliloquy, Beth smiled easily. Low-level currents surged through Matt. Though he said the feelings felt short of being any kind of "sparks" for his old flame, he couldn't help musing about how different their two lives had turned out. "She was always a family-oriented person," Matt said. "She was adventurous, but she always had that rock, her family." Now, more than twenty years later, Matt sat in front of Beth with his wife Colleen and their children Sean, fourteen, Riley, thirteen, Timothy, ten, and Madeleine, just a couple of days short of nine, the picture of a happy family. Indeed, Colleen Bresnahan would use one of the snapshots taken on Nantucket as the following year's Christmas card. And then there was Beth, the girl Matt was sure would end up happily married, all alone.

After an hour or so, the Bresnahan kids were getting a little restless—and who could blame them? Here it was a beautiful afternoon on Nantucket and they were stuck in a dark restaurant with Daddy, Mommy, and some lady who was cool but no match for the beach. The lunch ended as these things usually end, with promises to keep in touch.

Out on Main Street, Matt and Beth hugged one last time. As they walked away, both of them turned and had one last look at the other.

As is its wont, life had gone by fast for Beth. Had it really been almost twenty years and four kids ago that she had sat in the tree with Matt Bresnahan? Where did those days go when love was something that could be set on a shelf for later? Beth put on a brave face for the world. And, inwardly, she told herself over and over another chance would come, that love would step off the Fast Ferry and into her life. This time, she said, she would not be terrified of being hurt. Being hurt was worse than being alone. She, no doubt, remembered how she felt after Niall. But in those echoing moments when she awoke in the middle of the night alone, she wept. Around that time, an entry in her journal began: "I am a bit of a teary mess right now, but I know that each day I am a little stronger, and a little more certain of what I am doing. . . ."

And she kept running. August found Beth in Upstate New York in an aikido camp held at Colgate University, which brother Jim had once attended. Then there was a trip to Montreal to visit friends. In between, there were jaunts back and forth to New York and hosting yet another friend from her past.

The sight of Hilary Collins brought a flood of memories of an unfettered time in Beth's life. Over a glass of wine, they laughed about the diplomat and his wife, Mr. Wankie's, and the old Bull and Bear.

Hilary had come to Nantucket with her daughter. One day while Beth was changing into her bathing suit, Hilary's daughter noticed the tattoo. "Why does Beth have a doggie on the bum?" the daughter asked her mom. With Beth's aikido classes and her strict diet, the once ferocious rampant lion had shrunk along with her posterior.

August went by in a blink. In Athens, Olympic shot-putters competed in the same stadium they had in the fourth century B.C. Pictures of the presidential candidate, John Kerry, windsurfing off the coast of Nantucket were beamed around the planet. Four hundred thousand marched in protest as the Republicans met in their national convention in New York.

T he summer was over when Gene Mahon ran into Beth at yet another concert for the Nantucket Arts Council. This one was held at another church and featured folksinger Patty Larkin. During the performance, there were problems with the stage lighting that demanded Mahon's attention. Several times he had to walk down the aisle to fix the lights. Each time he did, he passed Beth and a very well dressed, good-looking man with blond hair. Mahon was a little jealous. Fifteen years older, several inches shorter, and balding, Mahon came to the conclusion that he had finished a distant second in the race for Beth's heart. He found himself staring at the happy couple during the performance. There was something in the way Beth leaned into the gentleman, something about her body language, which said to Mahon that she cared deeply for him. Mahon remembered the man as polite, but stopped short of saying he was friendly. When they spoke briefly after the concert, the man commented about how well Mahon handled the lighting problem.

Mahon was able to steer Beth away from her date and invited her to his birthday party to be held Saturday, October 23, two days before his birthday. A couple of days before the party, Beth e-mailed Mahon telling him that she didn't think she could make it, but that they could get together on Monday night for a drink.

By Monday night Beth would be dead.

CHAPTER
THIRTY-ONE

Guys disappear from the Dublin House all the time,"
said Bruce Kelly. "Maybe they need to sober up;
maybe they've met a woman. They usually come
back. Toolan did."

Several of the boys from the Dublin ran into Toolan over
the months of his sobriety. One day, after playing a softball
game, George Gross happened upon him in Central Park.
Toolan then was still dating Jessica Northrup and had her
dog in tow. According to Gross, the tiny pooch looked like a
snowball. Gross wasn't going to let an opportunity to razz
Toolan slip by. Gross slowly dropped his gaze from the towering Toolan to the little fluff of fur. "You kidding me?"
Gross remarked, slowly shaking his head for effect. "Look,
it's not mine," Toolan explained, his face a sunset red. "It's
my girlfriend's."

One of the bartenders at the Dublin had a chance meeting
with him outside of the New York Sports Club, a gym
around the corner from Toolan's apartment. The bartender
asked if Toolan was still "on the wagon," and received an
embarrassed shrug in response. But Toolan's sobriety was
conditional. He'd given up drinking for the sake of his relationship with Northrup. Any recovering alcoholic will tell
you, giving up drinking for someone else is a relapse waiting
to happen. With Northrup no longer his obsession, circumstances were in place for Toolan to "slip," the phrase AAers
use when one of theirs goes back to drinking.

◆ ◆ ◆

Why Toolan decided to travel to Nantucket the weekend after his breakup with Northrup is not completely clear. One, however, can make some educated guesses. The island held warm memories for him. According to Jessica Northrup, Toolan had a home movie of a long-ago Thanksgiving spent with the Mannixes in their Nantucket home. It was on Nantucket that Toolan once dreamt of an acting career, where, just after Columbia, his life brimmed with possibility.

But the island also had a pull that was not so idyllic for him. One of the strong suggestions Alcoholics Anonymous has for people early in sobriety is to stay away from "people, places, and things" that might act as a trigger to start them drinking again. Nantucket fell firmly into the "places" category for Toolan.

From the Summer House out in 'Sconset to Nelson Doubleday's 21 Federal in town, from the late night crowd at the Boarding House to the weekend bands at the Chicken Box, from the younger crowd shoulder to shoulder holding longneck Buds at the Gazebo on the Straight Warf to a champagne flute at Michael Sturgis's Cinco, from cocktails on the deck to beers on the beach, Nantucket is more than ever "the movable feast," as Beth's friend Paul Savage once called it. More alcohol is consumed per capita on Nantucket that any other place in Massachusetts, including all of Boston and the college towns. The *Boston Herald* calls Nantucket "the wine-lovers island of dreams." In the middle of May, the island holds a world-renowned wine festival. It's more of a weeklong party, and a way of kick-starting a drinking season that doesn't slow until after Labor Day.

For Toolan it was not only the island's ever-flowing fountain of booze that may have called to him. What Disney World is to a nine-year-old, Nantucket was to him. The island's stock market and banking wealth rolled by in Lexus SUV's, the spectacular sunsets seemed to shimmer in the balloon wineglasses. This was the province of the Masters of the Universe with battleship-sized yachts and island castles. Toolan just wasn't a Diet Coke, flip-flops and cutoffs kind of a guy. Perhaps it didn't seem fair that he was chained to this no drinking thing. With Northrup gone from his life, his pledge of sobriety may have seemed a bit extreme, a little monastic.

The exact moment when Toolan picked up a drink again is also not known. It might have been right after the breakup with Jessica Northrup, maybe at the Dublin House. Perhaps he waited until Labor Day weekend on Nantucket, a "geographic," as they call it in AA. Though the exact moment is hazy, the thoughts running through Tom Toolan's mind when he lifted that first beer are no secret. Just about every alcoholic could tell you what those thoughts were: *What's the harm in one beer? This time it will be different. This time I'll control it.* That same legion of alcoholics, the ones lucky enough to survive their relapses, can also tell you how horribly misguided that thinking is.

On the Sunday of Labor Day weekend, Toolan found himself once again in a Mannix home on Nantucket, this time at the house of Bernadette Mannix Feeney, the older sister of Toolan's childhood pal Jim Mannix.

In Bernadette's kitchen, Toolan brought his old Park Slope neighbor up to date on his life, perhaps editing out some of the rough spots. Perhaps Bernadette hadn't seen Toolan in some time, and no doubt would have noticed how well he looked. She had known him all his life. It is hard to imagine she hadn't heard some of the stories of his wild drinking. She had to know about his stealing her brother Jim's car. But that was ancient history now. Toolan may have told her about his breakup with Jessica Northrup. Maybe that was the moment when Bernadette thought about Beth. Perhaps that was the moment that set the horrible events into motion.

Bernadette and Beth had known each other only since the previous March. According to one published report, they met at a charity event for the Sharing Foundation, an organization that helps impoverished children in rural Cambodia.

Bernadette and her husband, Michael, have an adopted Cambodian child. Even though Beth and Bernadette spent many summers on the island, and even though they were both parishioners of the Church of St. Mary, Our Lady of the Isle, for most of their time on Nantucket they belonged to separate social circles. Coming from a very wealthy family, Bernadette was part of the Nantucket that was served; Bernadette's privilege came by way of birthright. Though, by the time she met Bernadette, Beth could hobnob with any of Nantucket's privileged class, she had earned that privilege.

Regardless of their differences, Beth was thrilled to have Bernadette in her life. She told her brothers and sister, that Bernadette was "her" friend, not a friend through her parents or brother Peter. Bernadette and Beth were about the same age, and it was comforting for Beth to have someone close by with whom to talk girl talk. Bernadette, of course, knew that Beth was looking for a guy. Perhaps in her enthusiasm to help Beth out, she overlooked Tom Toolan's disturbing past.

Bernadette picked up the phone and called her friend on Hawthorne Lane. "Come over and meet the man you're going to marry," she said to Beth.

For Beth, the circumstances were not fair. For the six months prior to meeting her, Toolan was clean and sober. Without the beer bloat, and working out at the New York Athletic Club several times a week, he had lost forty pounds. His addiction, with all of its accompanying character defects, was in remission. In the light of this sobriety, his inherent charm had blossomed. God, he was tall, handsome, smart, funny, and honest. Part of that honesty was not an act. Even if his involvement in the Twelve Steps was brief, the mere fact that he attended meetings is an expression of this self-honesty. And AA meetings encourage, even reward (with coins and applause), honesty. In the real world, AA honesty can be disarming and quite attractive. Toolan rode into Beth's life like a cross between Lancelot and Galahad, a choirboy with a crooked halo. Seven years younger than Beth, he was a trophy boyfriend—only with brains. Even his criminal past had an attraction. It wasn't like he had tried to stick up a gas station, for gosh sakes. He had tried to steal a Roman bust out of an art show! Beth thought her brothers would get a kick out of that one. Toolan was almost too good to be true.

By then, Beth had begun to leave the notion of predestination behind. She'd found the courage to attend an astrological camp where she again studied her "birth chart." At the camp she was frank to at least one other attendee about the lifelong fear she carried, but she also stated her resolve to work through that fear. Beth was tired of being alone. About six months before she met Toolan, for a memoir writing assignment, Beth wrote this about her life:

> *Is it that I so fear the lure of the negative, the hopeless, the twisted losers that I've very primly stayed on the clean and good side with my laces neatly tied and my clothes matching, behaving as I'm supposed to and being orderly? Is it the refusal to believe that world is a horrible place because then I'll just have to kill myself?*
>
> *So what I need to do is to go ahead and open Pandora's box. Let those wild things out, those slimy creatures that live in the bottom of my soul, that dark pit, that camouflaged hole, the frozen center. They will fly out and they will be horrifying. They will rush past me and whirl me around, snap at my head and bat at my shoulders, but in the end they can scare the shit out of me but they can't hurt me. . . .*
>
> *So I need to stand in the face of all the creatures when they fly out at me, and not die of shock and fear, or run away and hide.*

What began with elements of a fairy tale lasted only six weeks. In that time, Toolan and Beth were back and forth from his apartment in Manhattan to her cottage on Nantucket numerous times. They met each other's parents: Toolan's over dinner at the New York AC, Beth's at a couple of visits to John and Judy's home above the studio at 4 Fair Street. Judy had her suspicions of Toolan right off. She thought he talked too much, knew too many people, for her taste. She also thought his hair was "gross." John liked the fact that Toolan was Catholic, and he was happy that Beth seemed happy. But Beth's father didn't care for Jack that much. It takes some doing for a dog to get on the bad side of John, who has had dogs his entire life, but Jack managed it. He bit Beth's father—twice.

Toolan and Beth's lives intertwined, and the world spun. Suicide and roadside bombs killed U.S. soldiers and civilians in Iraq. The Red Sox stormed from behind to beat the hated Yankees for the American League championship. The presidential election was just weeks away, and John Kerry and George Bush were only a percentage point or so apart. And, on Nantucket, with the island seemingly all to themselves, they shared starlit nights on the beach and evenings in the cottage with Puccini on the stereo. There was laughter and shared bottles of good wine. And there were nights in the cottage when they walked hand in hand down the narrow hallway to Beth's bedroom.

People now ask why Beth didn't see through Toolan sooner. The simple answer is she didn't want to—at least for about four weeks she didn't want to. For four weeks, Beth wanted to believe that she'd met the man for whom she'd been waiting most of her life. She wanted to open her heart to him and not be afraid of being hurt. She felt the time had come for her to take that chance. She also felt the place was right. For Nantucket had always been her safe harbor: No one would ever hurt her there.

PART
THREE

CHAPTER
THIRTY-TWO

At approximately twelve noon, less than two hours after Tom Toolan stepped off a plane at Nantucket Airport, and less than an hour after a man wearing a topcoat bought a fishing knife in Brant Point Marine, Beth Lochtefeld lay dying in the living room of her cedar-shingled cottage on Hawthorne Lane. Beth's knuckles were cut and scraped raw from trying to beat her attacker away. There were nicks from the knife all over her arms. According to the coroner, at least six of the stab wounds in her body could have killed her. He had bashed her face with the handle end of the knife enclosed in his fist. One side of her face was a ghastly orange and purple. There was a wound in her throat, and one to the heart. Still, they say that even with a stab wound directly to the heart people can survive for a few seconds. Perhaps Beth could feel the blood spurt from the puncture in her chest as the torn muscle tried to keep her alive. Perhaps she knew she was about to die, that the worst of her fears had come true. Maybe the last living image Beth's eyes captured was her killer standing over her, the bloody knife still in his hand, the murderous rage in his face perhaps giving way to the frightening reality before him. Maybe the last thing that Beth Lochtefeld saw was the look of panic in his eyes.

In the bathroom mirror, the killer could see the splatter of Beth's blood on his face and shirt. He quickly looked away. That the murder weapon had only a four-inch blade gave the act a horrible intimacy. His hands were covered with Beth's still-warm blood. He could smell the blood; he could smell Beth's death. He ripped off the bloodstained shirt, and turned on the shower. His lungs fought for air. In the sink, the killer furiously washed his hands. He washed the knife. He held his head under the shower to wash Beth's blood from his hair. Bare-chested, water dripping, he staggered back into the living room where Beth's body lay. He was overwhelmed with urgency. But the moments crawled. He had to get out. His feet were leaden.

The crockery dishes of cassoulet Beth had made still sat on the kitchen table. Crickets sounded outside the open kitchen window, the sound incongruous to the horrible silence of the scene. He tried to settle his thoughts. He went back into Beth's office, for some reason he took her Palm Pilot and cell phone. He then stepped over Beth's body and turned the lock on the door. He pulled it closed behind him.

The escape route, no doubt, was down Hummock Pond Road past the high school where he turned on Surfside and then onto the Boulevard. The name of the route belies the characteristics of it. The Boulevard heads through a rather undeveloped part of the island. There are a few houses along the way, but for the most part the land is an expanse of tangled scrub oak.

The knife has never been found. Police searched exhaustively for it along the Boulevard. The density of the underbrush made the task almost impossible. The killer couldn't have found a better place to ditch the knife if he had dropped it into the ocean. There is one particularly remote spot where on either side of the road there are pull-offs; tire tracks of cars and trucks have worn down the grass. On a Monday afternoon in late October, you could park there for a half hour and not see another car come by. It was perhaps in this spot where the killer tossed the knife, bagged his bloody clothing, and began to think how he was going to get away with murder.

◆ ◆ ◆

ometime around 12:30 p.m. Barbara Kotalac looked over at the cottage and saw Beth's Subaru still parked in front. She remembered that Beth was supposed to pick up her nephew, Sam, from school. Just then, a series of previously disconnected thoughts began to assemble into a worrisome picture: Beth telling her about breaking up with her boyfriend, the strange man in the overcoat with deep voice, "He gave me a funny feeling. Why all of a sudden was this guy in the yard," she said. Barbara hurried into her house and dialed Peter Lochtefeld's number. "Call it a woman's intuition," she said.

On first try, Barbara got Peter's answering machine. She hung up, then thought better of it, and tried again. This time she began to leave a message. Just then Peter Lochtefeld walked into his house and heard Barbara Kotalac's voice on his answering machine. "There is a person in the yard," she said to Peter. For a split second there was silence on the other end of the line.

"Just hang up, Barbara," Peter said tersely. "I'm calling the police."

About the same time that the police broke down the front door of Beth's cottage, Tom Toolan was again in Nantucket Memorial Airport. Dave Murphy from the Hertz counter remembered him returning the car. A surveillance camera at the airport recorded Toolan placing a bag in a garbage can. Up to now, the bag has not been found. Unencumbered, Toolan boarded a 12:50 P.M. flight to Hyannis.

In Hyannis, Toolan rented a Chevrolet Impala. At some point, he stopped at a liquor store and bought a bottle of vodka and a few cans of 7-Up.

At about three thirty in the afternoon, as two Rhode Island State troopers sat in their cruiser on Route 3, just off Interstate 95 near Hopkinton, Rhode Island, a bulletin for Toolan's rented Impala came over the radio. One trooper asked his partner how long it would take to drive from Hyannis to where they sat. Two-and-a-half hours came the answer. "Then our suspect should be coming down the road in about ten minutes," the first trooper reportedly said. Almost exactly ten minutes later, a Chevrolet Impala that matched the description came flying onto Route 3 exit off of I-95. The Hopkinton and Connecticut State Police joined the Rhode Island troopers as they followed the Impala for about ten minutes. The Impala finally pulled to the side of the road. The half dozen or so cops, service weapons drawn, surrounded the car.

Less than four hours after Beth Lochtefeld was murdered, Tom Toolan was under arrest.

Throughout his life, Toolan rarely faced the consequences of his actions. In Paris as a high school junior, stealing his best friend's car, the jobs that he drank his way out of, the arrest for the stolen bust, firing the gun in front of his girlfriend in Atlanta, all of these incidents, and many, many more, he brushed off as if they were lint on the lapel of his double breasted blazer. His parents, his extended family, the family's influential friends, were always there to hold the safety net. But, as he sat in back of the troopers' car, perhaps he now finally realized there wasn't a net big enough to save him this time.

P olice had advised the Lochtefelds to wait until after a professional cleaning crew had a chance at the cottage. Tom Lochtefeld called an outfit on Cape Cod and was told that the earliest they could come was the following Monday. He couldn't wait that long. "I want to see what this bastard did to my sister," he told his brother Peter.

"The living room, dining room, kitchen, down the hall. Bathroom. The only room that wasn't affected by the struggle was her bedroom," said Beth's brother in an interview months after the murder. There were Luminol stains, the chemical used by forensic investigators to identify blood, everywhere he looked. There were dollops of dried blood still in Beth's office. "We could see where she drew her last breaths. The carpet was quite stained," he said, he voice quivering. "It was a very powerful moment for myself and my family."

How much, if any, aikido Beth tried to use in resisting her

attacker obviously doesn't matter. A common expression in aikido is "Yield to win." But practicing *tanto tori*, defending oneself against a knife attack, on a mat with a person using a wooden knife, is one thing, applying it while someone is trying to kill you, something completely different. Beth just hadn't been at it long enough, her sensei on Nantucket said.

Still, indications are Beth gave the killer as much as he could handle. Nicks from the knife covered both of Beth's arms. Her watch, the present from her cousin Eric, had deflected one of the blows. And when he was captured there were bruises on the killer's wrists and forearms, bruises on his neck. Beth had more courage than the killer expected. As one of the Nantucket cops told Tom Lochtefeld, Beth had put up one hell of a fight.

CHAPTER
THIRTY-THREE

Three days after his sister was murdered, Tom Lochte-feld sat at a window seat on the first Fast Ferry off of Nantucket. He'd volunteered to take the job of going to the coroner's office in Boston to identify Beth's remains. As he looked out into the fog bank that surrounded the island, the scenarios of the condition of Beth's body played like a horror movie in his thoughts. As they did, he began to wonder if he could do the grim task alone.

Today Tom is not sure whether he called his old college roommate, Brian Busconi, or Busconi called him. Either way, when Tom arrived at the coroner's office, Busconi was there—dressed in battle fatigues and a black beret.

A tough Boston "Southie," Busconi had played hockey for Harvard on a team that competed for the national championship. He went on to study medicine at the University of Massachusetts, became an orthopedic surgeon, and joined the medical staff of the Boston Red Sox. He was also a member of the National Guard and had been called up the previous June when he assumed the rank of lieutenant colonel. The sight of him there, in uniform, made Tom enormously grateful that Busconi was his friend.

The appointment at the coroner's was scheduled for 9:00 A.M. At ten Tom Lochtefeld was told it would be at least a couple of more hours. Then he was told to come back in the afternoon. An already excruciating day seemed only to be getting worse.

To get Tom's mind off of things, Busconi suggested they go to Fenway Park. The day before, Busconi's beloved Red "Sawx" had won the World Series in St. Louis. The crowd around the old Boston ballpark was immense, Sox fans reveling in their moment in history. They fought their way through the horde. Busconi didn't have his team ID. The security guard at the players' gate, however, did everything but salute the lieutenant colonel. Just like that, Tom was an underhand toss from first base. Magical at any time, the emerald field at Fenway was especially so in the afterglow of the championship. The famous Green Monster, Pesky Pole. Tom would later say that if his sister hadn't been murdered three days before, the moment would have been perfect. But Fenway couldn't allay his grief.

After some time, they left to have lunch at a local restaurant. At a nearby newsstand, Beth had again made the front page of the New York *Daily News;* this story was about how a reporter had been able to buy the same $13.95 knife that had apparently killed her.

In any other context, Tom might have laughed at the absurdity of his day. That morning he'd taken the Fast Ferry with his Uncle Jimmy, who was headed to Boston for a doctor's appointment. During the trip Jimmy told Tom that the undertaker who'd readied Beth's body to be shipped to the coroner had found a knife in the body bag. He removed it, thinking that the police had left the murder weapon there by mistake. Tom knew the police hadn't found the murder weapon yet, and he thought that the knife that had killed his sister had somehow made its way into the body bag. He immediately called Sergeant Robert Knott, the lead investigator on the case. On the ferry, it was hard to maintain a signal, and the cellular reception kept going in and out. Tom ended up in the bathroom of the ferry screaming into the cell that he knew where the murder weapon was. Knott was able to call back, and explained that the police had bought a knife just like the one the clerk at the fishing store said he sold to Toolan for use in the forensic autopsy.

Now the *Daily News* had bought another of the same knives. Brant Point Marine was having a regular run on them, Tom thought.

By two in the afternoon, Tom and Busconi were back in the coroner's office. But they were told there was still a delay. Tom kept thinking that he would wake up from the nightmare. Everywhere he looked, however, was the harsh reminder of reality. On a table in the waiting room, there was literature for families of victims of murders. A woman, her face showing the same forbidding expectancy as his, sat across from him. At some point, a police examiner came out. Of all the questions Tom felt compelled to ask, the one he did seemed the least likely. He asked if Beth really did have a tattoo of a lion on her butt. The examiner smiled and nodded yes. The examiner remarked on how pretty Beth was, and what great shape she'd been in. But the moment turned quickly sad. Fighting back tears, Tom asked how many of Beth's wounds were fatal. There were six that could have killed her, he was told.

The room was narrow and windowless, of course, with a pane of glass behind which were two panels. Someone, perhaps the same woman who had talked to Tom in the waiting room, though he's not sure, asked if he was ready. Tom nodded, and the panels opened. Beth lay on a table not four feet from him. Tom's breath caught in his throat. It was as though all the air in tiny room had been sucked out. At first, his stare was fixed on Beth's light brown hair with the golden highlights of a blonde. He wondered if the examiner had remembered to cut a lock. Beth's body was to be cremated, but the postmortem autopsy was going to delay the process for a few days. Tom wanted something of Beth in the funeral urn. Beth's head had been turned slightly away from him, to hide a wound to that side. Makeup had been applied to the side that he could see, but couldn't completely cover the yellow and purple bruises. A white sheet was pulled all the way up under her chin, to hide bruises and wounds to her throat. Tom went to his knees. Busconi put a viselike grip on Tom's arm and helped him to his feet. The question came from somewhere. It seemed so absurd that Tom's initial thought was: It wasn't being asked of him. His whole body shook. Busconi kept a reassuring hand on his old roommate's shoulder. The question came again. *Is that Beth behind the window?*

It had been only a week since Tom Lochtefeld had had dinner with Beth and her new boyfriend at the Harvard Club. One week since he saw her rushing toward him along the crowded sidewalk. She was smiling the thousand-watt smile of hers that always made him feel like a little brother: safe and comfortable. Only a week ago it seemed Beth's life was never fuller. Now, four feet from him, she lay on a gurney cold and dead, covered to her chin by a white sheet. "Oh, Beth, how did you get yourself in this situation," he uttered, as the tears streamed down his cheeks.

EPILOGUE

Throughout the writing of this book, and especially toward the end of it, there were numerous times when I felt the presence of Beth. When you spend nine months reporting and writing about someone's life and death, it is not unusual or otherworldly for the subject to become almost a physical presence. For all of that time, I had Beth's picture on my desk. I talked about her constantly, mostly to people who knew her well. Although a part of me wants to believe in communications with the other side, I'm not cut from stock that lends itself easily to the ways of the spirit world. I come from a family of three generations of New York City cops, and my inclination is toward the corporeal. But, several times, feelings came over me for which I have no explanation. One of these prompted a curious phone call.

For months I was too embarrassed to call John Lochtefeld, Beth's father. For a few weeks after Beth's murder, John and his family had come, literally, face-to-face with the great American tragedy machine that turns grief into newsprint and dollars. Tabloid reporters from New York, both newspaper and television, sneaked around his studio, one or two brazenly knocking on his door hoping for teary quotes. His family had been videotaped and photographed at the funeral, the memorial mass in Manhattan, and the burial on Nantucket.

Both the Boston and New York City papers squeezed all they could from the story. The news swell crested, perhaps, on November 15, 2004, when *People* gave Beth's murder its cover. "Murder in Nantucket. Every Woman's NIGHTMARE" shouted the headline. The press, especially the New York *Daily News*, tried to label Toolan with catchy lines like: "The Prince Charming Killer," and "The Fatal Attraction Killer." *The Globe* tried to keep the momentum rolling with follow-ups stories like "Stabbing Death has Nantucket on Edge," and "Slaying Shakes Nantucket Community."

Don't get me wrong: I'm not putting myself above my ink-stained brethren. I, like the rest, was a slave to the story, and the story seemed to have all the juicy elements: a lonely heart, a handsome murderer, the exclusive and wealthy island backdrop. Indeed, the idea to do this book was based on those very ingredients. And, for the most part, I did the work my job entails. I made the hard calls, to many who didn't want to talk to me, a few who called me a variety of names before they slammed the phone down. Most of those calls were easy. The idea of calling John Lochtefeld was hard.

Then I awakened one morning from a rather fitful night's sleep. I walked my dog, Bernie, got a coffee and a bagel from the local bagel shop, and sat in front of my computer— my normal routine. I was perhaps at the lowest point of the process of writing this book. Whatever words I wrote seemed stilted and labored. I was easily distracted. By midmorning I hadn't accomplished a thing. Next to my computer I kept a source list of phone numbers. John Lochtefeld's studio was one of the first I'd written down nine months before. For the umpteenth time, I looked at Beth's picture. Then I dialed John's number.

I asked nothing about the murder, and, as a matter of fact, we talked just a little about Beth. Instead, we went on some about his hunting, the deer population of the island, and the dogs he's had. John and his wife, Judy, had just come back from Notre Dame, he told me. There he'd attended his fiftieth reunion. At some point, John talked about his faith, and how he found his strength at his parish, the Church of St. Mary Our Lady of the Isle. Maybe it was the talk of faith

and God that prompted me. Lord knows, I've had my share
of hardwood pews and tight confessionals. Or maybe it was
Beth nudging me on. Either way, it seemed I had no control
over my mouth. The words came tumbling out. I said Beth
wanted him to know that she was in a good place, and that
she worried because he was worrying too much. For a moment, there was only silence. My reticence coming from the
realization that I'd just said my most presumptuous sentence
to date. John's silence was, I was sure, from being stunned
by my temerity. Then, both of us needing to fill in the embarrassing gap, began to speak at the same time. Both of our
voices quivered with emotion. Our conversation ended soon
after, but cordially. I told him I was truly sorry for his loss,
and that I was happy that I had gotten to know a bit about his
family and Beth.

A few months later, I was on Nantucket. I had taken the
first Fast Ferry over from Hyannis that morning. The
fog was so thick we were literally pulling into the
slip before I had my first glimpse of the harbor. By midmorning, though, the sun had dried off most of the haze.
Shafts of golden lights coursed through the window of 4 Fair
Street. The studio contained the tools of an artist's trade,
paint, brushes, canvas, and finished paintings. John Lochtefeld was seated in front of an easel, his back to me, his hand
delicately holding a brush. The painting he was working on
was the form of a crooked house, made up of multicolored
blocks. It made me smile, as most of John Lochtefeld's art
does. I knocked softly on the open door.

Tall, still powerful, wearing a crown of white hair, John
has a presence that fills his studio. But there is softness to
him. His eyes are especially gentle; Cathy, his surviving
daughter, calls their color "sea foam green." I introduced
myself, and it took a moment for him to place the name.
Then he smiled and pulled out a wooden chair and motioned
me to sit. I admitted to this being my first visit on the island.
I was getting the most out of it, I said. A friend who has a
home here met me at the dock. We spent a good part of the

morning getting an insider's look through the window of his
SUV. John laughed. We talked for almost two hours. In fact,
we were so engrossed in conversation that John almost forgot about lunch that his wife Judy had prepared upstairs. He
invited me to his home above the studio.

As I sat at the table at which the Lochtefeld family had
shared thousands of meals, dozens of images of Beth played
in my thoughts, like home movies. Because I had spanned
her life with reporting, I saw Beth sitting there at every age:
a smiling child, a precocious teen, a pretty college student,
and a confident woman. I saw Judy, still youthful looking,
but in my mind's eye a young mother, taping motivational
slogans to the refrigerator. I saw Beth's brothers and sister,
Cathy, sitting around the table, laughing about the swimming lessons at Children's Beach. I saw a younger John
Lochtefeld, the proud father, at the head of the table, those
gentle eyes filled with gratitude that his Nantucket dream
had come true.

After some time, John pulled a fishing hat onto his head
and led me down the outside stairs. We drove in his yellow
SUV, stopping first at the community garden, where John
turned off the water sprinkler. Beth and her father had
tended the garden together. When Beth was a child, John had
told her that he and his father kept a garden. The previous
spring, she had said that she wanted to do the same with
him.

The next stop was Beth's cottage. We idled on the gravel
drive of Hawthorne Lane for only a few moments. John
didn't want Barbara Kotalac, the landlord who lived in a
house next door, to feel obliged to come out. The cottage has
been rented for the season and showed the signs of summer
and life: fishing poles and an outdoor grill on the porch, a
window open with a curtain flapping in the breeze. The flowers and garden of the Kotalac house and cottage were in full
summer glory, the grass a felt green. As we sat there, John
became quiet, his eyes fixed on a spot somewhere in eternity,
his knuckles white against the steering wheel. Everything
about him in that moment seemed to be asking why.

◆ ◆ ◆

y thoughts went to another hard phone call I had
made, to Tom Toolan Jr., the accused murderer's
father. I had already sent a letter to his son, who
was awaiting trial in the Barnstable County jail on Cape
Cod. My letter had gone unanswered.

The phone rang only a few times before a man answered.
Despite the fact that I had practiced what I was going to say,
I tripped over my words. My voice trembled.

I managed to say something to the effect of wanting to
give him the chance to have input into my book. I reasoned
that the story of his son would be decidedly unflattering
without someone who could speak to the good points of Tom
Toolan III.

By then, I knew a little bit about the elder Toolan. I knew
he had been an English teacher; I knew he and his wife lived
in a nice building on Prospect Park West in Park Slope,
Brooklyn. My imagination had him sitting in an overstuffed
wing chair, reading Keats. After I finished my say, there was
a moment or two of silence, then a sigh. Like Beth's father,
Tom Toolan Jr. had already dealt with his share of tabloid reporters.

"Tell me why you are doing this?" he said, with a smooth
voice that had an English teacher's confidence. "Why must
you bring innocent people into this?"

I didn't expect Mr. Toolan to help me; I knew the call was
a long shot going in. I thought he might tell me not to call
again, or, perhaps, just slam the receiver down.

I didn't expect him to go on the offensive.

And he had me. I didn't know what to say. I backpedaled,
mumbled something about it being my job, in response to
which he suggested that I examine the virtue of such a profession. I hung up the phone wondering whether or not I
should do just that.

After about an hour the phone rang again. Mr. Toolan's
hard edge had softened considerably. In thinking about the
change afterward, I wondered if he had looked up my cre-
dentials as a writer, such as they are. Maybe he had come

across the book I'd written about my family of cops. Perhaps he thought I had been a police officer myself. (I was not; I often joke that I was closer to becoming a member of the Sopranos.) Though his manner was still a bit didactic, it was now as if he were talking to a student who, though bright, had become sidetracked or lost focus.

"Maybe it would be best if you put some thought into what you're doing," he said, slightly condescendingly. "Perhaps you might let your conscience guide you."

The cemetery is only a short distance from Hawthorne Lane, on the top of the hard turtle shell of the island. Judy Lochtefeld had tugged on my sleeve when her husband and I left the kitchen. She whispered that John hadn't been to the grave since the family had placed the headstone. As we stood over it, I felt a rush of emotions. I was honored, but a bit embarrassed at the intimacy of the moment. At one point, John picked up a pebble and placed it on the stone next to several others. He said that Beth's nephews and nieces had started the practice, which is a custom of the Jewish faith. The air was fragrant with sea, heather, and earth. Beams of sunlight streaked from between the clouds. A gentle breeze rippled at our shirts.

I was afraid to look at him, but I couldn't help myself. He stood, straight backed, his hands clasped in front of him holding his hat, his head bowed. The bottoms of those sea foam green eyes were filled with water. In that moment, I wondered if Beth had come back to Nantucket for him.

Of all my emotions that afternoon in that quiet place, the most overwhelming was a familiar one. Standing in front of Beth's grave, I felt the way I did the morning I first called John.

Just then the shafts of sunlight disappeared in the cloud clutter. The Nantucket sky can be like that. That morning I'd driven the fourteen miles from island's end to end and had encountered driving rain, bright sunshine, and misty fog. As we were sprinkled with rain,

John pulled his hat onto his head and slowly turned. As I followed him, I realized that all the words written about Beth, including the ones on these pages, didn't come close to capturing the emotions confined in the slumped shoulders of the man in front of me. That is, except for the words in marble, framed in rose quartz. I turned and had one last look at them:

ELIZABETH ANNE LOCHTEFELD
1960–2004
BELOVED DAUGHTER SISTER
AUNT AND FRIEND

UPDATE DECEMBER 2006

Justice moves at a glacial pace in the Commonwealth of Massachusetts. At the time of this writing, more than two years since Beth was stabbed to death in her sleepy, Nantucket cottage, Tom Toolan still awaits trial in the Barnstable House of Corrections on Cape Cod, where he is being held without bail.

At his arraignment, Toolan pled not guilty to the charge of first-degree murder. He has secured the services of Brockton, Massachusetts, defense attorney, Kevin Reddington. Mr. Reddington's past client list includes the first Catholic priest to admit guilt in the Boston Archdiocese sex scandal, Ronald H. Paquin, who pled guilty to three counts of child rape and is currently serving 12–15 years; and Michael "Mucko" McDermott, who stood trial for the shooting deaths of seven co-workers in the bloodiest mass murder in Massachusetts's history. During his trial, McDermott testified that St. Michael the Archangel sent him back in time to murder Hitler and six German generals. The jury found McDermott guilty and the judge sentenced him to seven life terms.

At a pre-trial hearing in Nantucket Superior Court, Mr. Reddington filed a motion for a change of venue. The defense attorney argued that "ongoing media scrutiny" coupled with "the unusual nature of an island community," would prevent Toolan from receiving a fair trial on Nantucket. As of this writing, the judge has not ruled on that motion.

If the case were heard on Nantucket, it would be the first trial of a premeditated murder on that island since the days of the whaling ships. The setting would also give appropriate closure to Beth's life story. It was in Nantucket where she found her innocence, her womanhood and finally her peace. It would be fitting for Beth also to find justice there.

If found guilty of murder in the first degree, Toolan could face a sentence of life without the possibility of parole.

ACKNOWLEDGMENTS

When I first started snooping around, Tom Lochtefeld contacted me to essentially head me off at the pass. Speaking for the Lochtefeld family, Tom had made the decision to talk to me only to ensure that I had my facts straight. I am very grateful for his help. I was continually amazed at the dignity and grace of all the Lochtefelds under such trying circumstances.

As far as the rest of my sourcing goes, Beth's memorial Web site, www.bethlochtefeld.org, proved invaluable and I would like to thank all of those I contacted from the site—whether you chose to talk to me or not. The compilation of the entries formed a montage of Beth's life that both moved and inspired me. I'd especially like to thank Vicky Taveras, Stuart Saft, Don and Dennis DeMarco, Paul Savage, Matt Bresnahan, Tony Maresco, John Gaccione, Karen Russo, Patti Engel Sambrana, Hilary Collins, Maura Abernathy, Jimmy Fleitz, Fran Sullivan Shultz, Louis Guarnaccia, Liz Mackey, and many more.

I am extremely grateful to the honesty and courage of the man I call Steve Doran in this book. I'd like to thank Liz Kelley for all her help on planes both temporal and ethereal. Also, I owe a debt of gratitude to David Tereshcuk, George Gross, Bruce Kelly, Terry Ferguson, Susan Breen, Mika Duffy, and Bob Burke. As my first reader, Joe Orso's suggestions and edits proved, once again, invaluable.

I'm grateful to Charlie Spicer from St. Martin's for his faith and support and to Michael Homler and Joe Cleeman for all their help. Finally, I'd like to thank my agent, Jane Dystel, who stays by me in thick and thin.

INDEX